Gaussian 98 User's Reference

Second Edition

Æleen Frisch

Michael J. Frisch

Gaussian, Inc.
Carnegie Office Park, Building 6
Pittsburgh, PA 15106 U.S.A.
Voice: 412-279-6700 ◆ *Fax:* 412-279-2118 ◆ *Email:* info@gaussian.com

ISBN: 0-9636769-7-0
Manual Version: 6.1 (corresponding to *Gaussian 98* Revision A.5)
January, 1999

Printed in the U.S.A.

Table of Contents

1

Introduction

This manual describes *Gaussian 98*, a connected system of programs for performing a variety of semi-empirical and ab initio molecular orbital (MO) calculations. It is designed as a complete reference to all of the program's capabilities.

Gaussian 98 is capable of predicting many properties of molecules and reactions, including:

- ◆ Molecular energies and structures
- ◆ Energies and structures of transition states
- ◆ Vibrational frequencies
- ◆ IR and Raman spectra
- ◆ Thermochemical properties
- ◆ Bond and reaction energies
- ◆ Reaction pathways
- ◆ Molecular orbitals
- ◆ Atomic charges
- ◆ Multipole moments
- ◆ NMR shielding and magnetic susceptibilities
- ◆ Vibrational circular dichroism intensities
- ◆ Electron affinities and ionization potentials
- ◆ Polarizabilities and hyperpolarizabilities
- ◆ Electrostatic potentials and electron densities

Computations can be carried out on systems in the gas phase or in solution, and in their ground state or in an excited state. Thus, *Gaussian 98* can serve as a powerful tool for exploring areas of chemical interest like substituent effects, reaction mechanisms, potential energy surfaces, and excitation energies.

The remainder of this chapter presents the literature citation for *Gaussian 98*, discusses its features in more technical detail and describes the contents of this manual and the rest of the *Gaussian 98* documentation set.

Literature Citation

Gaussian 98 represents further development of the *Gaussian 70*, *Gaussian 76*, *Gaussian 80*, *Gaussian 82*, *Gaussian 86*, *Gaussian 88*, *Gaussian 90*, *Gaussian 92*, *Gaussian 92/DFT* and *Gaussian 94* systems previously published [1-10]. The required citation for this work is:

> *Gaussian 98* (Revision A.1)[†], M. J. Frisch, G. W. Trucks, H. B. Schlegel, G. E. Scuseria, M. A. Robb, J. R. Cheeseman, V. G. Zakrzewski, J. A. Montgomery, R. E. Stratmann, J. C. Burant, S. Dapprich, J. M. Millam, A. D. Daniels, K. N. Kudin, M. C. Strain, O. Farkas, J. Tomasi, V. Barone, M. Cossi, R. Cammi, B. Mennucci, C. Pomelli, C. Adamo, S. Clifford, J. Ochterski, G. A. Petersson, P. Y. Ayala, Q. Cui, K. Morokuma, D. K. Malick, A. D. Rabuck, K. Raghavachari, J. B. Foresman, J. Cioslowski, J. V. Ortiz, B. B. Stefanov, G. Liu, A. Liashenko, P. Piskorz, I. Komaromi, R. Gomperts, R. L. Martin, D. J. Fox, T. Keith, M. A. Al-Laham, C. Y. Peng, A. Nanayakkara, C. Gonzalez, M. Challacombe, P. M. W. Gill, B. G. Johnson, W. Chen, M. W. Wong, J. L. Andres, M. Head-Gordon, E. S. Replogle and J. A. Pople, Gaussian, Inc., Pittsburgh PA, 1998.

The advances presented for the first time in *Gaussian 98* are the work of M. J. Frisch, G. W. Trucks, H. B. Schlegel, G. E. Scuseria, M. A. Robb, J. R. Cheeseman, V. G. Zakrzewski, J. A. Montgomery, R. E. Stratmann, J. C. Burant, S. Dapprich, J. M. Millam, A. D. Daniels, K. N. Kudin, M. C. Strain, O. Farkas, J. Tomasi, V. Barone, M. Cossi, R. Cammi, B. Mennucci, C. Pomelli, C. Adamo, S. Clifford, J. Ochterski, G. A. Petersson, P. Y. Ayala, Q. Cui, K. Morokuma, D. K. Malick, A. D. Rabuck, J. Cioslowski, G. Liu, A. Liashenko, P. Piskorz, and I. Komoromi.

Additional Citation Recommendations

In general, we recommend citing the original references describing the theoretical methods used when reporting results obtained from *Gaussian* calculations, as well as giving the citation for the program itself. These references are given in the discussions of the relevant keywords in chapter 3 of this manual. The only exceptions occur with long established methods such as Hartree-Fock theory which have advanced to the state of common practice and are essentially self-citing at this point.

In some cases, *Gaussian 98* output will display the references relevant to the current calculation type.

Gaussian 98 also includes the NBO program as link 607. If this program is used, it should be cited separately as:

> NBO Version 3.1, E. D. Glendening, A. E. Reed, J. E. Carpenter, and F. Weinhold.

The original literature references for NBO can also be cited [11-18].

[†] Note that you should replace "Revision A.1" with the identifier for the revision of the program that you actually use.

Gaussian 98 Capabilities

Gaussian 98 has been designed with the needs of the user in mind. All of the standard input is free-format and mnemonic. Reasonable defaults for input data have been provided, and the output is intended to be self-explanatory. Mechanisms are available for the sophisticated user to override defaults or interface their own code to the *Gaussian* system. The authors hope that their efforts will allow users to concentrate their energies on the application of the methods to chemical problems and to the development of new methods, rather than on the mechanics of performing the calculations.

The technical capabilities of the *Gaussian 98* system are listed in the subsections below (see chapter 3 for a discussion of the mappings between predicted quantities and calculation types).

Fundamental Algorithms

♦   Calculation of one- and two-electron integrals over any general contracted gaussian functions. The basis functions can either be cartesian gaussians or pure angular momentum functions, and a variety of basis sets are stored in the program and can be requested by name. Integrals may be stored in memory, stored externally, or be recomputed as needed [19-28]. The cost of computations can be linearized using fast multipole method (FMM) and sparse matrix techniques for certain kinds of calculations [29-34].

♦   Transformation of the atomic orbital (AO) integrals to the molecular orbital basis by "in-core" means (storing the AO integrals in memory), "direct" means (no integral storage required), "semi-direct" means (using some disk storage of integrals), or "conventional" means (with all AO integrals on disk).

Energies

♦   Molecular mechanics calculations using the AMBER [35], DREIDING [36] and UFF [37, 38] force fields.

♦   Semi-empirical calculations using the CNDO [39], INDO [40], MINDO/3 [41, 42], MNDO [41, 43-50], AM1 [41, 46, 47, 51, 52], and PM3 [53, 54] model Hamiltonians.

♦   Self-consistent field calculations using closed-shell (RHF) [55], unrestricted open-shell (UHF) [56], and restricted open-shell (ROHF) [57] Hartree-Fock wavefunctions.

♦   Correlation energy calculations using Møller-Plesset perturbation theory [58] carried to second, third [59], fourth [60, 61], or fifth[62] order. MP2 calculations use direct [20, 63] and semi-direct methods [22] to use efficiently however much (or little) memory and disk are available.

♦   Correlation energy calculations using configuration interaction (CI), using either all double excitations (CID) or all single and double excitations (CISD) [64].

- Coupled cluster theory with double substitutions (CCD)[65], coupled cluster theory with both single and double substitutions (CCSD) [66-69], Quadratic Configuration Interaction using single and double substitutions (QCISD) [70], and Brueckner Doubles Theory (BD) [71, 72]. A non-iterative triples contribution may also be computed (as well as quadruples for QCISD and BD).

- Density functional theory, including LSDA [73-76], BLYP [77-79], Becke's 1993 three-parameter hybrid method [80], Becke's 1996 one-parameter hybrid functional [81] and variations thereof [82, 83], and general, user-configurable hybrid methods of Hartree-Fock and DFT. See chapter 3 for a complete list of available functionals.

- Automated, high accuracy energy methods: G1 theory [84, 85], G2 theory [86] and G2(MP2) [87] theory; Complete Basis Set (CBS) [88-92] methods: CBS-4 [92], CBS-q [92], CBS-Q [92], CBS-Q//B3 [93], and CBS-QCI/APNO [91], as well as general CBS extrapolation.

- General MCSCF, including complete active space SCF (CASSCF) [94, 95], and allowing for the optional inclusion of MP2 correlation [96]. Algorithmic improvements [97, 98] allow up to twelve active orbitals in *Gaussian 98*.

- The Generalized Valence Bond-Perfect Pairing (GVB-PP) SCF method [99].

- Testing the SCF wavefunctions for stability under release of constraints, for both Hartree-Fock and DFT methods [100, 101].

- Excited state energies using the single-excitation Configuration Interaction (CI-Singles) method [102], the time-dependent method for HF and DFT [103-105], and the ZINDO semi-empirical method [106-114].

Gradients and Geometry Optimizations

- Analytic computation of the nuclear coordinate gradient of the RHF [115], UHF, ROHF, GVB-PP, CASSCF [116, 117], MP2 [21, 22, 118, 119], MP3, MP4(SDQ) [120, 121], CID [122], CISD, CCD, QCISD, Density Functional, and excited state CIS energies [102]. All of the post-SCF methods can take advantage of the frozen-core approximation.

- Automated geometry optimization to either minima or saddle points [115, 123-127], using internal or cartesian coordinates or a mixture of coordinates. Optimizations are performed by default using redundant internal coordinates [128], regardless of the input coordinate system used.

- Automated transition state searching using synchronous transit-guided quasi-Newton methods [129].

- Reaction path following using the intrinsic reaction coordinate (IRC) [130, 131].

- Two- or three-layer ONIOM [132-137] calculations for energies and geometry optimizations.

♦ Simultaneous optimization of a transition state and a reaction path [138].

♦ Conical intersection optimization using state-averaged CASSCF [139-141].

♦ IRCMax calculation which locates the point of maximum energy for a transition structure along a specified reaction path [142-150].

♦ Direct dynamics trajectory calculations in which the classical equations of motion are integrated using analytical second derivatives [151].

Frequencies and Second Derivatives

♦ Analytic computation of force constants (nuclear coordinate second derivatives), polarizabilities, hyperpolarizabilities, and dipole derivatives analytically for the RHF, UHF, DFT, RMP2, UMP2, and CASSCF methods [24, 25, 118, 152-159], and for excited states using CIS [160].

♦ Numerical differentiation of energies or gradients to produce force constants, polarizabilities, and dipole derivatives for the MP3, MP4(SDQ), CID, CISD, CCD, and QCISD methods [122, 161-163].

♦ Harmonic vibrational analysis and thermochemistry analysis using arbitrary isotopes, temperature, and pressure.

♦ Determination of IR and Raman intensities for vibrational transitions [153, 154, 156, 161, 164].

Molecular Properties

♦ Evaluation of various one-electron properties using the SCF, DFT, MP2, CI, CCD and QCISD methods, including Mulliken population analysis [165], multipole moments, natural population analysis, electrostatic potentials, and electrostatic potential-derived charges using the Merz-Kollman-Singh [166, 167], CHelp [168], or CHelpG [169] schemes.

♦ NMR shielding tensors and molecular susceptibilities using the SCF, DFT and MP2 methods [170-177].

♦ Vibrational circular dichroism (VCD) intensities [178].

♦ Atoms in Molecules [179] bonding analysis and atomic properties [179-183].

♦ Propagator methods for electron affinities and ionization potentials [184-190].

♦ Approximate spin orbit coupling between two spin states can be computed during CASSCF calculations [191-195].

Solvation Models

All of these models employ a self-consistent reaction field (SCRF) methodology for modeling systems in solution.

♦ Onsager model (dipole and sphere) [196-199], including analytic first and second derivatives at the HF and DFT levels, and single-point energies at the MP2, MP3, MP4(SDQ), CI, CCD, and QCISD levels.

♦ Polarized Continuum (overlapping spheres) model (PCM) of Tomasi and coworkers [200-208] for analytic HF, DFT, MP2, MP3, MP4(SDQ), QCISD, CCD, CID, and CISD energies and HF and DFT gradients.

♦ IPCM (static isodensity surface) model [209] for analytic energies at the HF and DFT levels.

♦ SCI-PCM (self-consistent isodensity surface) model [209] for analytic energies and gradients and numerical frequencies at the HF and DFT levels.

Overview of This Manual

In addition to this Introduction, this manual contains six chapters and four appendices:

♦ Chapter 2, "Running *Gaussian 98*," describes how to run the program under various operating systems.

♦ Chapter 3, "*Gaussian 98* Input," discusses the general structure of *Gaussian* input files and provides a reference for all supported keywords and options. Note that output is often edited for clarity and space reasons in the examples in this chapter.

♦ Chapter 4, "Efficiency Considerations," provides guidance on optimizing *Gaussian 98* performance. In doing so, it considers the features and limitations of the available algorithms and discusses the tradeoffs inherent in the various choices.

♦ Chapter 5, "Utility Programs," describes the set of utilities provided with *Gaussian 98*, including suggestions for their optimal use.

♦ Chapter 6, "Installation and Configuration," is designed for system administrators and discusses installing the *Gaussian 98* program and site-wide configuration of its operation.

♦ Appendix A, "Differences Between *Gaussian 98* and *Gaussian 94*," documents the additions to and changes in functionality of *Gaussian 98* with respect to the previous version of the program.

♦ Appendix B, "Program Limitations," documents the few hard limits in *Gaussian 98*.

♦ Appendix C, "Constructing Z-Matrices," explains how to create Z-matrix descriptions of molecular systems.

♦ Appendix D, "Additional Keywords," lists keywords and options which are obsolete, correspond to deprecated features, or are intended for use in program development contexts only.

The *Gaussian 98* Documentation Set

The *Gaussian 98* documentation set consists of these works:

♦ *Gaussian 98 User's Reference*, which discusses the mechanics of setting up input and running the program in full detail, documenting the available keywords and options. It also covers program installation, configuration, and performance considerations.

♦ *Gaussian 98 Programmer's Reference*, which is designed for programmers wanting to make modifications to *Gaussian 98,* or to interface their own programs to it. It documents implementation details, *Gaussian 98* system routines, all routes, overlays and internal options, and also provides other operating system-specific information of interest to programmers.

Users requiring detailed basic instruction on running *Gaussian*, including setting up jobs and interpreting Gaussian output, should consult the book *Exploring Chemistry with Electronic Structure Methods* [210].

♦ "*Gaussian 98* IOPs," a technical note documenting the defined options and their available settings for all of the *Gaussian 98* overlays. An up-to-date version of this article is available on our website (**www.gaussian.com/iops.htm**). The final chapter of the *Gaussian 98 Programmer's Reference* contains the version of this article that was current at press time.

Additions, updates, and clarifications to, and more detailed technical discussions of topics covered in the *Gaussian 98* documentation are included in each issue of ***Gaussian NEWS***. They are also available in the Technical Information area of our website (**www.gaussian.com/techinfo.htm**).

2

Running *Gaussian 98*

This chapter describes the operating system commands required to execute *Gaussian 98* on UNIX computer systems. See the additional instructions accompanying the program for the equivalent information for other operating systems. This chapter assumes that the program has already been installed as described in chapter 6. The final section of the chapter lists the component links of the *Gaussian 98* program.

Running *Gaussian 98* involves the following activities:

◆ Creating *Gaussian* input describing the desired calculation.
◆ Specifying the locations of the various scratch files.
◆ Specifying resource requirements.
◆ Initiating program execution, in either interactive or batch mode.

The first item is the subject of chapter 3. In this chapter, we will assume that a basic *Gaussian 98* input file has been created, and our discussion will examine the remaining three items on the list.

Specifying Scratch File Handling and Location

Gaussian 98 uses several scratch files in the course of its computation. They include:

◆ The Checkpoint file: *name*.chk
◆ The Read-Write file: *name*.rwf
◆ The Two-Electron Integral file: *name*.int
◆ The Two-Electron Integral Derivative file: *name*.d2e

By default, these files are given a name generated from the process ID of the *Gaussian 98* process, and they are stored in the scratch directory, designated by the GAUSS_SCRDIR environment variable (UNIX).[†] If the environment variable is unset, the location defaults to the current working directory of the *Gaussian 98* process.

[†] You may also see files of the form ***name*.inp** in this directory. These are the internal input files used by the program.

By default, these files are deleted at the end of a successful run. However, you may wish to save the checkpoint file for later use in another *Gaussian 98* job, for use by a visualization program, to restart a failed job, and so on. This may be accomplished by *naming* the checkpoint file, providing an explicit name and/or location for it, via a **%Chk** command within the *Gaussian* input file. Here is an example:

%Chk=water

This command, which is placed at the beginning of the input file (before the route section—see chapter 3 for details), gives the checkpoint file the name **water.chk**, overriding the usual generated name and causing the file to be saved at job conclusion. In this case, the file will reside in the current directory. However, a command like this one will specify an alternate directory location as well as filename:

%Chk=/chem/scratch2/water

If disk space in the scratch directory is limited, but space is available elsewhere on the system, you may want to split the scratch files among several disk locations. The following commands allow you to specify the names and locations of the other scratch files:

%RWF=path	*Read-Write file*
%Int=path	*Integral file*
%D2E=path	*Integral Derivative file*

In general, the read-write file is by far the largest, and so it is the one for which an alternate location is most often specified.

Splitting Scratch Files Across Disks
An alternate syntax is provided for splitting the Read-Write file, the Integral file, and/or the Integral Derivative file among two or more disks (or file systems). Here is the syntax for the **%RWF** command:

%RWF=*loc1,size1,loc2,size2, ...*

where each *loc* is a directory location or a file pathname, and each *size* is the maximum size for the file segment at that location. *Gaussian 98* will automatically generate unique filenames for any *loc* which specifies a directory only. On UNIX systems, directory specifications (without filenames) must include a terminal slash.

By default, the sizes are in units of words; the value may be followed by **KB**, **MB** or **GB** (without intervening spaces) to designate KB, MB or GB, respectively, or by **KW**, **MW** or **GW** to indicate units of kilowords, megawords or gigawords, respectively. Note that 1 MB = 1024^2 bytes = 1,048,576 bytes (not 1,000,000 bytes).

A value of **-1** for any size parameter indicates that any and all available space may be used, and a value of **0** says to use the current size of an existing segment. **-1** is useful only for the last file specified, for which it is the default.

For example, the following directive splits the Read-Write file across three disks:

%RWF=/dalton/s0/,60MW,/scratch/,800MB,/temp/s0/my_job,-1

The maximum sizes for the file segments are 480 MB, 800 MB, and unlimited, respectively. *Gaussian 98* will generate names for the first two segments, and the third will be given the name my_job. Note that the directory specifications include terminal slashes.

Due to limitations in current UNIX implementations, -1 should be used with caution, as it will attempt to extend a file segment beyond all remaining disk capacity on these systems; using it will also have the side effect of keeping any additional file segments included in the list from ever being used.

Saving and Deleting Scratch Files

By default, unnamed scratch files are deleted at the end of the *Gaussian 98* run, and named files are saved. The **%NoSave** command may be used to change this default behavior. When this directive is included in an input file, named scratch files whose directives appear in the input file *before* **%NoSave** will be deleted at the end of a run (as well as all unnamed scratch files). However, if the % directive naming the file appears *after* the **%NoSave** directive, the file will be retained. For example, these commands specify a name for the checkpoint file, and an alternate name and directory location for the read-write file, and cause only the checkpoint file to be saved at the conclusion of the *Gaussian 98* job:

```
%RWF=/chem/scratch2/water        Files to be deleted go here.
%NoSave
%Chk=water                       Files to be saved go here.
```

Initialization Files

The *Gaussian 98* system includes initialization files to set up the user environment for running the program. These files are:

```
$g98root/g98/bsd/g98.login          C shell
$g98root/g98/bsd/g98.profile        Bourne shell
```

Note that the g98root environment variable must be set up by the user. Thus, it is customary to include lines like the following within the .login or .profile file for *Gaussian 98* users:

.login *files*:
```
setenv g98root location
source $g98root/g98/bsd/g98.login
```

.profile *files*:
```
g98root=location
export g98root
. $g98root/g98/bsd/g98.profile
```

Once things are set up correctly, the **g98** command is used to execute *Gaussian 98* (see below).

Controlling Memory Usage

The **%Mem** command controls the amount of dynamic memory to be used by *Gaussian 98*. By default, 6 megawords words are used. This can be changed to *n* double-precision words by specifying:

%Mem=*n*

For example, the following command sets memory use to 64 million bytes:

%Mem=8000000

The value given to **%Mem** may also be followed by **KB**, **KW**, **MB**, **MW**, **GB** or **GW** (no intervening spaces) to denote other units. For example, the following command also sets the amount of dynamic memory to 64 MB:

%Mem=64MB

Even larger allocations may be needed for very large direct SCF calculations—at least $3N^2$ words, where *N* is the number of basis functions. Frequency and post-SCF calculations involving f functions should be given 6 MWords if possible (7 MWords on the Cray). Using more than 6 million words for moderate-sized calculations (i.e., a direct SCF with less than 500 basis functions) does not improve performance on most systems.

Warning: *Requesting more memory than the amount of physical memory actually available on a computer system will lead to very poor performance.*

If *Gaussian 98* is being used on a machine with limited physical memory, so that the default of 48 MB is not available, the default algorithms as well as the default memory allocation should be set appropriately during installation. See Chapter 4 for more details on using *Gaussian 98* efficiently.

Running *Gaussian 98* on UNIX Systems

Once all input and resource specifications are prepared, you are ready to run the program. *Gaussian 98* may be run interactively using one of two command styles:

g98 *job-name*   or   **g98** <*input-file* >*output-file*

In the first form, the program reads input from ***job-name***.com and writes its output to ***job-name***.log. When ***job-name*** is not specified, the program reads from standard input and writes to standard output, and these can be redirected or piped in the usual UNIX fashion. Either form of command can be forced in the background in the same manner as any shell command using &.

Scripts and *Gaussian 98*

Scripts designed to run *Gaussian 98* may also be created in several ways (we will use the C shell in these examples). First, **g98** commands like those above may be included in a shell script. Secondly, actual *Gaussian 98* input may be included in the script using the << construct:

```
#!/bin/csh
g98 <<END >water.log
%Chk=water
#RHF/6-31G(d)

water energy

0  1
O
H  1  1.0
H  1  1.0  2  120.0

END
echo "Job done. "
```

All lines preceding the string following the << symbols are taken as input to the **g98** command.

Finally, loops may be created to run several *Gaussian 98* jobs in succession. For example, the following script runs all of the *Gaussian 98* input files specified as its command line arguments, and it maintains a log of its activities in the file **Status**:

```
#!/bin/csh
echo "Current Job Status:" > Status
foreach file ($argv)
    echo "Starting file $file at 'date'" >> Status
    g98 < $file > $file:r.log
    echo "$file Done with status $status" >> Status
end
echo "All Done." >> Status
```

The following more complex script creates *Gaussian 98* input files on-the-fly from the partial input in the files given as the script's command line arguments. The latter are lacking full route sections; their route sections consist of simply a # sign or a # line containing special keywords needed for that molecular system, but no method, basis set, or calculation type.

The script creates a two-step job for each partial input file—a Hartree-Fock optimization followed by an MP2 single point energy calculation—consisting of both the literal commands included in the script and the contents of each file specified at script execution time (multi-step jobs are described in more detail in Chapter 3). It includes the latter by exploiting the *Gaussian 98* @ include file mechanism:

```
#!/bin/csh
echo "Current Job Status:" > Status
foreach file ($argv)
echo "Starting file $file at 'date'" >> Status
g98 <<END> $file:r.log
```

```
%Chk=$file:r
# HF/6-31G(d) FOpt
@$file/N

--Link1--
%Chk=$file:r
%NoSave
# MP2/6-31+G(d,p) SP Guess=Read Geom=AllCheck
END
echo "$file Done with status $status" >> Status
end    # end of foreach
echo "All Done." >> Status
```

See Chapter 3 for more details on multi-step jobs and the include file mechanism.

Batch Execution

Gaussian 98 may be run using the NQS batch facility on those UNIX systems that support it. The **subg98** command, defined in the initialization files, submits an input file to a batch queue. It has the following syntax:

subg98 *queue-name job-name* [**-scrdir** *dir1*] [**-exedir** *dir2*] [**-p** *n*]

The two required parameters are the queue and job names. Input is taken from ***job-name***.com and output goes to ***job-name***.**log**, just as for interactive runs. The NQS log file is sent to ***job-name***.batch-log. The optional parameters **-scrdir** and **-exedir** are used to override the default scratch and executable directories, respectively. Any other parameters are taken to be NQS options. In particular, **-p** *n* can be used to set the priority within the queue to *n*. This is priority for initiation (1 being lowest), and does not affect the run-time priority.

Running *Gaussian* 98 on Cray UniCOS Systems

The Cray version of *Gaussian 98* is very similar to the other UNIX versions. However, most Cray users use machines at central facilities and are encouraged to run their production jobs in batch mode.

Gaussian 98 is best run in a batch environment under the NQS queuing system. This gives some chance of restart should the Cray undergo an orderly shutdown, and allows better system management of resources like memory and disk. *Gaussian 98* also uses the NQS job control parameters to determine memory and time limits.

Submitting from an Interactive UniCOS Session

To submit an NQS job from an interactive session, a file like the following should be created:

```
# QSUB -r name -o name.out -eo
# QSUB -lt 2000 -lT 2100
# QSUB -lm 7mw -lM 7mw
g98 <name.com
```

where *name* should be replaced with names appropriate to your calculation. The first line names the running job, names the output file, and causes errors to be included in the output file. The time parameters are different to allow addition of job control for cleanup, (for example, archiving the checkpoint file in the event that the job exceeds its time limit). The memory parameters are used both for initial scheduling of your job for execution and by the program to determine dynamic memory use.

This job would then be submitted by issuing the command,

```
$ qsub name.job
```

and the output would be placed in your current working directory. Alternatively, the **subg98** command, provided with *Gaussian 98,* can be used.

Running Interactively

There may be some circumstances where it is desirable to run *Gaussian 98* interactively on the Cray. This can be done using a command like:

```
$ g98 input output
```

If no interactive memory limits are enforced, *Gaussian 98* supplies defaults. Error messages from such a job are returned to the screen.

Gaussian 98 and Cray Checkpoint Files

Please note that the *Gaussian 98* checkpoint file is distinct from the checkpoint facility provided by UniCOS. The *Gaussian 98* file may be used by later *Gaussian* runs to recover intermediate results, but it will not have any influence on whether a job restarts after an NQS shutdown. You can force an NQS job not to restart by including the following line within the job file:

```
# QSUB -nr
```

Then you can modify your input to allow *Gaussian 98* to read its own checkpoint file and resubmit the job. This is particularly useful for optimizations and numeric frequency calculations.

Memory Management under UniCOS

UniCOS is a non-virtual memory implementation of UNIX. As a result, questions of memory management are more important. Efficient vector execution of *Gaussian 98* can require a sizable amount of memory. However, for most calculations, excess memory is underutilized and thus adds unnecessarily to the cost of the job on the Cray. For Hartree-Fock energies and optimizations, 6 Megawords is a good value, while for post-SCF procedures, 6-8 Megawords is adequate. However, a large amount of memory is still needed for all calculations including f functions, and post-Hartree-Fock procedures require more memory as the basis set size increases.

Gaussian 98 Links

The following table lists the component programs of *Gaussian 98*—known as *links*—along with their primary functions:

Link	Function
L0	Initializes program and controls overlaying
L1	Processes route section, builds list of links to execute, and initializes scratch files
L101	Reads title and molecule specification
L102	FP optimization
L103	Berny optimizations to minima and TS, STQN transition state searches
L105	MS optimization
L106	Numerical differentiation of forces/dipoles to obtain polarizability/hyperpolarizability
L107	Linear-synchronous-transit (LST) transition state search
L108	Potential energy surface scan
L109	Newton-Raphson optimization
L110	Double numerical differentiation of energies to produce frequencies
L111	Double num. diff. of energies to compute polarizabilities & hyperpolarizabilities
L113	EF optimization using analytic gradients
L114	EF numerical optimization (using only energies)
L115	Follows reaction path using the intrinsic reaction coordinate (IRC)
L116	Numerical self-consistent reaction field (SCRF)
L117	Post-SCF SCRF
L118	Trajectory calculations
L120	Controls ONIOM calculations
L202	Reorients coordinates, calculates symmetry, and checks variables
L301	Generates basis set information
L302	Calculates overlap, kinetic, and potential integrals
L303	Calculates multipole integrals
L308	Computes dipole velocity and $Rx\nabla$ integrals
L309	Computes ECP integrals
L310	Computes spdf 2-electron integrals in a primitive fashion
L311	Computes sp 2-electron integrals
L314	Computes spdf 2-electron integrals
L316	Prints 2-electron integrals
L319	Computes 1-electron integrals for approximate spin orbital coupling
L401	Forms the initial MO guess
L402	Performs semi-empirical and molecular mechanics calculations
L405	Initializes an MCSCF calculation
L502	Iteratively solves the SCF equations (conven. UHF & ROHF, all direct methods, SCRF)
L503	Iteratively solves the SCF equations using direct minimization
L506	Performs an ROHF or GVB-PP calculation
L508	Quadratically convergent SCF program
L510	MC-SCF
L601	Population and related analyses (including multipole moments)
L602	1-electron properties (potential, field, and field gradient)

Link	Function
L604	Evaluates MOs or density over a grid of points
L607	Performs NBO analyses
L608	Non-iterative DFT energies
L609	Atoms in Molecules properties
L701	1-electron integral first or second derivatives
L702	2-electron integral first or second derivatives (sp)
L703	2-electron integral first or second derivatives (spdf)
L709	Forms the ECP integral derivative contribution to gradients
L716	Processes information for optimizations and frequencies
L801	Initializes transformation of 2-electron integrals
L802	Performs integral transformation (N^3 in-core)
L803	Complete basis set (CBS) extrapolation
L804	Integral transformation
L811	Transforms integral derivatives & computes their contributions to MP2 2nd derivatives
L901	Anti-symmetrizes 2-electron integrals
L902	Determines the stability of the Hartree-Fock wavefunction
L903	Old in-core MP2
L905	Complex MP2
L906	Semi-direct MP2
L908	OVGF (closed shell)
L909	OVGF (open shell)
L913	Calculates post-SCF energies and gradient terms
L914	CI-Singles, RPA and Zindo excited states; SCF stability
L915	Computes fifth order quantities (for MP5, QCISD(TQ) and BD(TQ))
L918	Reoptimizes the wavefunction
L1002	Iteratively solves the CPHF equations; computes various properties (including NMR)
L1003	Iteratively solves the CP-MCSCF equations
L1014	Computes analytic CI-Singles second derivatives
L1101	Computes 1-electron integral derivatives
L1102	Computes dipole derivative integrals
L1110	2-electron integral derivative contribution to F^x
L1111	2 PDM and post-SCF derivatives
L1112	MP2 second derivatives
L9999	Finalizes calculation and output

3

Gaussian 98 Input

This chapter describes *Gaussian 98* input. The first section discusses input files in general, and the remainder of the chapter documents the available keywords and options.

Gaussian 98 input consists of a series of lines in an ASCII text file. The basic structure of a *Gaussian 98* input file includes several different sections:

Input File Section	Purpose	Blank-line Terminated?
Link 0 Commands	Locate and name scratch files	no
Route section (# lines)	Specify desired calculation type, model chemistry and other options	yes
Title section	Brief description of the calculation	yes
Molecule specification	Specify molecular system to be studied	yes
Optional additional sections	Input needed for specific job types	usually yes

Many *Gaussian 98* jobs will include only the second, third, and fourth sections. Here is an example of such a file, which requests a single point energy calculation on water:

```
# HF/6-31G(d)                                    Route section

water energy                                     Title section

0   1                                            Molecule specification
O  -0.464    0.177    0.0                         (in Cartesian coordinates)
H  -0.464    1.137    0.0
H   0.441   -0.143    0.0
```

In this job, the route and title sections each consist of a single line. The molecule specification section begins with a line giving the charge and spin multiplicity for the molecule: 0 charge (neutral molecule) and spin multiplicity 1 (singlet) in this case. The charge and spin multiplicity line is followed by lines describing the location of each atom in the molecule; this example uses Cartesian coordinates to do so. Molecule specifications are discussed in more detail later in this chapter.

The following input file illustrates the use of Link 0 commands and an additional input section:

```
%Chk=heavy                              Link 0 section
#HF/6-31G(d) Freq=ReadIsotopes          Route section

Heavy water frequencies                 Title section

0    1                                   Molecule Specification section
atomic coordinates ...

298.15    1.0                            Additional input section for the
  16                                     Freq=ReadIsotopes keyword
   2
   2
```

This job requests a frequency calculation on water using alternate isotopes for the hydrogen atoms. The job also specifies a name for the checkpoint file.

Link 0 commands were introduced in the last chapter and are discussed individually in the penultimate section of this chapter. The remaining input sections are discussed in the subsequent subsections of this introductory section. For convenience, the table on the following page lists all possible sections that might appear within a *Gaussian 98* input file, along with the keywords associated with each one.

General Input Syntax

In General, *Gaussian 98* input is subject to the following syntax rules:

♦ Input is free-format and case-insensitive.

♦ Spaces, tabs, commas, or forward slashes can be used in any combination to separate items within a line. Multiple spaces are treated as a single delimiter.

♦ Options to keywords may be specified in any of the following forms:

> *keyword = option*
> *keyword(option)*
> *keyword=(option1, option2, ...)*
> *keyword(option1, option2, ...)*

Multiple options are enclosed in parentheses and separated by any valid delimiter (commas are conventional and are shown above). The equals sign before the opening parenthesis may be omitted, or spaces may optionally be included before and/or after it.

Note that some options also take values; in this case, the option name is followed by an equals sign: for example, **CBSExtrap(NMin=6)**.

Gaussian 98 Input Section Ordering

Section	Keywords	Final blank-line?
Link 0 commands	% *commands*	no
Route Section (# lines)	*all*	yes
Extra Overlays	**ExtraOverlays**	yes
Title section	*all*	yes
Molecule specification	*all*	yes
Modifications to coordinates	**Opt=ModRedundant**	yes
Connectivity specifications	**Geom=Connect** *or* **ModConnect**	yes
2nd title[†] and molecule specification	**Opt=QST2** *or* **QST3**	yes
Modifications to 2nd set of coordinates	**Opt=ModRedun** *and* **QST2** *or* **QST3**	yes
Connectivity specifications for 2nd set of coordinates	**Geom=Connect** *or* **ModConnect** *and* **Opt=ModRedun** *and* **QST2** *or* **QST3**	yes
3rd title[†] and initial TS structure	**Opt=QST3**	yes
Modifications to 3rd set of coordinates	**Opt=(ModRedun, QST3)**	yes
Connectivity specifications for 3rd set of coordinates	**Geom=Connect** *or* **ModConnect** **Opt=(ModRedun, QST3)**	yes
Initial force constants (Cartesian)	**Opt=FCCards**	yes
Accuracy of energy & forces	**Opt=ReadError**	no
Trajectory input (multiple sections depending on options selected)	**Trajectory**	yes
Atomic masses	**IRC=ReadIsotopes**	yes
Basis set specification	**Gen, ExtraBasis**	yes
Basis set alterations	**Massage**	yes
ECP specification	**ExtraBasis, Pseudo=Cards**	yes
Background charge distribution	**Charge**	yes
Finite field coefficients	**Field=Read**	yes
Symmetry types to combine	**Guess=LowSymm**	no
Orbital specifications[‡]	**Guess=Cards**	yes
Orbital alterations[‡]	**Guess=Alter**	yes
Solvation model parameters	**SCRF**	no
PCM solvation model input	**SCRF=(PCM,Read)**	yes
Weights for CAS state averaging	**CASSCF=StateAverage**	no
States of interest for spin orbit coupling	**CASSCF=Spin**	no
# orbitals/GVB pair	**GVB**	no
Alternate atomic radii	**Pop=ReadRadii** *or* **ReadAtRadii**	yes
Data for electrostatic properties	**Prop=Read** *or* **Opt**	yes
Cube filename (& spec. for Cards option)	**Cube**	yes
NBO input	**Pop=NBORead**	no
Orbital freezing information	**ReadWindow** *option*	yes
OVGF obitals to refine	**R/UOVGF IOp(9/11=100)**	yes
Temperature, pressure, atomic masses	**Freq=ReadIsotopes**	no
PROAIMS wavefunction filename	**Output=WFN**	no

[†] A blank line also separates the second or third title section from the corresponding molecule specification.

[‡] UHF jobs use separate α and β sections (themselves separated by a blank line).

♦ All keywords and options may be shortened to their shortest unique abbreviation within the entire *Gaussian 98* system. Thus, the **Conventional** option may be abbreviated to **Conven**, but not to **Conv** (due to the presence of the **Convergence** option). This holds true whether or not both **Conventional** and **Convergence** happen to be valid options for any given keyword.

♦ The contents of an external file may be included within a *Gaussian 98* input file using the following syntax: *@filename*. This causes the entire file to be placed at the current location in the input stream. Appending **/N** to such commands will prevent the included file's contents from being echoed at the start of the output file.

♦ Comments begin with an exclamation point (!), which may appear anywhere on a line. Separate comment lines may appear anywhere within the input file.

Gaussian 98 Job Types

The route section of a *Gaussian 98* input file specifies the type of calculation to be performed. There are three key components to this specification:

♦ The job type
♦ The method
♦ The basis set

The following table lists the job types available in *Gaussian 98*:

Keyword	Type of Job
SP	Single point energy
Opt	Geometry optimization
Freq	Frequency and thermochemical analysis
IRC	Reaction path following
Scan	Potential energy surface scan
Polar	Polarizabilities and hyperpolarizabilities
Trajectory	Direct dynamics trajectory calculation
Force	Compute forces on the nuclei
Stable	Test wavefunction stability
Volume	Compute molecular volume
Density=Checkpoint	Recompute population analysis only
Guess=Only	Print initial guess only; recompute population analysis
ReArchive	Extract archive entry from checkpoint file only

In general, only *one* job type keyword should be specified. The exceptions to this rule are:

♦ **Polar** and **Opt** may be combined with **Freq** (although **SCRF** may not be combined with **Opt Freq**). In the latter case, the geometry optimization is automatically followed by a frequency calculation at the optimized structure.

◆ **Opt** may be combined with **IRCMax** in order to specify options for the optimization portion of the calculation.

When no job type keyword is specified within the route section, the default calculation type is usually a single point energy calculation (**SP**). However, in *Gaussian 98*, a route section of the form: *method2/basis2 // method1/basis1* may be used to request an optimization calculation (at *method1/basis1*) followed by a single point energy calculation (at *method2/basis2*) at the optimized geometry. For example, the following route section requests a HF/6-31G(d) geometry optimization followed by a single point energy calculation using the QCISD/6-31G(d) model chemistry:

```
# QCISD/6-31G(d)//HF/6-31G(d) Test
```

In this case, the **Opt** keyword is optional and is the default. Note that **Opt Freq** calculations may *not* use this syntax.

Predicting Molecular Properties

The following table provides a mapping between commonly-desired predicted quantities and the *Gaussian 98* keywords that will produce them:

Property	*Keyword*
Atomic charges	Pop, AIM
Atoms in Molecules properties	AIM
Bond order analysis	AIM
Dipole moment	Pop
Electron affinities via propagator methods	*OVGF
Electron density	Cube=Density
Electrostatic potential	Cube=Potential, Prop
Electrostatic-potential derived charges	Pop
High accuracy energies	G2, CBS-4, CBS-QB3, CBS-Q
Hyperfine coupling constants (anisotropic)	Prop
Hyperpolarizabilities	Freq, Polar
Ionization potentials via propagator methods	*OVGF
IR and Raman Spectra	Freq
Magnetic properties	NMR
Molecular orbitals	Pop=Regular
Multipole moments	Pop
NMR properties	NMR
Polarizabilities	Freq, Polar
Thermochemical analysis	Freq
UV/Visible spectra	CIS, Zindo, TD
Vibrational circular dichroism	Freq=VCD

Model Chemistries

The combination of method and basis set specifies a model chemistry to *Gaussian 98*, specifying the *level of theory*. Every *Gaussian 98* job must specify both a method and basis set. This is usually accomplished via two separate keywords within the route section of the input file, although a few method keywords imply a choice of basis set.

Methods

The following table lists methods which are available in *Gaussian 98*, along with the job types for which each one may be used. Note that the table lists only *analytic* optimizations, frequencies, and polarizability calculations; numerical calculations are often available for unchecked methods (see the discussion of the specific keyword in question for details).

Method Availabilities in *Gaussian 98*

	SP[a]	Opt[b]	Freq[c]	IRC	Traj	ONIOM	Polar	Stable
HF	∗	∗	∗	∗	∗	∗	∗	∗
CASSCF	∗	∗	∗	∗	∗		∗	
GVB	∗	∗		∗				
MP2	∗	∗	∗	∗		∗	∗	
MP3, MP4(SDQ)	∗	∗		∗		∗		
MP4(SDTQ)	∗					∗		
MP5	∗					∗		
CI	∗	∗		∗				
QCISD, CCD	∗	∗		∗		∗		
QCISD(T) or (TQ), CCSD	∗					∗		
BD	∗					∗		
*OVGF	∗							
Density Functional Methods	∗	∗	∗	∗	∗	∗	∗	∗
G1, G2, G2MP2	∗							
Complete Basis Set Methods	∗							
CIS	∗	∗	∗	∗			∗	
ZINDO, TD	∗							
Semi-Empirical Methods (ground state)	∗	∗	d	∗	∗	∗		
Molecular Mechanics Methods	∗	∗	d			∗		

[a] Note that the availability for **Scan** is the same as that for **SP**.

[b] Refers to the availability of analytic gradients. Note that the availability for **Force** and the IRC portion of **IRCMax** is the same as that for **Opt**.

[c] Refers to the availability of analytic second derivatives.

[d] Frequencies are computed numerically but options such as **Opt=CalcFC** are still valid.

If no method keyword is specified, **HF** is assumed. Most method keywords may be prefaced by **R** for closed-shell restricted wavefunctions, **U** for unrestricted open-shell wavefunctions, or **RO** for restricted open-shell wavefunctions: for example, **ROHF**, **UMP2**, or **RQCISD**. **RO** is available only for Hartree-Fock, all Density Functional methods, AM1, MINDO3 and MNDO semi-empirical energies and gradients, and MP2 energies; note that analytic **ROMP2** gradients are *not* yet available.

In general, *only a single method keyword should be specified*, and including more than one of them will produce *bizarre* results. However, there are exceptions:

♦ **CASSCF** may be specified along with **MP2** to request a CASSCF calculation including electron correlation.

♦ **ONIOM** and **IRCMax** jobs require multiple method specifications. However, they are given as options to the corresponding keyword.

♦ The form *model2 // model1* described previously may be used to generate an automatic **Opt+SP** computation.

Basis Sets

Most methods require a basis set be specified; if no basis set keyword is included in the route section, then the STO-3G basis will be used. The exceptions consist of a few methods for which the basis set is defined as an integral part of the method; they are listed below:

♦ All semi-empirical methods (including Zindo for excited states)
♦ All molecular mechanics methods
♦ **G1**, **G2** and **G2MP2**
♦ **CBS-4**, **CBS-Lq**, **CBS-Q**, **CBS-QB3** and **CBS-APNO**

The following basis sets are stored internally in the *Gaussian 98* program (see references cited for full descriptions), listed below by their corresponding *Gaussian 98* keyword (with two exceptions):

♦ **STO-3G** [211, 212]
♦ **3-21G** [213-218]
♦ **6-21G** [213, 214]
♦ **4-31G** [219-222]
♦ **6-31G** [219-224]
♦ 6-31G†: *Gaussian 98* also includes the 6-31G† and 6-31G†† basis sets of George Petersson and coworkers, defined as part of the Complete Basis Set methods [89, 225]. These are accessed via the **6-31G(d')** and **6-31G(d',p')** keywords, to which single or double diffuse functions may also be added.
♦ 6-311G: Specifies the 6-311G basis for first-row atoms and the McLean-Chandler (12s,9p) → (621111,52111) basis sets for second-row atoms [226, 227] (note that the basis sets for P, S, and Cl are those called "negative ion" basis sets by McLean and Chandler; these were deemed to give better results for neutral molecules as well), the Wachters-Hay

[228, 229] all electron basis set for the first transition row, using the scaling factors of Raghavachari and Trucks [230], and the 6-311G basis set of McGrath, Curtiss and coworkers for the other elements in the third row [224, 231, 232]. Note that Raghavachari and Trucks recommend both scaling and including diffuse functions when using the Wachters-Hay basis set for first transition row elements; the **6-311+G** form must be specified to include the diffuse functions. MC-311G is a synonym for **6-311G.**

♦ **D95V**: Dunning/Huzinaga valence double-zeta [233].

♦ **D95**: Dunning/Huzinaga full double zeta [233].

♦ **SHC**: D95V on first row, Goddard/Smedley ECP on second row [233, 234]. Also known as **SEC**.

♦ **CEP-4G**: Stevens/Basch/Krauss ECP minimal basis [235-237].

♦ **CEP-31G**: Stevens/Basch/Krauss ECP split valance [235-237].

♦ **CEP-121G**: Stevens/Basch/Krauss ECP triple-split basis [235-237].
  Note that there is only one CEP basis set defined beyond the second row, and all three keywords are equivalent for these atoms.

♦ **LanL2MB**: STO-3G [211, 212] on first row, Los Alamos ECP plus MBS on Na-Bi [238-240].[†]

♦ **LanL2DZ**: D95 on first row [233], Los Alamos ECP plus DZ on Na-Bi [238-240].

♦ **SDD**: **D95V** on the first row [233] and Stuttgart/Dresden ECP's on the remainder of the periodic table [241-264].

♦ **SDDAll**: Selects Stuttgart potentials for Z > 2.

♦ **cc-pVDZ, cc-pVTZ, cc-pVQZ, cc-pV5Z, cc-pV6Z**: Dunning's correlation consistent basis sets [265-269] (double, triple, quadruple, quintuple-zeta and sextuple-zeta, respectively). These basis sets have had redundant functions removed and have been rotated [270] in order to increase computational efficiency. As so altered, they produce identical energetic results to the **cc*** basis sets in *Gaussian 94*.

These basis sets include polarization functions by definition. The following table lists the valence polarization functions present for the various atoms included in these basis sets:

Atoms	cc-pVDZ	cc-pVTZ	cc-pVQZ	cc-pV5Z	cc-pV6Z
H	2s,1p	3s,2p,1d	4s,3p,2d,1f	5s,4p,3d,2f,1g	6s,5p,4d,3f,2g,1h
He	2s,1p	3s,2p,1d	4s,3p,2d,1f	5s,4p,3d,2f,1g	*not available*
B-Ne	3s,2p,1d	4s,3p,2d,1f	5s,4p,3d,2f,1g	6s,5p,4d,3f,2g,1h	7s,6p,5d,4f,3g,2h,1i
Al-Ar	4s,3p,1d	5s,4p,2d,1f	6s,5p,3d,2f,1g	7s,6p,4d,3f,2g,1h	*not available*

These basis sets may be augmented with diffuse functions by adding the **AUG-** prefix to the basis set keyword (rather than using the + and ++ notation—see below). However, the elements He, Mg, Li, Be, and Na do not have diffuse functions defined within these basis sets.

♦ **Dcc-pVDZ** and **Dcc-pVTZ**: Dunning's correlation consistent basis sets as above using Davidson's contraction scheme [270] and reduces the number of primitives in the s and p contracted functions. Energies computed with these basis sets will differ slightly from those computed with the corresponding standard **cc** basis set.

♦ **SV, SVP** and **TZV** of Ahlrichs and coworkers [271, 272].

♦ MIDI! of Truhlar and coworkers [273]. The **MidiX** keyword is used to request this basis set.

[†] *Gaussian 98* also includes the **LanL1MB** and **LanL1DZ** basis sets. However, their use is strongly discouraged.

♦ **EPR-II** and **EPR-III**: The basis sets of Barone [274] which are optimized for the computation of hyperfine coupling constants by DFT methods (particularly B3LYP). EPR-II is a double zeta basis set with a single set of polarization functions and an enhanced s part: (6,1)/[4,1] for H and (10,5,1)/[6,2,1] for B to F. EPR-III is a triple-zeta basis set including diffuse functions, double d-polarizations and a single set of f-polarization functions. Also in this case the s-part is improved to better describe the nuclear region: (6,2)/[4,2] for H and (11,7,2,1)/[7,4,2,1] for B to F.

Adding Polarization and Diffuse Functions

Single first polarization functions can also be requested using the usual * or ** notation. Note that (**d,p**) and ** are synonymous—**6-31G**** is equivalent to **6-31G(d,p)**, for example—and that the 3-21G* basis set has polarization functions on second row atoms only. The + and ++ diffuse functions [275] are available with some basis sets, as are multiple polarization functions [276]. The keyword syntax is best illustrated by example: **6-31+G(3df,2p)** designates the 6-31G basis set supplemented by diffuse functions, 3 sets of d functions and one set of f functions on heavy atoms, and supplemented by 2 sets of p functions on hydrogens.

When the **AUG-** prefix is used to add diffuse functions to the **cc-pV*Z** basis sets, one diffuse function of each function type in use for a given atom is added [265, 266]. For example, the **AUG-cc-pVTZ** basis places one s, one d, and one p diffuse functions on hydrogen atoms, and one d, one p, one d, and one f diffuse functions on B through Ne and Al through Ar.

Adding a single polarization function to **6-311G** (i.e. **6-311G(d)**) will result in one d function for first and second row atoms and one f function for first transition row atoms, since d functions are already present for the valence electrons in the latter. Similarly, adding a diffuse function to the **6-311G** basis set will produce one s, one p, and one d diffuse functions for third-row atoms.

When a frozen-core calculation is done using the **D95** basis, both the occupied core orbitals and the corresponding virtual orbitals are frozen. Thus while a **D95**** calculation on water has 26 basis functions, and a **6-31G**** calculation on the same system has 25 functions, there will be 24 orbitals used in a frozen-core post-SCF calculation involving either basis set.

The following table lists polarization and diffuse function availability and the range of applicability for each built-in basis set in *Gaussian 98*:

Basis Set	*Applies To*	*Polarization Functions*	*Diffuse Functions*
STO–3G	H-Xe	*	
3-21G	H-Xe	* *or* **	+
6-21G	H-Cl	(**d**)	
4-31G	H-Ne	(**d**) or (**d,p**)	
6-31G	H-Kr	(**3df,3pd**)	++
6-311G	H-Kr	(**3df,3pd**)	++
D95	H-Cl[†]	(**3df,3pd**)	++
D95V	H-Ne	(**d**) *or* (**d,p**)	++

Basis Set	Applies To	Polarization Functions	Diffuse Functions
SHC	H-Cl	*	
CEP-4G	H-Rn	*	
CEP-31G	H-Rn	*	
CEP-121G	H-Rn	*	
LanL2MB	H-Ba, La-Bi		
LanL2DZ	H, Li-Ba, La-Bi		
SDD, SDDAll	all but Fr and Ra		
cc–pV{DTQ5}Z Dcc-pV{DT}Z	H-He, B-Ne, Al-Ar	included in definition	added via AUG– prefix
cc-pV6Z	H, B-Ne	included in definition	added via AUG– prefix
SV	H-Kr		
SVP	H-Kr	included in definition	
TZV	H-Kr	(3df,3pd)	
MidiX	H, C, N, O, F, P, S, Cl	included in definition	
EPR-II,III	H, B, C, N, O, F	included in definition	

† Na and Mg are not included for this basis set.

Additional Basis Set-Related Keywords

The following additional keywords are useful in conjunction with these basis set keywords:

♦ **5D** and **6D**: Use 5 or 6 d functions (pure vs. Cartesian d functions), respectively.

♦ **7F** and **10F**: Use 7 or 10 f functions (pure vs. Cartesian f functions), respectively. These keywords also apply to all higher functions (g and beyond).

Other basis sets may also be input to the program using the **ExtraBasis** and **Gen** keywords. The **ChkBasis** keyword indicates that the basis set is to read from the checkpoint file (defined via the **%Chk** command). See the individual descriptions of these keywords later in this chapter for details.

Issues Arising from Pure vs. Cartesian Basis Functions

Gaussian users should be aware of the following points concerning pure vs. Cartesian basis functions:

♦ All of the built-in basis sets use pure f functions. Most also use pure d functions; the exceptions are 3-21G, 6-21G, 4-31G, 6-31G, 6-31G†, 6-31G††, D95 and D95V. The preceding keywords may be used to override the default pure/Cartesian setting. Note that basis functions are generally converted to the other type automatically when necessary, for example, when a wavefunction is read from the checkpoint file for use in a calculation using a basis consisting of the other type [277].

♦ Cartesian and pure functions of the same angular momentum (i.e., d vs f and higher) may not be mixed within a single calculation in *Gaussian 98*.

♦ When using the **ExtraBasis** and **Gen** keywords, the basis set explicitly specified in the route section *always* determines the default form of the basis functions (for **Gen**, these are **5D** and **7F**). For example, if you use a general basis set taking some functions from the 3-21G and 6-31G basis sets, pure functions will be used unless you explicitly specify **6D** in the route section in addition to **Gen**. Similarly, if you add basis functions for a transition metal from the 6-311G(d) basis set via **ExtraBasis** to a job that specifies the 6-31G(d) basis set in the route section, Cartesian d functions will be used. Likewise, if you want to add basis functions for Xe from the 3-21G basis set to the 6-311 basis set via the **ExtraBasis** keyword, the Xe basis functions will be pure functions.

The Job Title Section

This section is required in the input, but is not interpreted in any way by the *Gaussian 98* program. It appears in the output for purposes of identification and description. Typically, this section might contain the compound name, its symmetry, the electronic state, and any other relevant information. The title section cannot exceed five lines and must be followed by a terminating blank line. Since archive entries resulting from calculations using a general basis set or the **ReadWindow** keyword do not contain the original input data for these options, it is strongly recommended that the title sections for these jobs include a complete description of the basis set or frozen-core selection used.

The following characters should be avoided in the title section, especially if the *Browse Quantum Chemistry Database System* is in use: @ # ! – _ \ all control characters, and *especially* ^G.

Overview of Molecule Specifications

This input section specifies the nuclear positions and the number of electrons of α- and β-spin. There are several ways in which the nuclear configuration can be specified: as a Z-matrix, as Cartesian coordinates, or as a mixture of the two (note that Cartesian coordinates are just a special case of the Z-matrix).

The first line of the molecule specification section specifies the net electric charge (a signed integer) and the spin multiplicity (a positive integer). Thus, for a neutral molecule in a singlet state, the entry **0 1** is appropriate. For a radical anion, **-1 2** would be used. This is the only molecule specification input required if **Geom=CheckPoint** is used. The entire molecule specification (and title section) may be omitted by including **Geom=AllCheck** in the route section.

The remainder of the molecule specification gives the element type and nuclear position for each atom in the molecular system. The lines within it usually have one of these forms:

Element-label, x, y, z
Element-label, atom 1, bond-length, atom 2, bond-angle, atom 3, dihedral-angle

Although these examples use commas to separate items within a line, any valid separator may be used. The first form specifies the atom in Cartesian coordinates, while the second uses internal coordinates. Lines of both types may appear within the same molecular specification.

Element-label is a character string consisting of either the chemical symbol for the atom or its atomic number. If the elemental symbol is used, it may be optionally followed by other alphanumeric characters to create an identifying label for that atom. A common practice is to follow the element name with a secondary identifying integer: C1, C2, C3, and so on; this technique is useful in following conventional chemical numbering.

In the first form, the remaining items on each line are Cartesian coordinates specifying the position of that nucleus. In the second form, *atom1, atom2, atom3* are the labels for previously-specified atoms which will be used to define the current atoms' position (alternatively, the other atoms' line numbers within the molecule specification section may be used for the values of variables, where the charge and spin multiplicity line is line 0).

The position of the current atom is then specified by giving the length of the bond joining it to *atom1*, the angle formed by this bond and the bond joining *atom1* and *atom2*, and the dihedral (torsion) angle formed by the bond joining *atom2* and *atom3* with the plane containing the current atom, *atom1* and *atom2*.

Here are two molecule specification sections for ethane:

```
0    1                                    0,1
C    0.00    0.00    0.00                 C1
C    0.00    0.00    1.52                 C2,C1,1.5
H    1.02    0.00   -0.39                 H3,C1,1.1,C2,111.2
H   -0.51   -0.88   -0.39                 H4,C1,1.1,C2,111.2,H3,120.
H   -0.51    0.88   -0.39                 H5,C1,1.1,C2,111.2,H3,-120.
H   -1.02    0.00    1.92                 H6,C2,1.1,C1,111.2,H3,180.
H    0.51   -0.88    1.92                 H7,C2,1.1,C1,111.2,H6,120.
H    0.51    0.88    1.92                 H8,C2,1.1,C1,111.2,H6,-120.
```

The version on the left uses Cartesian coordinates while the one on the right represents a sample Z-matrix (illustrating element labels). Note that the first three atoms within the Z-matrix do not use the full number of parameters; only at the fourth atom are there enough previously-defined atoms for all of the parameters to be specified.

Here is another Z-matrix form for this same molecule:

```
0    1
C1
C2    C1    RCC
H3    C1    RCH    C2    ACCH
H4    C1    RCH    C2    ACCH    H3    120.
H5    C1    RCH    C2    ACCH    H3   -120.
H6    C2    RCH    C1    ACCH    H3    180.
H7    C2    RCH    C1    ACCH    H6    120.
H8    C2    RCH    C1    ACCH    H6   -120.
      Variables:
RCH  = 1.5
RCC  = 1.1
ACCH = 111.2
```

In this Z-matrix, the literal bond lengths and angle values have been replaced with variables. The values of the variables are given in a separate section following the specification of the final atom. Variable definitions are separated from the atom position definitions by a blank line or a line like the following:

```
Variables:
```

This Z-matrix form may be used at any time, and it is required as the starting structure for a geometry optimization using internal coordinates (i.e., **Opt=Z-matrix**). In the latter case, the variables indicate the items to be optimized; see the examples for the **Opt** keyword for more details.

The preceding discussion is designed to present only a basic overview of molecule specification options. See Appendix B for additional details on Z-matrix construction.

Molecule specifications for molecular mechanics calculations may also include atom typing information. See the discussion of the "Molecular Mechanics Methods" later in this chapter for details.

Multi-Step Jobs

Multiple *Gaussian 98* jobs may be combined within a single input file. The input for each successive job is separated from that of the preceding job step by a line of the form:

```
--Link1--
```

Here is an example input file containing two job steps:

```
%Chk=freq
# HF/6-31G(d) Freq

Frequencies at STP
```

Molecule specification

```
--Link1--
%Chk=freq
%NoSave
# HF/6-31G(d) Geom=AllCheck Guess=Read Freq=(ReadFC,ReadIsotopes)

300.0  2.0
```
Isotope specifications

This input file computes vibrational frequencies and performs thermochemical analysis at two different temperatures and pressures: first at 298.15 K and 1 atmosphere, and then again at 300 K and 2 atmospheres. Note that a blank line *must* precede the **--Link1--** line.

Gaussian 98 Keywords

This section discusses the available *Gaussian 98* keywords and their options. Keywords are generally arranged in alphabetical order, with the following exceptions:

♦ Basis set keywords are not present; see the preceding section on basis sets for information about available basis sets and their associated keywords. Note, however, that the **ChkBasis**, **ExtraBasis**, **Gen**, and **Pseudo** keywords *are* discussed in this section.

♦ All DFT-related keywords are collected under the heading **DFT Methods**.

♦ Link 0 commands are placed after all alphabetic keywords (i.e., following the discussion of **ZINDO**), forming the penultimate section of this chapter.

♦ Keywords related to specifying alternate routes—**ExtraLinks**, **ExtraOverlays**, **NonStd**, **Skip**, and **Use**—are discussed in the final section of this chapter, "Specifying Nonstandard Routes." Related information is also presented in the discussion of the **testrt** utility in chapter 5.

Within the discussion of a specific keyword, options are listed in order of importance and frequency of use, rather than in strictly alphabetical order.

 #

DESCRIPTION
The route section of a *Gaussian 98* job is initiated by a pound sign (#) as the first non-blank character of a line. The remainder of the section is in free-field format. For most jobs, all of the information can be placed on this first line, but overflow to other lines (which may but need not begin with a # symbol) is permissible. The route section must be terminated by a blank line.

If no keywords are present in the route section, the calculation defaults to **HF/STO-3G SP**.

ALTERNATE FORMS
#N	Normal print level; this is the default.
#P	Additional output is generated. This includes messages at the beginning and end of each link giving assorted machine-dependent information (including execution timing data), as well as convergence information in the SCF.
#T	Terse output: output is reduced to essential information and results.

➤ AIM

DESCRIPTION

The **AIM** properties keyword may be used to request molecular properties predicted via the theory of Atoms in Molecules [179] and extensions thereto; the implementation in *Gaussian 98* is due to Cioslowski and coworkers [180-183, 278-281], and these workers should be cited in papers using this method. By default, the **AIM** keyword computes Atom in Molecules atomic charges. Its various options may be specified to request other or additional properties.

The use of **AIM** implies **SCF(Conver=8)**. On non-Hartree-Fock jobs, use **Density=Current** to specify the density of the specified method as the one desired for analysis (the default without this keyword is the SCF density).

OPTIONS

Charges   Compute atomic charges only.

AtomicProp   Compute atomic properties: atomic charges, dipole moments, kinetic energy, and traceless quadrupole moments. This option may be abbreviated as **AP**. This is the default mode of operation.

BondOrders   Compute covalent bond orders, localized orbitals, and atomic charges, but no other atomic properties. This option may be abbreviated as **BO**. This option implies **Tight** as well.

CriticalPoints   Compute critical points only. This option may be abbreviated as **CP**.

AtomicSurfaces   Compute atomic surfaces only. This option may be abbreviated as **AS**.

All   Compute all available properties.

Tight   Compute results to higher numerical accuracy.

RELATED KEYWORDS
SCF(Conver), Population, Density

AVAILABLILTY
Basis sets used with **AIM=Tight** may contain only s, p, and d functions.

EXAMPLES
The following route section illustrates the use of the **AIM** keyword:

```
#P UMP2/6-31G* Density=Current AIM=All
```

We will consider selections from the output that would result from the preceding route section. The output from the **AIM** keyword, which follows the population analysis section, begins with this banner:

```
--------------------------------------------------------------------
This link is based on concepts and algorithms described in:
CPL 219 (1994) 151,   CPL 203 (1993) 137,    CPL 194 (1992) 73,
JACS 114 (1992) 4392, THEOCHEM 255 (1992) 9, JACS 113 (1991) 4142,
IJQC S24 (1990) 15.  Additional citations required when reporting results from this feature.

Alpha and beta electrons analyzed separately.          Indicates an open shell calc.
...
*************************************************************************

       Properties of atoms in molecules using the MP2 density.

*************************************************************************
```

The first section of the **AIM** output lists the *attractors* (they usually correspond to atomic nuclei):

I. ATTRACTORS

```
-----------------------------------------------------------------------
Attr.  Cartesian Coords     Nucleus             Density
        X      Y      Z    (Distance)       Total        Spin
-----------------------------------------------------------------------
  1   0.00   2.12  -1.31  F  (0.000006)   0.41922E+03  -.31228E-01
  2   0.00   0.00   0.30  C  (0.000009)   0.11765E+03  -.89128E-01
  3   0.00   0.00   2.71  O  (0.000009)   0.29086E+03  -.71134E-01
  4   0.00  -2.12  -1.31  F  (0.000006)   0.41922E+03  -.31228E-01
-----------------------------------------------------------------------
```

The atom corresponding to each attractor is given in the fifth column, following the Cartesian coordinates of the attractor. Attractor numbers must be used to identify "atoms" throughout the rest of the **AIM** output.

Section II of the AIM output lists critical points and zero-flux (atomic) surfaces for the molecular system. Section III reports atomic properties. Here is the portion which gives atomic charges:

```
---------------------------------------------------------------
Attr.      Number of electrons          Charge
            total          spin
---------------------------------------------------------------
  1        9.680777      -0.063631      -0.680777
  2        4.404421      -0.612270       1.595579      carbon atom
  3        9.233734      -0.260448      -1.233734      oxygen atom
  4        9.680777      -0.063631      -0.680777
---------------------------------------------------------------
Total   32.999709      -0.999981      -0.999709      overall molecule
---------------------------------------------------------------
```

Other atomic properties follow the charges in section III. The final section (IV) of the **AIM** output lists localized orbitals and covalent bond orders. Here are the covalent bond orders for this molecule (derived from the atomic overlap matrix):

```
******* AOM-Derived covalent bond orders (all electrons) *******
-------------------------------------------------
          F  1      C  2      O  3      F  4
-------------------------------------------------
   F  1   9.00567
   C  2   0.74634   2.87410
   O  3   0.13843   1.33411   8.23439
   F  4   0.13328   0.74634   0.13843   9.00567
-------------------------------------------------
```

To determine the predicted bond order for a given bond of interest, find the entry for the intersection of the two atoms in this table, selecting the column corresponding to the lower of the two attractor numbers, and the row for the other attractor. For example, the predicted bond order for the C-O bond in this molecule is given as the second number in the column labelled **C 2**: 1.33411.

LIMITATIONS

The current code virtually always results in errors in atomic charges of less than $2.0*10^{-4}$ per atom. In practice, the errors are usually much smaller, varying between $1.0*10^{-5}$ and $5.0*10^{-5}$. The L values are usually between 10^{-4} and 10^{-5}.

When the **AIM** code fails, it is usually for one of the following reasons:

♦ The electron density has a very unusual topology. The algorithm can handle non-nuclear attractors, but cannot handle bond lines connecting ring points (instead of attractors). When there is some trouble of this sort (e.g. B_2H_6 at some levels of theory), the program terminates with the message: **THE HOPF-POINCARE RELATION CANNOT BE SATISFIED.**

♦ When molecules with rings and cages have atoms with *very* curved surfaces (again indicating that the electron density has a very unusual topology: for example, nitrocyclopropane at the MP2/6-31+G(d) level of theory). In such cases, the program terminates with the message: **NEWTON-RAPHSON STEP FAILED.** This indicates that the atomic surface sheet cannot be determined due to iterative divergence.

♦ When the zero-flux surfaces are curved strongly enough to generate a very large number of rays (> 100,000). This sort of problem is seen very occasionally with some C-F and B-F bonds; such jobs fail with the message: **TOO MANY INTEGRATION DOMAINS.**

➤ AM1

DESCRIPTION
This method keyword requests a semi-empirical calculation using the AM1 Hamiltonian [41, 46, 47, 51, 52]. No basis set keyword should be specified.

AVAILABILITY
Energies, "analytic" gradients, and numerical frequencies.

EXAMPLES
The AM1 energy appears in the output file as follows (followed by the x, y, and z components of the dipole moment):

```
Energy=    -.091965532835 NIter=  10.
Dipole moment=    .000000    .000000  -.739540
```

The energy is as defined by the AM1 model. Note that energy differences computed from the values in semi-empirical calculations are in Hartrees and may be compared directly with energy differences computed from jobs using other methods.

➤ AMBER

See **Molecular Mechanics Methods** *below.*

➤ Archive

DESCRIPTION
This keyword directs *Gaussian 98* to place the results from the calculation into the site archive (results database) if the job completes successfully. The **GAUSS_ARCHDIR** environment variable specifies the location of the archive files. Refer to the *Browse Quantum Chemistry Database System User's Guide* for information on making use of the archive entries. The **Test** keyword may be used to suppress automatic archiving. In this case, archive entries are still listed at the end of the output file (from which they may be extracted at a later time if desired). **NoTest** is a synonym for **Archive**.

Not all job types may be archived. See the discussion of the individual keywords for such limitations. Archiving is also disabled by default whenever the **IOp** keyword is used to set internal program options; the **Archive** keyword can override this.

RELATED KEYWORDS
Rearchive, Test

EXAMPLES
Here is a sample archive entry, as it appears at the conclusion of a *Gaussian 98* output file:

```
1\1\GINC-DALTON\SP\RHF\STO-3G\H2O1\GWTRUCKS\24-Oct-1994\0\\#T TEST
POP=NONE\\Water single point energy\\0,1\O\H,1,1.\H,1,1.,2,120.\\V
ersion=IBM-RS6000-G98RevA.1\HF=-74.9490523\RMSD=5.447e-04\PG=C02V
[C2(O1),SGV (H2)]\\@
```

The lines of the archive entry are wrapped without regard to word breaks. Fields within the archive entry are separated by backslashes, sections are separated by multiple backslashes, and the entry ends with an at sign (@). The archive entry records the site, user, date, and program version used for the calculation, as well as the route section and the title section for the job. It also contains the molecule specification or optimized geometry and all of the calculation's essential results. Note, however, that it does not include quantities which can be rapidly recomputed from them (such as thermochemistry results for a frequency calculation).

For those job types which cannot be archived, the following line will appear in the output file in place of the archive entry:

```
This type of calculation cannot be archived.
```


➤ BD

DESCRIPTION
This method keyword requests a Brueckner Doubles calculation [71, 72].

OPTIONS

T   Requests a Brueckner Doubles calculation with a triples contribution [71] added. **BD-T** is a synonym for **BD(T)**.

TQ   Requests a Brueckner Doubles calculation with triples and quadruples contributions [62] added.

FC   This indicates "frozen-core," and it implies that inner-shells are excluded from the correlation calculation. This is the default calculation mode. **Full** specifies the inclusion of all electrons, and **RW** and **Window** allow you to input specific information about which orbitals to retain in the post-SCF calculation (see the discussion of the **MPn** keywords for an example).

MaxCyc=n   Specifies the maximum number of cycles.

AVAILABILITY

Analytic energies, numerical gradients, and numerical frequencies.

EXAMPLES

The BD energy appears in the output labeled E(CORR), following the final correlation iteration:

```
DE(CORR)=  -.55299518D-01    E(CORR)=      -.75019628089D+02
```

The energy is given in Hartrees. If triples (or triples and quadruples) were requested, the energy including these corrections appears after the above:

```
Brueckner Doubles with Triples and Quadruples (BD(TQ))
========================================================
Saving the triples amplitudes on disk, using 192 words of disk.
   T4(aaa)=    .00000000D+00
   T4(aab)=   -.40349028D-04
   T4(abb)=   -.40349028D-04
   T4(bbb)=    .00000000D+00
Time for triples=           .10 seconds.
Disk space used for TT scratch files  :          512 words
E5TTaaa =     .00000000D+00
E5TTaab =    -.12350750D-04
E5TTabb =    -.12350750D-04
E5TTbbb =     .00000000D+00
E5TT     =   -.24701500D-04
E5TQ2    =    .68473650D-05
EQQ2     =   -.44495423D-04
DE5   =  -.62349557751D-04 BD(TQ)    =   -.75019771137D+02
```

The section gives information about the computation of the non-iterative triples and quadruples correction. The final energy appears in the last line, labeled BD(TQ).

➤ **B1B96**
➤ **B1LYP**
➤ **B3LYP**
➤ **B3PW91**
➤ **B96**
➤ **BLYP**

See **DFT Methods** below.

➤ CASSCF

DESCRIPTION

This method keyword requests a Complete Active Space Multiconfiguration SCF (MC-SCF) [94, 95, 116, 117, 155, 282]. An MC-SCF calculation is a combination of an SCF computation with a full CI involving a subset of the orbitals; this subset is known as the *active space*. The number of electrons (N) and the number of orbitals (M) in the active space for a CASSCF *must* be specified following the keyword: **CASSCF**(N,M). Note that options may be interspersed with N and M in any order.

By default, the active space is defined assuming that the electrons come from the highest occupied orbitals in the initial guess determinant and that the remaining orbitals required for the active space come from the lowest virtuals of the initial guess. Thus, for a 4-electron, 6-orbital CAS—specified as **CASSCF(4,6)**—on a closed-shell system, the active space would consist of:

♦ Enough occupied orbitals from the guess to provide 4 electrons. Thus, the 2 highest occupied MOs would be included.

♦ Enough virtual orbitals to make a total of 6 orbitals. Since 2 occupied orbitals were included, the lowest 4 virtual orbitals would become part of the active space.

Similarly, a 4 electron, 6 orbital CAS on a triplet would include the highest 3 occupied orbitals (one of which is doubly occupied and two singly occupied in the guess determinant) and the lowest 3 virtual orbitals. In *Gaussian 98*, algorithmic improvements make an active space of up to about 12 orbitals feasible [97, 98]. Above 8 orbitals, the CASSCF code automatically uses this new direct method for matrix elements.

Normally, **Guess=Alter** is necessary to ensure that the orbitals which are selected involve the electrons of interest and that they are correlated correctly. A prior run with **Guess=Only** can be used to quickly determine the orbital symmetries (see the first example below). Alternatively, a full Hartree-Fock single point calculation may be done, and the subsequent job will include (**Guess=Read,Alter**) in order to retrieve and then modify the computed initial guess from the checkpoint file. You need to include **Pop=Regular** in the route section of the preliminary job in order to include the orbital coefficient information in the output (use **Pop=Full** for cases where you need to examine more than just the few lowest virtual orbitals). You may also choose to view the orbitals in a visualization package.

By default, CASSCF calculations use a direct algorithm to avoid disk storage of integrals. A conventional algorithm may be selected by including **SCF=Conven** in the route section.

CAS is a synonym for **CASSCF**.

Use **#P** in the route section to include the final eigenvalues and eigenvectors in addition to the energy and one-electron density matrix in the CASSCF output.

A brief overview of the CASSCF method is given in chapter 9 (exercises 5 and 6) and appendix A of *Exploring Chemistry with Electronic Structure Methods* [210]. See reference [117] for a detailed discussion on the choice of an active space. See chapter 5 for a discussion of efficiency considerations for CASSCF calculations.

Note: CASSCF is a powerful but advanced method with many subtleties. We strongly recommend that you study the cited references before attempting to run production CASSCF calculations (this is especially true for **CASSCF MP2**). Example applications are discussed in references [283-289].

VARIATIONS

♦ An MP2-level electron correlation correction to the CASSCF energy may be computed during a CASSCF calculation by specifying the **MP2** keyword in addition to **CASSCF** within the route section [96].

♦ Calculations on excited states of molecular systems may be requested using the **NRoot** option. Note that a value of 1 specifies the ground state, not the first excited state (in contrast to usage with the **CIS** keyword).

♦ State-averaged CASSCF calculations may be performed using the **StateAverage** and **NRoot** options to specify the states to be used.

♦ Conical intersections and avoided crossings may be computed by including **Opt=Conical** in the route section of a CASSCF job (see the examples) [139-141].

♦ Approximate spin orbit coupling between two spin states can be computed during CASSCF calculations by including the **Spin** option [191-195]. The method used in *Gaussian 98* is based on reference [195]. It is available for the elements H through Cl.

In order to compute the spin orbit coupling, the integrals are computed in a one-electron approximation involving relativistic terms, and then effective charges are used that scale the Z value for each atom to empirically account for 2 electron effects. Note that such calculations will be state-averaged by default, using the state specified by the **NRoot** option (or the ground state by default), and the next higher state.

OPTIONS

NRoot=j Requests that the jth root of the CI be used, so that an excited state is obtained when $j > 1$. The option defaults to the ground state ($j=1$). The state specified by **NRoot** is referred to as the "state of interest."

StateAverage Used to specify a state-averaged CASSCF calculation. All states up to **NRoot** are averaged. This option requires the weighting for the various states to be input in format nF10.8 (no trailing blank line). **StateAverage** is not allowed in combination with **Opt=Conical** or **CASSCF=Spin**, both of which perform state-averaged calculations by default.

Spin Compute approximate spin orbit coupling between the two states, specified on a single additional input line (no following blank line). Implies a state-averaged CASSCF calculation. Spin orbit coupling may be computed for the elements H through Cl only.

OrbLocal[=n] Localize the first n strongly-occupied orbitals (the default is to localize all active orbitals).

DavidsonDiag   Requests the use of the Davidson diagonalization method for the CI matrix instead of the Lanczos iterations. Lanczos is the default for **NRoot** values of 1 or 2; otherwise, Davidson is the default.

FullDiag   Requests the use of the full (Jacobi) diagonalization method for the CI matrix instead of Lanczos or Davidson iterations. The default is full diagonalization if there are 6 or fewer active orbitals. **NoFullDiag** suppresses the use of the full diagonalization method.

The full Jacobi diagonalization method must be used if quadratic converence is required (see the **QC** option below), and when one knows nothing at all about the CI eigenvector (in the latter case, specify **FullDiag** for calculations involving more than 6 active orbitals)

StateGuess=k Set the starting vector for the Lanczos method to configuration k. For example, this option can be useful for selecting a configuration of the correct symmetry for a desired excited state (different from that of the ground state). In such cases, running a preliminary calculation to determine the orbital symmetries may be required.

k may also be set to the special value **Read**, which says to read in the entire eigenvector from the input stream (format: N_Z, $(Ind(I), C(Ind(I)), I=1, N_Z)$).

The default diagonalization method is most efficient if the size of the CI problem is greater than about 50, or the user can identify one or more dominant components in the eigenvector from the onset of the calculation, via the initial trail vector. By default, the starting vector is initialized in $j+1$ positions, where j is the value given to the **NRoot** option (or its default value). The positions correspond to the lowest $j+1$ energy diagonal elements of the CI Hamiltonian. This usually results in good convergence for the lowest j roots.

The **StateGuess** option (below) may be used to change this default. **CASSCF**(...,**StateGuess=**k) sets $C(k)$ to 1.0. The central requirement for this vector is that it not be deficient in the eigenvector that is required. Thus, if the CI eigenvector is dominated by configuration k, setting the **StateGuess** option to k will generate a good starting vector (e.g., **StateGuess=1** is appropriate if the CI vector is dominated by the SCF wavefunction). However, if the coefficient of configuration k is exactly zero (e.g., by symmetry) in the desired root, then that eigenvector will be missing, and the calculation will converge to a higher state.

OrbRot   **OrbRot** includes and **NoCPMCSCF** excludes the orbital rotation derivative contributions from the CP-MC-SCF equations in an **Opt=Conical** calculation. **OrbRot** is the default.

SlaterDet   Use Slater determinants in the CASSCF calculation. This option is needed to locate a conical intersection/avoided crossing between a singlet state and a triplet state.

HWDet   Use Hartree-Waller determinants instead of Slater. This is the default for CAS calculations involving 10 or more orbitals. It implies **NoFullDiag**.

RFO	Requests the RFO quadratic step. At most, one of **QC** and **RFO** should be specified.
QC	Requests a quadratically convergent algorithm for the CAS. This option should be used with caution; it works well only with a very good guess. Only one of **QC** and **RFO** should be specified.
UNO	Requests that the initial orbitals for the CAS be produced from the natural orbitals generated from a previous UHF calculation [290, 291]. Normally used with **Guess=Read**.

The UNO guess must be used with caution. Often, some of the natural orbitals which have modest occupation are not the important ones for the process of interest. Consequently, unless the entire valence space is being correlated (which is usually prohibitively expensive), one normally runs one job which does a UHF calculation with **Pop=NaturalOrbital**, and then examines the resulting orbitals. The orbitals which belong in the active space are then selected, and a single-point **CASSCF(...,UNO) Guess=(Read, Alter)** calculation is performed. The resulting converged orbitals are then examined to verify that the correct active space has been located, and finally an optimization can be run with **CASSCF(...,UNO) Guess=Read**. For singlets, this entire process depends on the user being able to coax the UHF wavefunction to converge to the appropriate broken spin-symmetry (non-RHF) result.

NPairs=n	Number of GVB pairs outside of the CAS active space in a GVBCAS calculation [292].
Restart	Restart a CASSCF calculation. Note that **SCF=Restart** performs the same function.

CASSCF MP2-SPECIFIC OPTIONS

DoOff	Include off diagonal contributions within the computation.
Thresh=n	Set the cutoff for CI vector components that are included to 10^n.
MP2States=*mask*	Compute the MP2 correction for the specified states. *Mask* is interpreted as a binary bit mask specifying the desired states. For example, *mask*=1011 means to compute states 1, 2 and 4. The default is to compute the correction only for the state of interest.
NFC=n	Set the number of frozen core orbitals.
NFV=n	Set the number of frozen virtual orbitals.

Note: **NFC** and **NFV** provide analogous functionality to the **Window** option for regular MP2 calculations.

UseL906	Use the **CAS MP2** facility that was the default in *Gaussian 94*.

AVAILABILITY AND RESTRICTIONS
Energies, analytic gradients, and analytic and numerical frequencies. CASSCF may not be combined with any semi-empirical method.

Analytic polarizabilites may not be performed with the CASSCF method. Use **CASSCF Polar=Numer**.

When restarting a CASSCF optimization, the keywords **CASSCF Opt=Restart Extralinks=L405** must be included in the job's route section.

RELATED KEYWORDS
Opt=Conical, MP2, Guess, Pop, SCF

EXAMPLES
We will consider several of the most important uses of the CASSCF method in this section.

Preliminary Examination of the Orbitals (Guess=Only). The following route section illustrates one method of quickly examining the orbitals in order to determine their symmetries and any alterations needed to produce the desired initial state. We include **Pop=Reg** to obtain the molecular orbital output in the population analysis section:

```
# HF/3-21G Guess=Only Pop=Reg Test
```

The molecule being investigated is 1,3-cyclobutadiene, a singlet with D_{2h} symmetry. We are going to run a 4x4 CAS, so there will be four orbitals in the active space: 2 occupied and 2 virtual. We want all four orbitals to be π orbitals.

The HOMO is orbital 14; therefore, orbitals 13 through 16 will comprise the active space. When we examine these orbitals, we see that only orbitals 14 and 15 are of the correct type. The molecule lies in the YZ-plane, so π orbitals will have significantly non-zero coefficients in the X direction. Here are the relevant coefficients for orbitals 10 and 13-16:

```
Molecular Orbital Coefficients
                         10          13          14          15          16
                          O           O           O           V           V
    3  1 C    2PX      0.29536     0.00000     0.34716     0.37752     0.00000
    7         3PX      0.16911     0.00000     0.21750     0.24339     0.00000
   12  2 C    2PX      0.29536     0.00000     0.34716    -0.37752     0.00000
   16         3PX      0.16911     0.00000     0.21750    -0.24339     0.00000
   21  3 C    2PX      0.29536     0.00000    -0.34716    -0.37752     0.00000
   25         3PX      0.16911     0.00000    -0.21750    -0.24339     0.00000
   30  4 C    2PX      0.29536     0.00000    -0.34716     0.37752     0.00000
   34         3PX      0.16911     0.00000    -0.21750     0.24339     0.00000
```

Orbital 10 is clearly also a π orbital. If we look at higher virtual orbitals, we will find that orbital 19 is also a π orbital. We have found our four necessary orbitals, and can now use **Guess=Alter** to move them into the active space. Here is the input file for the CASSCF calculation:

```
# CASSCF(4,4)/3-21G Guess=Alter Pop=Reg  Test

1,3-Cyclobutadiene Singlet, D2H, Pi 4x4 CAS

0 1
```
molecule specification

| 10,13 | *Interchange orbitals 10 and 13.* |
| 16,19 | *Interchange orbitals 16 and 19.* |

CASSCF Energy and the One-Electron Density Matrix. When we run this CASSCF calculation on cyclobutadiene, we will obtain a prediction for the energy. It appears in the CASSCF output as follows:

```
TOTAL                  -152.836259
 ...                 energy at each iteration
 ITN=  9 MaxIt= 64 E=   -152.8402786733 DE=-1.17D-05 Acc= 1.00D-05
 ITN= 10 MaxIt= 64 E=   -152.8402826495 DE=-3.98D-06 Acc= 1.00D-05
 ...
DO AN EXTRA-ITERATION FOR FINAL PRINTING
```

The value of E for the final iteration is the predicted energy: -152.8402826495 hartrees in this case.

It is also important to examine the one-electron density matrix, which appears next in the output:

```
Final one electron symbolic density matrix:
            1              2              3              4
  1   0.191842D+01
  2  -0.139172D-05  0.182680D+01
  3   0.345450D-05  0.130613D-05  0.172679D+00
  4   0.327584D-06  0.415187D-05  0.564187D-06  0.820965D-01
MCSCF converged.
```

The diagonal elements indicate the approximate occupancies for each successive orbital in the active space. If any of these values is (essentially) zero, then that orbital was empty throughout the calculation; similarly, if any of them is essentially 2, then that orbital was doubly occupied throughout the CAS. In either case, there were no excitations into or out of the orbital in question, and there is probably a problem with the CASSCF calculation. In our case, the two "occupied" orbitals have values less than 2, and the other two orbitals in the active space have non-zero occupancies, so things are fine.

CASSCF MP2 Energy. When you run a CASSCF calculation with correlation (**CASSCF MP2** in the route section), the following additional lines will appear in the CASSCF output (with the first one coming significantly before the second):

```
MP2 correction to the MCSCF energy is computed        Indicates a CASSCF MP2 job.
...
E2 = -0.2635549296D+00 EUMP2 = -0.15310383973610D+03
                       Electron correlation-corrected energy.
```

The string EUMP2 labels the energy; in this case, the value is -153.1038397361 hartrees.

CAS Configuration Information. The beginning of the CASSCF output lists the configurations, in the following format:

```
PRIMARY BASIS FUNCTION=   1   2   1   2
                      2                      SYMMETRY TYPE   = 0
                          1       3
                          1       2
                      3                      SYMMETRY TYPE   = 0
                          2       3
                          1       2
```

The first line indicates the electron assignments for the lowest configuration. This is a 4x4 CAS, so the primary basis function output indicates that there is an α and β electron in both orbitals 13 and 14 (the numbers refer to the orbitals in the active space, from lowest to highest, and the electron order in the output is: α α β β). In configuration 2, the α electron in orbital 13 remains there, the α electron from orbital 14 has been excited to orbital 15, the β electron in orbital 13 remains there, as does the β electron in orbital 14. Similarly, in configuration 3, there is a β electron in orbital 13, an α (from 13) and β electron in orbital 14, and a β electron in orbital 15.

Using CASSCF to Study Excited States. The following two-step job illustrates one method for studying excited state systems using the CASSCF method. The first step assumes that a preliminary Hartree-Fock single point calculation has been done in order to examine the orbitals; it takes advantage of the initial guess computation done by that job, which it retrieves from the checkpoint file:

```
%chk=CAS1
# CASSCF(2,4) 6-31+G(D) Guess=(Read,Alter) Pop=NaturalOrbital Test
Geom=Check

Alter the guess so that the three LUMOs are all the desired
symmetry, and run the CAS

0,1
```

orbital alterations

```
--Link1--
%chk=CAS1
%nosave
# CASSCF(2,4,NRoot=2) 6-31+G(D) Guess(Read) Pop(NaturalOrbital)
Geom=Check Test

Excited state calculation

0,1
```

The second job step uses the **NRoot** option to **CASSCF** to specify the first excited state. The first excitation energy for the system will then be computed by taking the energy difference between the two states (see exercise 5 in chapter 9 of *Exploring Chemistry with Electronic Structure Methods* [210] for a more detailed discussion of this technique).

Predicting Conical Intersections. Including **Opt=Conical** keyword in the route section changes the job from an optimization of the specified state using CASSCF to a search for a conical intersection or avoided crossing involving that state. The optimized structure will be that of the conical intersection or avoided crossing. Distinguishing between these two possibilities may be accomplished by examining the final eigenvalues in the CASSCF output for the final optimization step (it precedes the optimized structure):

```
FINAL EIGENVALUES AND EIGENVECTORS
  VECTOR EIGENVALUES      CORRESPONDING EIGENVECTOR

     state     energy
       1   -154.0503161      0.72053292        -0.48879229        . . .
                            -0.16028934E-02     0.31874441E-02     . . .

            . . .
       2   -154.0501151      0.45467877         0.77417416        . . .
```

If the two eigenvalues (the first entry in the lines labelled with a state number) are essentially the same, then the energies of the two states are the same, and it is a conical intersection. Otherwise, it is an avoided crossing.

Spin Orbit Coupling. Here is the output from a CASSCF calculation where the spin orbit coupling has been requested with the **Spin** option (the coupling is between the state specified to the **NRoot** option and the next lower state):

```
****************************
  spin-orbit coupling program
****************************
Number of configs= 4
1st state is 1        Identifies the two states between which the spin orbit coupling is computed.
2nd state is 2
Transition Spin Density Matrix
              1              2
   1   .000000D+00    .141313D+01
   2   .553225D-01    .000000D+00
magnitude in x-direction=       .0000000  cm-1
magnitude in y-direction=       .0000000  cm-1
magnitude in z-direction=     55.2016070  cm-1
total magnitude=     55.2016070  cm-1        Spin orbit coupling.
MCSCF converged.
```

The spin orbit coupling is broken down into X, Y, and Z components, followed by its total magnitude, which in this case is 55.2016070 cm^{-1}.

➤ CBS-4
➤ CBS-Lq
➤ CBS-Q
➤ CBS-QB3
➤ CBS-APNO

DESCRIPTION

These method keywords specify the various Complete Basis Set (CBS) methods of Petersson and coworkers for computing very accurate energies [88-93, 225]. The keywords refer to the CBS-4 [92], CBS-q [90] (i.e., **Lq** for "little q"), CBS-Q [92], CBS-Q//B3 [93] and CBS-APNO [92] methods, respectively. No basis set should be specified with any of these keywords.

These methods are complex energy computations involving several to many pre-defined calculations on the specified system. All of these distinct steps are performed automatically when one of these keywords is specified, and the final computed energy value is displayed in the output.

Either of the **Opt=Maxcyc=**n or **QCISD=Maxcyc=**n keywords may be used in conjunction with any of the these keywords to specify the maximum number of optimization or QCISD cycles, respectively. Note, however, that they may not be combined with the **Restart** option.

OPTIONS

ReadIsotopes Specify alternate temperature, pressure, and/or isotopes (the defaults are 298.15 K, 1 atmosphere, and the most abundant isotopes). This information appears in a separate input section having the format:

> temp pressure [scale]   Values must be real numbers.
> isotope mass for atom 1
> isotope mass for atom 2
> ...
> isotope mass for atom n

where temp, pressure, and scale are the desired temperature, pressure, and an optional scale factor for frequency data when used for thermochemical analysis (the default value of $1/1.12$ (≈ 0.8929) if scale is omitted or set to 0.0). The remaining lines hold the isotope masses for the various atoms in the molecule, arranged in the same order as they appeared in the molecule specification section. If integers are used to specify the atomic masses, the program will automatically use the corresponding actual exact mass (e.g., 18 specifies O^{18}, and Gaussian 98 uses the value 17.99916).

Restart Restart from the checkpoint file from a previous CBS calculation. If the previous calculation did not complete, it will be completed. May also be used to quickly substitute different temperature, pressure, or isotopes with a previously-completed calculation (without doing any additional expensive calculations), in which case **ReadIso** must also be specified.

AVAILABILITY

Energies only. **CBS-4**, **CBS-Lq**, **CBS-Q** and **CBS-QB3** are available for first and second row atoms; **CBS-APNO** is available for first row atoms only.

EXAMPLES

The output from each step of a CBS method calculation is included in the output file. The final section of the file contains a summary of the results of the entire run.

CBS Summary Output. Here is the output from a CBS-Q calculation on CH_2 (triplet state):

```
Complete Basis Set (CBS) Extrapolation:
 G. Petersson and M. A. Al-Laham, JCP 94, 6081 (1991)
 G. Petersson, T. Tensfeldt & J. A. Montgomery, JCP 94, 6091 (1991)
 additional references ...

 Temperature=     298.150000   Pressure=           1.000000
 E(ZPE)=              .016835   E(Thermal)=          .019690
 E(SCF)=          -38.936531    DE(MP2)=            -.114652
 DE(CBS)=            -.011929   DE(MP34)=           -.018702
 DE(QCI)=            -.002781   DE(Int)=             .004204
 DE(Empirical)=      -.005891
 CBS-Q (0 K)=     -39.069447    CBS-Q Energy=      -39.066592
 CBS-Q Enthalpy=  -39.065647    CBS-Q Free Energy= -39.043444
```

The temperature and pressure are given first, followed by the components terms of the CBS-Q energy. The second-to-last line gives the CBS-Q energy values (reading across): at 0 K and at the specified temperature (298.15 K by default). The final line gives the CBS-Q enthalpy (including the thermal correction for the specified temperature) and the Gibbs free energy computed via the CBS-Q method (i.e., the CBS-Q energy including the frequency job free-energy correction). All of the energies are in hartrees.

Rerunning the Calculation at a Different Temperature. The following two-step job illustrates the method for running a second (very rapid) CBS calculation at a different temperature. This job computes the CBS-4 energy at 298.15 K and then again at 300 K:

```
%Chk=cbs
# CBS-4 Test

CBS-4 on formaldehyde

0 1
molecule specification

--Link1--
%Chk=cbs
%NoSave
# CBS-4(Restart,ReadIso) Geom=AllCheck Test

300.0 1.0
isotope specifications
```

➤ CBSExtrapolate

DESCRIPTION
This keyword requests a general Complete Basis Set extrapolation of the MP2 energy [88-90, 225]. The method requires two parameters: the minimum number of pair natural orbitals and the integration grid. The first can be specified with the **NMin** option, and it defaults to 5 for the 6-31G**, 6-31G†† and 6-311G** basis sets (with or without diffuse functions), and to 10 for the 6-311G basis set with (2df,p) or (3df,p) polarization functions (again, with or without diffuse functions). **NMin** *must* be specified in all other cases, or an error will result.

The default integration grid is the (99,302) grid; an alternate grid can be specified with the **Int=Grid** keyword. The integration portion is a small part of the total CBS extrapolation computation, so this relatively large grid was chosen. See the description of the **Integral** keyword for a full discussion of the available grids.

OPTIONS

NMin=*N*	Specifies *N* as the minimum number of pair natural orbitals.
PopLocal	Use population localization [293]; this is the default.
BoysLocal	Use Boys localization [294-296].
NoLocal	Do not use any localization.
NRPopLocal	Newton-Raphson population localization.
NRBoysLocal	Newton-Raphson Boys localization.

AVAILABILITY
Single point energy calculations only, using any electron correlation method.

RELATED KEYWORDS
Int=Grid

➤ CCD
➤ CCSD

These method keywords request a coupled cluster [65, 297] calculations, using double substitutions from the Hartree-Fock determinant for **CCD** [65], or both single and double substitutions for **CCSD** [66-69]. **CC** is a synonym for **CCD**.

OPTIONS

T Include triple excitations non-iteratively [70] (**CCSD** only). **CCSD-T** is a synonym for **CCSD(T)**.

E4T Used with the **T** option to request inclusion of triple excitations for both the complete MP4 and to form CCSD(T).

T1Diag Computes the T1 diagnostic of T. J. Lee and coworkers [298] (**CCSD** only).

FC This indicates "frozen-core," and it implies that inner-shells are excluded from the correlation calculation. This is the default calculation mode. **Full** specifies the inclusion of all electrons, and **RW** and **Window** allow you to input specific information about which orbitals to retain in the post-SCF calculation (see the discussion of the **MP***n* keywords for an example).

Conver=*N* Sets the convergence calculations to 10^{-N} on the energy and $10^{-(N+2)}$ on the wavefunction. The default is $N=7$ for single points and $N=8$ for gradients.

MaxCyc=*n* Specifies the maximum number of cycles for **CCSD** calculations.

AVAILABILITY
Analytic energies, analytic gradients for CCD and numerical gradients for the other methods, and numerical frequencies.

RELATED KEYWORDS
MP4, Transformation

EXAMPLES
The Coupled Cluster energy appears in the output as follows (following the final correlation iteration):

```
DE(CORR)=   -.54979226D-01       E(CORR)=       -.75019641794D+02
...
CCSD(T)=   -.75019717665D+02
```

The CCSD energy is labeled E(CORR), and the energy including the non-iterative triples contribution is given in the final line.

➤ CID
➤ CISD

DESCRIPTION

These method keywords request a Hartree-Fock calculation followed by configuration interaction with all double substitutions (**CID**) or all single and double substitutions (**CISD**) from the Hartree-Fock reference determinant [59, 122, 163]. **CIDS** and **CI** are synonyms for **CISD**.

OPTIONS

FC   This indicates "frozen-core," and it implies that inner-shells are excluded from the correlation calculation. This is the default calculation mode. **Full** specifies the inclusion of all electrons, and **RW** and **Window** allow you to input specific information about which orbitals to retain in the post-SCF calculation (see the discussion of the **MP**n keywords for an example).

Conver=N Sets the convergence calculations to 10^{-N} on the energy and $10^{-(N+2)}$ on the wavefunction. The default is $N=7$ for single points and $N=8$ for gradients.

MaxCyc=n Specifies the maximum number of cycles for **CISD** calculations.

AVAILABILITY

Analytic energies, analytic gradients, and numerical frequencies.

RELATED KEYWORDS
Transformation

EXAMPLES

The CI energy appears in the output as follows:

```
DE(CI)=      -.48299990D-01           E(CI)=          -.75009023292D+02
NORM(A) =     .10129586D+01
```

The output following the final CI iteration gives the predicted total energy.

The second output line displays the value of Norm(A). Norm(A)–1 gives a measure of the correlation correction to the wavefunction; the coefficient of the HF configuration is thus 1/Norm(A). Note that the wavefunction is stored in intermediate normalization; that is:

$$\Psi^{CISD} = \Psi^0 + \sum_{ia} T_{ia} \Psi(i \rightarrow a) + \sum_{ijab} T_{ijab} \Psi(ij \rightarrow ab)$$

where Ψ^0 is the Hartree-Fock determinant and has a coefficient of 1 (which is what intermediate normalization means). Norm(A) is the factor by which to divide the wavefunction as given above to fully normalize it. Thus:

$$\text{Norm}(A) = \sqrt{1 + \sum_{ia} T_{ia} T_{ia} + \sum_{ijab} T_{ijab} T_{ijab}}$$

The coefficient of the Hartree-Fock determinant in the fully normalized wavefunction is then $1/\text{Norm}(A)$, the coefficient of singly-excited determinant $\Psi_{i \to a}$ is $T_{ia}/\text{Norm}(A)$, and so on.

➤ Charge

DESCRIPTION
The **Charge** keyword requests that a background charge distribution be included in the calculation. The charge distribution is made up of point charges [299, 300].

By default, the charges are read from the input stream, one per line, in this format:

x y z charge   point charge format

Coordinates are in the units specified by the **Units** keyword (defaulting to Angstroms) and in the input orientation. This is a change in behavior with respect to earlier versions of *Gaussian*.

OPTIONS
Angstroms   Indicates that input charge locations are specified in Angstroms.

Bohrs   Indicates that input charge locations are specified in Bohrs.

StandardOrientation
     Indicates that the input charges are specified in the standard orientation rather than the input orientation. Use the **%KJob=L301** Link 0 command to quickly determine the standard orientation for a molecule.

Check   Reads the background charge distribution from the checkpoint file.

AVAILABILITY
Not valid with semi-empirical methods.

RELATED KEYWORDS
%Kjob, Units

➤ ChkBasis

DESCRIPTION

The **ChkBasis** keyword requests that the basis set be read from the checkpoint file, and is useful in compound jobs involving general basis sets by allowing them to have only one copy of the basis set in the input stream (see the discussion of the **Gen** keyword below). Note, however, that **ChkBasis** can be used to retrieve *whatever* basis set exists in a checkpoint file, regardless of how it was originally specified. ECP's specified in the basis set are also retrieved.

Of course, no basis set keyword should be specified with **ChkBasis**.

CheckPointBasis, **ReadBasis**, and **RdBasis** are all synonyms for **ChkBasis**.

RELATED KEYWORDS
Gen, ExtraBasis

➤ CIS

DESCRIPTION

This method keyword requests a calculation on excited states using single-excitation CI (CI-Singles) [102, 160]. Chapter 9 of *Exploring Chemistry with Electronic Structure Methods* [210] provides a detailed discussion of this method and its uses.

CI-Singles jobs will also usually include the **Density** keyword; without options, this keyword causes the population analysis to use the current (CIS) density rather than its default of the Hartree-Fock density.

STATE SELECTION OPTIONS

Singlets Solve only for singlet excited states. Only effective for closed-shell systems, for which it is the default.

Triplets Solve only for triplet excited states. Only effective for closed-shell systems.

50-50 Solve for half triplet and half singlet states. Only effective for closed-shell systems.

Root=N Specifies the "state of interest" to be optimized in geometry optimizations, for which the generalized density is to be computed. The default is the first excited state ($N=1$).

NStates=M Solve for M states (the default is 3). If **50-50** is requested, **NStates** gives the number of each type of state for which to solve (i.e., the default is 3 singlets *and* 3 triplets).

Add=N Read converged states off the checkpoint file and solve for an additional N states.

Densities   Compute the one-particle density for each state.

TransitionDensities

Compute the transition densities between the ground state and each excited state. The oscillator strengths are then reported automatically. This is the default.

AllTransitionDensities

Computes the transition densities between every pair of states.

PROCEDURE- AND ALGORITHM-RELATED OPTIONS

Direct   Forces solution of the CI-Singles equation using AO integrals which are recomputed as needed. **CIS=Direct** should be used only when the approximately $4O^2N^2$ words of disk required for the default (**MO**) algorithm are not available, or for very large calculations (over 200 basis functions).

MO   Forces solution of the CI-Singles equations using transformed two-electron integrals. This is the default algorithm in *Gaussian 98*. The transformation attempts to honor the **MaxDisk** keyword, thus further moderating the disk requirements.

AO   Forces solution of the CI-Singles equations using the AO integrals, avoiding an integral transformation. The AO basis is seldom an optimal choice, except for small molecules on systems having very limited disk and memory.

FC   This indicates "frozen-core," and it implies that inner-shells are excluded from the correlation calculation. This is the default calculation mode. **Full** specifies the inclusion of all electrons, and **RW** and **Window** allow you to input specific information about which orbitals to retain in the post-SCF calculation (see the discussion of the **MP**n keywords for an example).

Conver=N   Sets the convergence calculations to 10^{-N} on the energy and $10^{-(N+2)}$ on the wavefunction. The default is $N=4$ for single points and $N=6$ for gradients.

Read   Reads initial guesses for the CI-Singles states off the checkpoint file. Note that unlike the SCF, an initial guess for one basis set cannot be used for a different one.

Restart   Restarts the CI-Singles iterations off the checkpoint file.

RWFRestart   Restarts the CI-Singles iterations off the read-write file. Useful when using non-standard routes to do successive CI-Singles calculations.

DEBUGGING OPTIONS

ICDiag   Forces in-core full diagonalization of the CI-Singles matrix formed in memory from transformed integrals. This is mainly a debugging option.

MaxDiag=N Limits the submatrix diagonalized in the Davidson procedure to dimension N. This is mainly a debugging option. **MaxDavidson** is a synonym for this option.

AVAILABILITY

Energies, analytic gradients, and analytic frequencies.

RELATED KEYWORDS

ZINDO, TD, Density, MaxDisk, Transformation

EXAMPLES

There are no special features or pitfalls with CI-Singles input. Output from a single point CI-Singles calculation resembles that of a ground-state CI or QCI run. An SCF is followed by the integral transformation and evaluation of the ground-state MP2 energy. Information about the iterative solution of the CI problem comes next; note that at the first iteration, additional initial guesses are made, to ensure that the requested number of excited states are found regardless of symmetry. After the first iteration, one new vector is added to the solution for each state on each iteration.

The change in excitation energy and wavefunction for each state is printed for each iteration (in the **#P** output):

```
Iteration  3 Dimension    27
 Root  1 not converged, maximum delta is    0.002428737687607
 Root  2 not converged, maximum delta is    0.013107675296678
 Root  3 not converged, maximum delta is    0.030654755631835
 Excitation Energies [eV] at current iteration:
 Root  1 :    3.700631883679401   Change is   -0.001084398684008
 Root  2 :    7.841115226789293   Change is   -0.011232152003400
 Root  3 :    8.769540624626156   Change is   -0.047396173133051
```

The iterative process can end successfully in two ways: generation of only vanishingly small expansion vectors, or negligible change in the updated wavefunction.

When the CI has converged, the results are displayed, beginning with this banner:

```
*******************************************************************
   Excited States From <AA,BB:AA,BB> singles matrix:
*******************************************************************
```

The transition dipole moments between the ground and each excited state are then tabulated. Next, the results on each state are summarized, including the spin and spatial symmetry, the excitation energy, the oscillator strength, and the largest coefficients in the CI expansion (use **IOp(9/40=**N**)** to request more coefficients: all that are greater than 10^{-N}):

```
Excitation energies and oscillator strengths:
                        symmetry        excitation energy                    oscillator strength
  Excited State    1:    Singlet-A"      3.7006 eV  335.03 nm   f=0.0008
        8 ->  9            0.69112                   CI expansion coefficients for each excitation.
Excitation is from orbital 8 to orbital 9.
This state for opt. and/or second-order corr.        ⇒ This is the "state of interest."
Total Energy, E(Cis) =  -113.696894498        CIS energy is repeated here for convenience.
```

➤ CNDO

DESCRIPTION
This method keyword requests a semi-empirical calculation using the CNDO Hamiltonian [39]. No basis set keyword should be specified.

AVAILABILITY
Energies, "analytic" gradients, and numerical frequencies.

EXAMPLES
The CNDO energy appears in the output file as follows (followed by the x, y, and z components of the dipole moment):

```
 Energy=    -19.887711334547 NIter=   10.
 Dipole moment=    .000000    .000000   -.739540
```

The energy is as defined by the CNDO model. Note that energy differences computed from the values in semi-empirical calculations are in Hartrees and may be compared directly with energy differences computed from jobs using other methods.

➤ Complex

DESCRIPTION
This keyword allows the molecular orbitals to become complex. It may only be used for closed-shell singlet states.

AVAILABILITY
Analytic energies for Hartree-Fock and MP2 only, analytic HF gradients, and numerical HF frequencies.

RELATED KEYWORDS
SCF

➤ CPHF

DESCRIPTION
This keyword selects the algorithm used for solving the CPHF equations [301-310].

OPTIONS

Grid=*grid*   Specify the integration grid for the CPHF portion of the calculation. The syntax is the same as for the **Integral=Grid** option. The argument to this option may be a grid keyword (**Fine, UltraFine**, and so on) or a specific grid. See the discussion of **Integral=Grid** later in this manual for full details on grid specification.

The default grid used depends on the one used for integral evaluation. If any specific grid is specified to the **Integral** keyword, then that grid is also used for the CPHF. Otherwise, when the latter uses the **SG1** or **Fine** grid, the **Coarse** grid is used for the CPHF (a pruned (35,11)), and when **UltraFine** is used for the integrals, then **SG1** is used for the CPHF.

Simultaneous   Use one expansion space for all variables. This is faster than using separate spaces, but is slightly less accurate. This is the default.

Separate   Use a separate expansion space for each variable in the CPHF (the opposite of **Simultaneous**).

ZVector   Use the Z-Vector method [119, 311, 312] for post-SCF gradients. Allowed and the default if Hartree-Fock 2nd derivatives are not also requested. The **NoZVector** keyword says to use the full 3 x N_{Atoms} CPHF for post-SCF gradients.

AO   Solve CPHF in the atomic orbital basis [302, 305, 308, 309]. This is the default for Hartree-Fock second derivatives (which is also the only calculation type for which it is valid).

MO   Solve in the molecular orbital basis. It is the default and only legal value for PSCF gradients.

MaxInv=*N*   Specifies the largest reduced space for in-core inversion during simultaneous solution (up to dimension *N*). Larger reduced problems are solved by a second level of DIIS. The default is as large a space as memory permits.

Conver=*N*   Set the CPHF convergence criterion to 10^{-N}. The default is *N*=9 for **CPHF=Separate** and *N*=10 for **CPHF=Simultaneous** (the default).

RELATED KEYWORDS
SCF

➤ Cube

DESCRIPTION

The **Cube** properties keyword can be used to evaluate molecular orbitals, the electrostatic potential, the electron density, density gradient, the norm of the density gradient, and Laplacian of the density over a 3 dimensional grid (cube) of points. Which density is used is controlled by the **Density** keyword; use **Density=Current** to evaluate the cube over the density from a correlated or CI-Singles wavefunction instead of the default Hartree-Fock density.

Note that only one of the available quantities can be evaluated within any one job step. Save the checkpoint file (using **%Chk**), and include **Guess=(Read,Only) Density=Checkpoint** in the route section of a subsequent job (or job step) in order to evaluate a different quantity without repeating any of the other steps of the calculation.

Gaussian 98 provides reasonable defaults for grids, so **Cube** no longer requires that the cube be specified by the user. However, the output filename must still always be provided (see below).

Alternatively, **Cube** may be given a parameter specifying the number of points to use per "side" (the default is 80). For example, **Cube=100** specifies a grid of 1,000,000 points (100^3), evenly distributed over the rectangular grid generated by the program (which is not necessarily a cube). In addition, the input format used by earlier versions of *Gaussian* is still supported; **Cube=Cards** indicates that a grid will be input. It may be used to specify a grid of arbitrary size and shape.

The options **Coarse**, **Medium** and **Fine** may also be specified as the parameter to **Cube**. They correspond to values of 40, 80 and 100, respectively. These options are designed to facilitate uniform quality in grid sampling across the range of molecular sizes.

The files created by **Cube** can be manipulated using the **cubman** utility, described in chapter 5.

Note that **Pop=None** will inhibit cube file creation.

INPUT FORMAT

When the user elects to provide it, the grid information is read from the input stream. The first line—required for all **Cube** jobs—gives a file name for the cube file. Subsequent lines, which are included only with **Cube=Cards**, must conform to format (I5,3F12.6), according to the following syntax:

Output-file-name	*Required in all* **Cube** *jobs.*
IFlag, X_O, Y_O, Z_O	*Output unit number and initial point.*
N_1, X_1, Y_1, Z_1	*Number of points and step-size in the X-direction.*
N_2, X_2, Y_2, Z_2	*Number of points and step-size in the Y-direction.*
N_3, X_3, Y_3, Z_3	*Number of points and step-size in the Z-direction.*

If $N_1<0$ the input cube coordinates are assumed to be in Bohr, otherwise, they are interpreted as Angstroms (this keyword is not affected by the setting of the **Units** keyword). $|N_1|$ is used as the number of X-direction points in any case. Note that the three axes are used exactly as specified; they are not orthogonalized, so the grid need not be rectangular.

If the **Orbitals** option is selected, the cube filename (or cube filename and cube specification input) is followed by one or more lines listing of the orbitals to evaluate, in free-format, terminated by a blank line. In addition to numbers for the orbitals (with β orbitals numbered starting at $N+1$), the following abbreviations can appear in the list:

HOMO	The highest occupied molecular orbital
LUMO	The lowest unoccupied molecular orbital
OCCA	All occupied (α) orbitals
OCCB	All β occupied orbitals for UHF
ALL	All orbitals
VALENCE	All occupied non-core orbitals
VIRTUALS	All virtual orbitals

OUTPUT FILE FORMATS

Using the default input to **Cube** produces an unformatted output file (you can use the **cubman** utility to convert it to a formatted version if you so desire; see chapter 5). When the **Cards** option is specified, then the *IFlag* parameter's sign determines the output file type. If *IFlag*>0, the output is unformatted. If *IFlag*<0, the output is formatted. All values in the cube file are in atomic units, regardless of the input units.

For density and potential grids, unformatted files have one row per record (i.e., $N_1{}^*N_2$ records each of length N_3). For formatted output, each row is written out in format (6E13.5). In this case, if N_3 is not a multiple of six, then there may be blank space in some lines.

The norm of the density gradient and the Laplacian are also scalar (i.e., one value per point), and are written out in the same manner. Density+gradient grids are similar, but with two writes for each row (of lengths N_3 and $3{}^*N_3$).

For example, for a density cube, the output file looks like this:

```
NAtoms, X-Origin, Y-Origin, Z-Origin
N1, X1, Y1, Z1                              # of increments in the slowest running direction
N2, X2, Y2, Z2
N3, X3, Y3, Z3                              # of increments in the fastest running direction
IA1, Chg1, X1, Y1, Z1              Atomic number, charge, and coordinates of the first atom
...
IAn, Chgn, Xn, Yn, Zn             Atomic number, charge, and coordinates of the last atom
(N1*N2) records, each of length N3          Values of the density at each point in the grid
```

Note that a separate write is used for each record.

For molecular orbital output, NAtoms will be less than zero, and an additional record follows the data for the final atom (in format 10I5 if the file is formatted):

NMO, (MO(I),I=1,NMO)   *Number of MOs and their numbers*

If N_{MO} orbitals were evaluated, then each record is $N_{MO}*N_3$ long and has the values for all orbitals at each point together.

READING CUBE FILES WITH FORTRAN PROGRAMS

If one wishes to read the values of the density, Laplacian, or potential back into an array dimensioned $X(N_3,N_2,N_1)$ code like the following Fortran loop may be used:

```
      Do 10 I1 = 1, N1
      Do 10 I2 = 1, N2
         Read(n,'(6E13.5)') (X(I3,I2,I1),I3=1,N3)
10    Continue
```

where n is the unit number corresponding to the cube file.

If the origin is (X_0,Y_0,Z_0), and the increment is (X_1,Y_1,Z_1), then point (I_1,I_2,I_3) has the coordinates:

X-coordinate:	$X_0+(I_1-1)*X_1+(I_2-1)*X_2+(I_3-1)*X_3$
Y-coordinate:	$Y_0+(I_1-1)*Y_1+(I_2-1)*Y_2+(I_3-1)*Y_3$
Z-coordinate:	$Z_0+(I_1-1)*Z_1+(I_2-1)*Z_2+(I_3-1)*Z_3$

The output is similar if the gradient or gradient and Laplacian of the charge density are also requested, except that in these cases there are two or three records, respectively, written for each pair of I_1, I_2 values. Thus, if the density and gradient are to be read into arrays $D(N_3,N_2,N_1)$, $G(3,N_3,N_2,N_1)$, $RL(N_3,N_2,N_1)$ from a formatted output file, a correct set of Fortran loops would be:

```
      Do 10 I1 = 1, N1
      Do 10 I2 = 1, N2
         Read(n,'(6F13.5)')  (D(I3,I2,I1),I3=1,N3)
         Read(n,'(6F13.5)')  ((G(IXYZ,I3,I2,I1),IXYZ=1,3), I3=1,N3)
10    Continue
```

where again n is the unit number corresponding to the cube file.

GRID-RELATED OPTIONS

N	Number of points to use per "side" (the default is 80). For example, **Cube=100** specifies a grid of 1,000,000 points (100^3), evenly distributed over the rectangular grid generated by the program (which is not necessarily a cube).
Coarse	Corresponds to *N*=40.
Medium	Corresponds to *N*=80.
Fine	Corresponds to *N*=100.

CUBE CONTENTS OPTIONS

Density　　　　Compute just the density values.

Potential　　　Compute the electrostatic potential at each point.

Gradient　　　Compute the density and gradient.

Laplacian　　Compute the Laplacian of the density ($\nabla^2\rho$). **Divergence** is a synonym for **Laplacian**.

NormGradient　Compute the norm of the density gradient at each point.

Orbitals　　　Compute the values of one or more molecular orbitals at each point.

FrozenCore　　Remove the SCF core density. This is the default for the density, and is not allowed for the potential.

Full　　　　　Evaluate the density including all electrons.

Total　　　　Use the total density. This is the default.

Alpha　　　　Use only the alpha spin density.

Beta　　　　　Use only the beta spin density.

Spin　　　　　Use the spin density (difference between alpha and beta densities).

Cards　　　　Read grid specification from the input stream (as described above).

RELATED KEYWORDS
Density

➤ Density

DESCRIPTION
By default, population and other analysis procedures use the SCF density. The generalized densities for the MP2, MP3, MP4(SDQ), QCISD, CCD, CID and CISD methods are available. These are based on the Z-Vector [119, 311-313], and hence yield multipole moments which are the correct analytical derivatives of the energy. The unrelaxed densities at second order (*not* the same as MP2) can also be used but are not recommended.

The options of the **Density** keyword select which density to analyze. The **Density** keyword without an option is equivalent to **Density=Current**.

OPTIONS

Current   Use the density matrix for the current method. This is the default when no option is given to **Density**.

All   Use all available densities. This is allowed for population analysis but not for electrostatics or density evaluation. Note that this option does not produce densities for all of the excited states in a CI-Singles calculation, only the density for the state of interest (see the examples below for a method of doing the former).

HF   Use the SCF density. **SCF** is a synonym for **HF**.

MP2   Use the generalized density corresponding to the second-order energy.

Transition=N[,M]

Use the CIS transition density between state M and state N. M defaults to 0, which corresponds to the ground state.

AllTransition   Use all available CIS transition densities.

CI   Use the generalized density corresponding to the CI energy.

QCI   Use the generalized density corresponding to the QCI (or coupled cluster) energy. **CC** is a synonym for **QCI**.

RhoCI   Use the one-particle density computed using the CI wavefunction for state N. This is *not* the same as the CI density [313], and its use is discouraged! Chapter 9 of *Exploring Chemistry with Electronic Structure Methods* discusses this issue [210].

Rho2   Use the density correct to second-order in Møller-Plesset theory. This is *not* the same as the MP2 density, and its use is discouraged! [313]

CIS=N   Use the total unrelaxed CIS density for state N. Note that this is *not* the same as the density resulting from **CIS(Root=N,...)** **Density=Current**, which is to be preferred [313].

Checkpoint   Recover the density from the checkpoint file for analysis. Implies **Guess=Only CheckBasis**: the calculation does not recompute new integrals, SCF, and so on, and retrieves the basis set from the checkpoint file.

RELATED KEYWORDS
Guess, ChkBasis

EXAMPLES
The following route section specifies a CI-Singles calculation which predicts the first six excited states of the molecule under investigation. The population and other analyses will use the CIS density corresponding to the lowest excited state:

```
%Chk=benzene
# CIS(NStates=6)/6-31+G(d,p) Density=Current Pop=CHelpG
```

The following route section may be used to rerun the post-CIS analyses for the other excited states:

```
%Chk=benzene
# CIS(Read,Root=N) Density=Current Pop=CHelpG
# Guess=Read Geom=AllCheck
```

This route picks up the converged CIS and CIS wavefunction from the checkpoint file, and performs the necessary CPHF calculation to produce the relaxed density for state N, which is then used in the population and other analyses.

➤ Density Functional (DFT) Methods

DESCRIPTION

Gaussian 98 offers a wide variety of Density Functional Theory (DFT) [73, 74, 314, 315] models (see also [314, 316-327] for discussions of DFT methods and applications). Energies [76], analytic gradients, and true analytic frequencies [157-159] are available for all DFT models.[‡] The same optimum memory sizes given by **freqmem** (see chapter 5) are recommended for the more general models.

The self-consistent reaction field (SCRF) can be used with DFT energies, optimizations, and frequency calculations to model systems in solution.

The next subsection presents a very brief overview of the DFT approach. Following this, the specific functionals available in *Gaussian 98* are given. The final subsections discuss considerations related to accuracy and stability in DFT calculations.

BACKGROUND

In Hartree-Fock theory, the energy has the form:

$$E_{HF} = V + <hP> + 1/2<PJ(P)> - 1/2<PK(P)>$$

where: V is the nuclear repulsion energy,
   P is the density matrix,
   $<hP>$ is the one-electron (kinetic plus potential) energy,
   $1/2<PJ(P)>$ is the classical coulomb repulsion of the electrons, and
   $-1/2<PK(P)>$ is the exchange energy resulting from the quantum (fermion) nature of electrons.

In density functional theory, the exact exchange (HF) for a single determinant is replaced by a more general expression, the exchange-correlation functional, which can include terms accounting for both exchange energy and the electron correlation which is omitted from Hartree-Fock theory:

[‡]   Polarizability derivatives (Raman intensities) and hyperpolarizabilities are not computed during DFT frequency calculations.

$$E_{KS} = V + <hP> + 1/2<PJ(P)> + E_X[P] + E_C[P]$$

where $E_X[P]$ is the exchange functional, and $E_C[P]$ is the correlation functional.

Hartree-Fock theory is really a special case of density functional theory, with $E_x[P]$ given by the exchange integral $-1/2<PK(P)>$ and $E_c=0$. The functionals normally used in density functional are integrals of some function of the density and possibly the density gradient:

$$E_X[P] = \int f(\rho_\alpha(r),\rho_\beta(r),\nabla\rho_\alpha(r),\nabla\rho_\beta(r))dr$$

where the methods differ in which function f is used for E_x and which (if any) f is used for E_C. In addition to pure DFT methods, *Gaussian 98* supports hybrid methods in which the exchange functional is a linear combination of the Hartree-Fock exchange and a functional integral of the above form. Proposed functionals lead to integrals which cannot be evaluated in closed form and are solved by numerical quadrature.

KEYWORDS FOR DFT METHODS

Names for the various pure DFT models are given by combining the names for the exchange and correlation functionals. In some cases, standard synonyms used in the field are also available as keywords.

Exchange Functionals. The following exchange functionals available in *Gaussian 98*:

		Keywords	
Name	*Description*	*Used Alone*	*Comb. Form*
Slater	$\rho^{4/3}$ with the theoretical coefficient of 2/3, also referred to as Local Spin Density exchange [73-75].	**HFS**	**S**
Xα	$\rho^{4/3}$ with the empirical coefficient of 0.7, usually used when this exchange functional is used without a correlation functional [73-75].	**XAlpha**	**XA**
Becke 88	Becke's 1988 functional, which includes the Slater exchange along with corrections involving the gradient of the density [78].	**HFB**	**B**
Perdew-Wang 91	The exchange component of Perdew and Wang's 1991 functional [328-332].	*N/A*	**PW91**
Barone's Modified PW91	The Perdew-Wang 1991 exchange functional as modified by Adamo and Barone [333].	*N/A*	**MPW**
Gill96	The 1996 exchange functional of Gill [83, 334].	*N/A*	**G96**

The combination forms are used when one of these exchange functionals is used in combination with a correlation functional (see below).

Correlation Functionals. The following correlation functionals are available:

Name	Description	Comb. Form
VWN	Vosko, Wilk, and Nusair 1980 correlation functional fitting the RPA solution to the uniform electron gas, often referred to as Local Spin Density (LSD) correlation [335] (functional III in the paper).	VWN
VWN V	Functional V from the VWN80 paper which fits the Ceperley-Alder solution to the uniform electron gas (this is the functional recommended in the paper) [335].	VWN5
LYP	The correlation functional of Lee, Yang, and Parr, which includes both local and non-local terms [77, 79].	LYP
Perdew Local	The local (non-gradient corrected) functional of Perdew (1981) [336].	PL
Perdew 86	The gradient corrections of Perdew, along with his 1981 local correlation functional [337].	P86
Perdew/Wang 91	Perdew and Wang's 1991 gradient-corrected correlation functional [328-332].	PW91
Becke 96	Becke's 1996 gradient-corrected correlation functional (part of his one parameter hybrid functional [81].	B96

All of the keywords for these correlation functionals must be combined with the keyword for the desired exchange functional. For example, **BLYP** requests the Becke exchange functional and the LYP correlation functional. **SVWN** requests the Slater exchange and the **VWN** correlation functional, and is known in the literature by its synonym LSDA (Local Spin Density Approximation).

LSDA is a synonym for **SVWN**. Some other software packages with DFT facilities use the equivalent of **SVWN5** when "LSDA" is requested. Check the documentation carefully for all packages when making comparisons.

Hybrid Functionals. Three *hybrid functionals,* which include a mixture of Hartree-Fock exchange with DFT exchange-correlation, are available via keywords:

Name	Description	Keywords
Becke's Three Parameter Hybrid Functional Using the LYP Correlation Functional	This is Becke's 3 parameter functional [80], which has the form: $$A*E_X^{Slater}+(1-A)*E_X^{HF}+B*\Delta E_X^{Becke}+E_C^{VWN}+C*\Delta E_C^{non-local},$$ where the non-local correlation is provided by the LYP expression, and VWN is functional III (not functional V). The constants A, B, and C are those determined by Becke by fitting to the G1 molecule set.[†] Since LYP includes both local and non-local terms, the correlation functional used is actually: $C*E_C^{LYP}+(1-C)*E_C^{VWN}$. In other words, VWN is used to provide the excess local correlation required, since LYP contains a local term essentially equivalent to VWN.	B3LYP
Becke's Three Parameter Hybrid Functional with Perdew 86	This is Becke's 3 parameter functional as above, with the non-local correlation provided by the Perdew 86 expression. The constants A, B, and C are again those determined by Becke.	B3P86
Becke's Three Parameter Hybrid Functional with Perdew/Wang 91	This is Becke's 3 parameter functional as above, with the non-local correlation provided by the Perdew 91 expression. The constants A, B, and C are again those determined by Becke.	B3PW91
Becke's One Parameter Hybrid Functional with Becke's 1996 Correlation Functional	This is Becke's one-parameter hybrid functional as defined in the original paper [81].	B1B96
Becke's One Parameter Hybrid Functional with LYP Correlation	Becke's one parameter hybrid functional using the LYP correlation functional (as described for B3LYP above) as implemented by Adamo and Barone [81, 82].	B1LYP
One Parameter Hybrid Functional with Modified Perdew-Wang Exchange and Correlation	Barone and Adamo's Becke-style one parameter functional using modified Perdew-Wang exchange and Perdew-Wang 91 correlation [333].	MPW1PW91
One Parameter Hybrid Functional with Gill 96 Exchange and LYP Correlation	Barone and Adamo's Becke-style one parameter functional using Gill96 exchange and LYP correlation [83].	G961LYP

| Half-and-half Functionals | These keywords implement the following functionals:

BHandH: $\quad 0.5^*E_X^{HF} + 0.5^*E_X^{LSDA} + E_C^{LYP}$

BHandHLYP: $\ 0.5^*E_X^{HF} + 0.5^*E_X^{LSDA} + 0.5^*\Delta E_X^{Becke88} + E_C^{LYP}$

Note that these are *not* the same as the "half-and-half" functionals proposed by Becke (*J. Chem. Phys.* **98** (1993) 1372). These functionals are included for backward-compatibility. | **BHandH**
BHandHLYP |

[†] Becke determined the values of the three parameters by fitting to the 56 atomization energies, 42 ionization potentials, 8 proton affinities, and 10 first-row atomic energies in the G1 molecule set [80, 84, 85], computing values of A=0.80, B=0.72, and C=0.81. He used LDA densities and the Perdew/Wang 1991 correlation functional rather than VWN functional III and LYP.

User-Defined Models. *Gaussian 98* can use any model of the general form:

$$P_2E_X^{HF} + P_1(P_4E_X^{Slater} + P_3\Delta E_x^{non-local}) + P_6E_C^{local} + P_5\Delta E_C^{non-local}$$

Currently, the only available local exchange method is *Slater* (**S**), which should be used when only local exchange is desired. The available non-local exchange corrections (which include Slater local exchange) are Becke (**B**), Perdew-Wang 91 (**PW91**), Barone's modified PW91 (**MPW**) and Gill 96 (**G96**). One of these prefixes should be combined with one of the available correlation functional suffixes given in the following table:

E_C^{local}	$E_C^{non-local}$	Suffix
VWN	*LYP*	**LYP**
VWNV	none	**VWN5**
Perdew Local	*Perdew 86*	**P86**
Perdew/Wang 91	*Perdew/Wang 91*	**PW91**
Becke 96	*Becke 96*	**B96**

You specify the values of the six parameters with various non-standard options to the program:

♦ **IOp(5/45=***mmmmnnnn***)** sets P_1 to *mmmm*/1000 and P_2 to *nnnn*/1000. P_1 is usually set to either 0.0 or 1.0, depending on whether an exchange functional is desired or not, and any scaling is accomplished using P_3 and P_4.

♦ **IOp(5/46=***mmmmnnnn***)** sets P_3 to *mmmm*/1000 and P_4 to *nnnn*/1000.

♦ **IOp(5/47=***mmmmnnnn***)** sets P_5 to *mmmm*/1000 and P_6 to *nnnn*/1000.

For example, **IOp(5/45=10000500)** sets P_1 to 1.0 and P_2 to 0.5. Note that all values must be expressed using four digits, adding any necessary leading zeros.

Here is a route section specifying the functional corresponding to the **B3LYP** keyword:

```
# BLYP IOp(5/45=10000200) IOp(5/46=07200800) IOp(5/47=08101000)
```

ACCURACY CONSIDERATIONS
A DFT calculation adds an additional step to each major phase of a Hartree-Fock calculation. This step is a numerical integration of the functional (or various derivatives of the functional). Thus in addition to the sources of numerical error in Hartree-Fock calculations (integral accuracy, SCF convergence, CPHF convergence), the accuracy of DFT calculations also depends on number of points used in the numerical integration.

The "fine" integration grid (corresponding to **Int=FineGrid**) is the default in *Gaussian 98*. This grid greatly enhances calculation accuracy at minimal additional cost. We do not recommend using any smaller grid in production DFT calculations. Note also that it is important to use the *same* grid for all calculations where you intend to compare energies (e.g., computing energy differences, heats of formation, and so on).

Larger grids are available when needed (e.g. tight optimization of certain kinds of systems). An alternate grid may be selected by including **Int(Grid=N)** in the route section (see the discussion of the **Integral** keyword for details).

DFT single point energy calculations involving basis sets which include diffuse functions should always use the **SCF=Tight** keyword to request tight SCF convergence criteria.

CONVERGENCE AND STABILITY
The Kohn-Sham equations for the optimal DFT density are similar to the Hartree-Fock equations, and for both cases it is possible to have SCF convergence problems and/or to converge to a saddle point in *wavefunction* space, rather than a minimum.

In general, the convergence properties of the hybrid methods are similar to Hartree-Fock: most cases converge readily with the standard methods. Pure DFT methods (i.e., without any Hartree-Fock exchange) tend to give small HOMO-LUMO gaps, and consequently convergence problems are much more frequent than for Hartree-Fock or hybrid methods. We recommend the following techniques for difficult DFT cases:

- ♦ Level shifting, using the **SCF=VShift** keyword, is useful for many problem cases. Note that you need to make sure that the final wavefunction respresents the desired electronic state, as this can change with level shifting.

- ♦ Use **SCF=QC** if the SCF procedure fails even with level shifting.

Using either method, you will want to use stability testing (**Stable=Opt**) to confirm that the solution is a local minima in wavefunction space [100, 101]. See the discussion of the **Stable** keyword for details.

AVAILABILITY
Energies, analytic gradients, and analytic frequencies.

RELATED KEYWORDS
IOp, Int=Grid, SCF=(VShift,QC), Stable

EXAMPLES

The energy is reported in DFT calculations in a form similar to that of Hartree-Fock calculations. Here is the energy output from a **Becke3LYP** calculation:

```
SCF Done:   E(RB+HF-LYP) =   -75.3197099428     A.U. after    5 cycles
```

The item in parentheses following the E denotes the method used to obtain the energy. The output from a **BLYP** calculation is labeled similarly:

```
SCF Done:   E(RB-LYP) =   -75.2867073414     A.U. after    5 cycles
```

➤ DREIDING

See **Molecular Mechanics Methods** *below*.

➤ ExtraBasis

DESCRIPTION

This keyword indicates that additional basis functions are to be added to the basis set specified in the route section for the calculation. These basis functions appear in a separate section in the input stream, using any of the valid formats (which are described in detail in the discussion of the **Gen** keyword).

RELATED KEYWORDS

Gen, Pseudo

EXAMPLES

The following job uses the 6-31G(d,p) basis set along with an additional (diffuse) function on all of the carbon atoms:

```
# HF/6-31G(d,p) ExtraBasis …
```

title section

molecule specification

```
C 0
SP 1 1.00
 0.4380000000D-01   0.1000000000D+01   0.1000000000D+01
****
```

The following job uses the 6-311G(d,p) basis set for Cr and the 6-31G(d,p) for all other atoms (Cr is not present in 6-31G):

```
# HF/6-31G(d,p) ExtraBasis ...
```

title section

molecule specification

```
Cr 0
6-311G(d,p)
****
```

➤ Field

DESCRIPTION
The **Field** keyword requests that a finite field be added to calculation. In *Gaussian 98*, the field can either involve electric multipoles (through hexadecapoles) or a Fermi contact term. **Field** requires a parameter in one of these two formats:

$$M \pm N \quad \text{or} \quad F(M)N$$

where M designates a multipole, and $F(M)$ designates a Fermi contact perturbation for atom M (following the ordering in the molecule specification section of the input file). $N*0.0001$ specifies the magnitude of the field in atomic units in the first format, and specifies the magnitude of the Fermi contact perturbation in the second format.

Thus, **Field=X+10** applies an electric dipole field in the X direction of 0.001 au, while **Field=XXYZ–20** applies the indicated hexadecapole field with magnitude 0.0020 au and direction opposite to the default (which is determined by the standard orientation). Similarly, **Field=F(3)27** applies a perturbation of 0.0027 times the spin density on atom 3.

Note that the coefficients are those of the Cartesian operator matrices; be careful of the choice of sign convention when interpreting the results.

The field specification parameter may be placed among any other options as desired. Archiving is disabled when **Field** is specified.

OPTIONS

Read   Reads the coefficients of 35 electric multipole components from the input stream, using format 3D20.10. The first component is a charge, and other field components follow in lower trangular/tetrahedral/... order.

RWF   Takes the 35 multipole components from the read-write file.

ERWF	Extracts only the three electric dipole field components from the read-write file.
Checkpoint	Reads the 35 multipole components from the checkpoint file. **Chk** is a synonym for **Checkpoint**.
EChk	Extracts only the three electric dipole field components from the checkpoint file.

AVAILABILITY
Single point energy, **Force**, and **Scan** calculations only.

LIMITATIONS
Note that if symmetry is left on during a GVB calculation, the finite field will or will not lead to correct numerical derivatives, depending on whether the selected field breaks molecular symmetry. To be safe, use **Guess=NoSymm** whenever using **Field** with **GVB**.

➤ FMM

DESCRIPTION
Force the use of the fast multipole method [29-33, 338-340] if possible. Using FMM is recommended for large calculations involving pure DFT functionals.

OPTIONS

LMax=N	Specifies the maximum order multipole. The defaults are 12 for single point calculations and 18 for other calculation types.
Levels=N	Specifies the number of levels to use in the FMM. The default is 8.
Tolerance=N	Specifies the accuracy level as 10^{-N}. The default values for N are 8 for single point energy calculations and 10 for other calculation types.
BoxLen=N	Sets the minimum box length (size) to $N/10$ Bohrs. By default, N is 30.

AVAILABILITY
Energies, gradients and frequencies for pure DFT methods.

RELATED KEYWORDS
Sparse

➤ FormCheck

The **FormCheck** keyword requests that a formatted version of the checkpoint file be written at the end of a successful run. This is useful for users who wish to interface the output of the program to various front-ends. Currently, the formatted checkpoint file always has the name Test.FChk (note the mixed case), and it is placed into the default directory from which the job is run.

This keyword cannot store transition densities or natural orbitals in the formatted checkpoint file.

FChk and **FCheck** are synonyms for **FormCheck**.

OPTIONS

All   Write everything to the formatted checkpoint file.

ForceInt   Write forces in internal coordinates.

ForceCart   Write forces in Cartesian coordinates.

EField   Write the electric field properties (in Cartesian coordinates).

OptInt   Write the intermediate structures from an optimization in internal coordinates.

OptCart   Write the intermediate structures from an optimization in Cartesian coordinates.

Basis   Write the basis set data (exponents, coefficients, etc.).

MO   Write the Molecular orbitals.

DENSITY-RELATED OPTIONS

Spin   If densities are requested, write separate α and β components (the default is the total density).

UseNO   If densities are requested, use the natural orbital representation (the default is the density lower triangle).

SCFDensity   Write the SCF density.

CurrentDensity Write the generalized density for the current method.

AllDensities   Write all available densities.

CurrTrans   Write the transition density between the ground and current state.

GroundTrans   Write the transition densities between the ground and all excited states.

GroundCurrTrans Write all transition densities involving *either* the ground or the current state.

AllTrans	Write all transition densities.
CurrEx1PDM	Write the CI-Singles 1PDM for the current state.
AllEx1PDM	Write all CI-Singles 1PDMs.

RELATED KEYWORDS
Output, **%Chk**; see also the discussion of the **formchk** utility in chapter 5.

➤ Force

DESCRIPTION
This calculation type keyword requests a single calculation of the forces on the nuclei (i.e., the gradient of the energy). The dipole moment is also computed (as a proper analytic derivative of the energy for MP2, CC, QCI and CI) [163, 313].

OPTIONS

EnOnly   Compute the forces by numerically differentiating the energy once. It is the default for all methods for which analytic gradients are unavailable. Note that this procedure exhibits some numerical instability, so care must be taken that an optimal step size is specified for each case.

Restart   Restarts numerical evaluation of the forces.

StepSize=*N*   Sets the step size used in numerical differentiation to 0.0001*N*. The units are Angstroms by default unless **Units=Bohr** has been specified. The default step size is 0.01 Å. **StepSize** is valid only in conjunction with **EnOnly**.

AVAILABILITY
Analytic gradients are available for all SCF wavefunctions, all DFT methods, CIS, MP2, MP3, MP4(SDQ), CID, CISD, CCD, QCISD, CASSCF, and all semi-empirical methods. For other methods, the forces are determined by numerical differentiation.

EXAMPLES
The forces on the nuclei appears in the output as follows (this sample is from a calculation on water):

```
***** AXES RESTORED TO ORIGINAL SET *****
---------------------------------------------------------------
Center     Atomic                Forces (Hartrees/Bohr)
Number     Number         X              Y              Z
---------------------------------------------------------------
   1          8       -.049849321     .000000000    -.028780519
   2          1        .046711997     .000000000    -.023346514
```

3		1		.003137324		.000000000		.052127033

	MAX	.052127033	RMS	.031211490

Internal Coordinate Forces (Hartree/Bohr or radian)

Cent	Atom	N1	Length/X	N2	Alpha/Y	N3	Beta/Z	J

1	O							
2	H	1	-.023347(1)					
3	H	1	-.023347(2)	2	-.088273(3)			

	MAX	.088272874	RMS	.054412682

The forces are determined in the standard orientation, but are restored to the original (Z-matrix) set of axes before printing (as noted in the output). This is followed by a display of the corresponding derivatives with respect to the internal coordinates (lengths and angles used in the Z-matrix) when internal coordinates are in use. The forces are followed in each case by their maximum and root-mean-square values.

➤ Freq

DESCRIPTION
This calculation type keyword computes force constants and the resulting vibrational frequencies. Intensities are also computed. By default, the force constants are determined analytically if possible (for RHF, UHF, MP2, CIS, all DFT methods, and CASSCF), by single numerical differentiation for methods for which only first derivatives are available (MP3, MP4(SDQ), CID, CISD, CCD, QCISD, and all semi-empirical methods), and by double numerical differentiation for those methods for which only energies are available. When frequencies are done analytically, polarizabilities are also computed automatically; when numerical differentiation is required, polarizabilities must be explicitly requested using the **Polar** keyword (e.g., **QCISD Freq Polar**).

The **VCD** option may be used to compute the vibrational circular dichroism (VCD) intensities in addition to the normal frequency analysis [178].

Vibrational frequencies are computed by determining the second derivatives of the energy with respect to the Cartesian nuclear coordinates and then transforming to mass-weighted coordinates. *This transformation is only valid at a stationary point!* Thus, it is *meaningless* to compute frequencies at any geometry other than a stationary point *for the method used for frequency determination.* For example, computing 3-21G frequencies at a STO-3G optimized geometry produces meaningless results. It is also incorrect to compute frequencies for a correlated method using frozen-core at a structure optimized with all electrons correlated, or vice-versa. The recommended practice is to compute frequencies following a previous geometry optimization using the same method. This may be accomplished automatically by specifying both **Opt** and **Freq** within the route section for a job.

Note also that the coupled perturbed Hartree-Fock (CPHF) method used in determining analytic frequencies is not physically meaningful if a lower energy wavefunction of the same spin multiplicity exists. Use the **Stable** keyword to test the stability of Hartree-Fock and DFT wavefunctions.

The keyword **Opt=CalcAll** requests that analytic second derivatives be done at every point in a geometry optimization. Once the requested optimization has completed all the information necessary for a frequency analysis is available. Therefore, the frequency analysis is performed and the results of the calculation are archived as a frequency job.

OPTIONS

VCD   Compute the vibrational circular dichroism (VCD) intensities in addition to the normal frequency analysis [178]. This option is valid for SCF and DFT methods.

Raman   Compute Raman intensities in addition to IR intensities. This is the default for SCF frequency calculations. It may be specified for DFT and MP2 calculations in order to produce Raman intensities by numerical integration.

NoRaman   Skips the extra steps required to compute the Raman intensities during analytic frequency calculations, saving 10-30% in CPU time. This option is operative only for the **HF** method.

ReadIsotopes   Specify alternate temperature, pressure, and/or isotopes (the defaults are 298.15 K, 1 atmosphere, and the most abundant isotopes). This information appears in a separate input section having the format:

            temp pressure [scale]   *Must be floating point numbers.*
            isotope mass for atom 1
            isotope mass for atom 2
            ...
            isotope mass for atom n

where *temp*, *pressure*, and *scale* are the desired temperature, pressure, and an optional scale factor for frequency data when used for thermochemical analysis (the default value of $1/1.12$ (≈ 0.8929) if *scale* is omitted or set to 0.0). The remaining lines hold the isotope masses for the various atoms in the molecule, arranged in the same order as they appeared in the molecule specification section. If integers are used to specify the atomic masses, the program will automatically use the corresponding actual exact isotopic mass (e.g., 18 specifies O^{18}, and *Gaussian 98* uses the value 17.99916).

ReadFC   Requests that the force constants from a previous frequency calculation be read from the checkpoint file, and the normal mode and thermochemical analysis be repeated, presumably using a different temperature, pressure, or isotopes, at minimal computational cost. Note that since the basis set is read from the checkpoint file, no general basis should be input.

HPModes   Include the high precision format (to five figures) vibrational frequency eigenvectors in the frequency output in addition to the normal three-figure output.

Analytic   This specifies that the second derivatives of the energy are to be computed analytically. This option is available only for RHF, UHF, CIS, CASSCF, MP2, and all DFT methods, and it is the default for those cases.

Numerical   This requests that the second derivatives of the energy are to be computed numerically using analytically calculated first derivatives. It can be used with any method for which gradients are available and is the default for those for which gradients but not second derivatives are available. **Freq=Numer** can be combined with **Polar=Numer** in one job step.

EnOnly   This requests double numerical differentiation of energies to produce force constants. It is the default and only choice for those methods for which no analytic derivatives are available. This option is not available for the restricted open shell (RO) methods, for the semi-empirical methods, or for the CI methods. **EnergyOnly** is a synonym for **EnOnly**.

Cubic   Requests numerical differentiation of analytic second derivatives to produce third derivatives.

Step=*N*   Specifies the step-size for numerical differentiation to be 0.0001*N (in Angstoms unless **Units=Bohr** has been specified). If **Freq=Numer** and **Polar=Numer** are combined, N also specifies the step-size in the electric field. The default is 0.001 Å for Hartree-Fock and correlated **Freq=Numer**, 0.005 for GVB and CASSCF **Freq=Numer**, and 0.01 Å for **Freq=EnOnly**.

Restart   This option restarts a numerical frequency calculation after the last completed geometry (analytic frequency calculations are not restartable). A failed numerical frequency job may be restarted from its checkpoint file by simply repeating the route section of the original job, adding the **Restart** option to the **Freq** keyword. No other input is required.

Projected   For a point on a mass-weighted reaction path (IRC), compute the projected frequencies for vibrations perpendicular to the path. For the projection, the gradient is used to compute the tangent to the path. Note that this computation is very sensitive to the accuracy of the structure and the path [341]. Accordingly, the geometry should be specified to at least 5 significant digits. This computation is not meaningful at a minimum.

HindRot   Requests the identification of internal rotation modes during the harmonic vibrational analysis [342]. If any normal modes are identified as internal rotation, hindered or free, the thermodynamic functions are corrected. The identification of the rotating groups is made possible by the use of redundant internal coordinates. Thus, redundant internal coordinates *must* be used for the **HindRot** option to function properly. Because some structures, such as transition states, may have a specific bonding pattern not automatically recognized, the set of redundant internal coordinates may need to be altered via the **Geom=Modify** keyword.

   If the force constants are available on a previously generated checkpoint file, additional vibrational/internal rotation analyses may be performed by specifying **Freq=(ReadFC, HindRot)**. Since **Opt=CalcAll** automatically performs a vibrational analysis on the optimized structure, **Opt=(CalcAll, HindRot)** may also be used.

ReadInfo   Specify parameter values for a **Freq=HindRot** calculation (default values are automatically assigned by the program) via the additional input lines below:

VMax
J K N1 N2 N3   *Repeated as needed.*
...
        Blank line terminates input.

VMax is the maximum value (in kcal/mol) of the estimated barrier for identification of internal rotation. If it is set to zero, the default value of 20.0 kcal/mol is used.

Additional input lines specify the periodicity of the model potential (*N1*), the symmetry number for the rotating group (*N2*), and number of wells to be considered (*N3*) for rotation about the bond joining atom numbers *J* and *K*. Setting any of the parameters *N1*, *N2* or *N3* to zero retains the automatically assigned value; setting any one parameters to a negative value will cause rotation about this bond to be treated as a vibration. Input is terminated by a blank line.

AVAILABILITY
Analytic frequencies are available for the HF, DFT, MP2, CIS and CASSCF methods. Numerical frequencies are available for MP3, MP4(SDQ), CID, CISD, CCD and QCISD.

RELATED KEYWORDS
Polar, Opt, Stable

EXAMPLES
The following two-step job contains an initial frequency calculation followed by a second thermochemistry analysis using a different temperature, pressure, and selection of isotopes:

```
%Chk=freq
# HF/6-31G(d,p) Freq Test

Frequencies for test 34

molecule specification

--Link1--
%Chk=freq
%NoSave
# HF/6-31G(d,p) Freq(ReadIso,ReadFC) Geom=AllCheck Test

300.0 1.0
16
 2
 3
...
```

Note also that the **freqchk** utility (described in chapter 5) may be used to rerun the thermochemical analysis from the frequency data stored in a *Gaussian* checkpoint file.

The basic components of the output from a frequency calculation are discussed in detail in chapter 4 of *Exploring Chemistry with Electronic Structure Methods* [210].

You may be surprised to see output that looks like it belongs to a geometry optimization at the beginning of a frequency job:

```
GradGradGradGradGradGradGradGradGradGradGradGradGradGradGrad
Berny optimization.
Initialization pass.
```

Link 103, which performs geometry optimizations, is executed at the beginning and end of all frequency calculations. This is done so that the quadratic optimization step can be computed using the correct second derivatives. Occasionally an optimization will complete according to the normal criterion using the approximate Hessian matrix, but the step size is actually larger than the convergence criterion when the correct second derivatives are used. The next step is printed at the end of a frequency calculation so that such problems can be identified. If you think this concern is applicable, use **Opt=CalcAll** instead of **Freq** in the route section of the job, which will complete the optimization if the geometry is determined not to have fully converged (usually, given the full second derivative matrix near a stationary point, only one additional optimization step is needed), and will automatically perform a frequency analysis at the final structure.

Specifying **#P** in the route section produces some additional output for frequency calculations. Of most importance are the polarizability and hyperpolarizability tensors (they still may be found in the archive entry in normal print-level jobs). They are presented in lower triangular and lower tetrahedral order, respectively (i.e., α_{XX}, α_{XY}, α_{YY}, α_{XZ}, α_{YZ}, α_{ZZ} and β_{XXX}, β_{XXY}, β_{XYY}, β_{YYY}, β_{XXZ}, β_{XYZ}, β_{YYZ}, β_{XZZ}, β_{YZZ}, β_{ZZZ}), in the standard orientation:

```
Dipole          = 2.37312183D-16 -6.66133815D-16 -9.39281319D-01
Polarizability= 7.83427191D-01   1.60008472D-15   6.80285860D+00
                -3.11369582D-17   2.72397709D-16   3.62729494D+00
HyperPolar      = 3.08796953D-16 -6.27350412D-14   4.17080415D-16
                 5.55019858D-14 -7.26773439D-01 -1.09052038D-14
                -2.07727337D+01   4.49920497D-16 -1.40402516D-13
                -1.10991697D+01
```

#P also produces a bar-graph of the simulated spectra for small cases.

Thermochemistry analysis follows the frequency and normal mode data. The zero-point energy output in *Gaussian 98* has been expanded over that produced by previous versions:

```
Zero-point correction=                         .023261 (Hartree/Particle)
Thermal correction to Energy=                  .026094
Thermal correction to Enthalpy=                .027038
Thermal correction to Gibbs Free Energy=       .052698
Sum of electronic and zero-point Energies=    -527.492    E₀=E_elec+ZPE
Sum of electronic and thermal Energies=       -527.489    E= E₀+ E_vib+ E_rot+ E_trans
Sum of electronic and thermal Enthalpies=     -527.488    H=E+RT
Sum of electronic and thermal Free Energies=  -527.463    G=H–TS
```

The raw zero-point energy correction and the thermal corrections to the total energy, enthalpy, and Gibbs free energy (all of which include the zero-point energy) are listed, followed by the corresponding corrected energy. The analysis uses the standard expressions for an ideal gas in the canonical ensemble. Details can be found in McQuarrie [343] and other standard statistical mechanics texts. In the output, the various quantities are labeled as follows:

E (Thermal)	Contributions to the thermal energy correction
CV	Constant volume molar heat capacity
S	Entropy
Q	Partition function

The thermochemistry analysis treats all modes other than the free rotations and translations as harmonic vibrations. For molecules having hindered internal rotations, this can produce slight errors in the energy and heat capacity at room temperatures and can have a significant effect on the entropy. The contributions of any very low frequency vibrational modes are listed separately so that if they are group rotations and high accuracy is needed, their harmonic contributions can be subtracted from the totals, and their correctly computed contributions included. Expressions for hindered rotational contributions to these terms can be found in Benson [344]. The partition functions are also computed, with both the bottom of the vibrational well and the lowest (zero-point) vibrational state as reference.

➤ G1
➤ G2
➤ G2MP2

DESCRIPTION

These method keywords request the Gaussian-1 (more colloquially known as G1) [84, 85] and Gaussian-2 (G2) [86] methods for computing very accurate energies. **G2MP2** requests the modified version of G2 known as G2(MP2), which uses MP2 instead of MP4 for the basis set extension corrections [87], and is nearly as accurate as the full G2 method at substantially reduced computational cost. All of these methods are complex energy computations involving several pre-defined calculations on the specified molecular system. All of the distinct steps are performed automatically when one of these keywords is specified, and the final computed energy value is displayed in the output. No basis set keyword should be specified with these keywords.

Either of the **Opt=Maxcyc=**n or **QCISD=Maxcyc=**n keywords may be used in conjunction with any of the these keywords to specify the maximum number of optimization or QCISD cycles, respectively. Note, however, that they may not be combined with the **Restart** option.

OPTIONS

ReadIsotopes   Specify alternate temperature, pressure, and/or isotopes (the defaults are 298.15 K, 1 atmosphere, and the most abundant isotopes). This information appears in a separate input section having the format:

> *temp pressure [scale]*   *Must be real numbers.*
> *isotope mass for atom 1*
> *isotope mass for atom 2*
> *...*
> *isotope mass for atom n*

where *temp*, *pressure*, and *scale* are the desired temperature, pressure, and an optional scale factor for frequency data when used for thermochemical analysis (the default value of 1/1.12 ($\approx$ 0.8929) if *scale* is omitted or set to 0.0). The remaining lines hold the isotope masses for the various atoms in the molecule, arranged in the same order as they appeared in the molecule specification section. If integers are used to specify the atomic masses, the program will automatically use the corresponding actual exact mass (e.g., 18 specifies O^{18}, and *Gaussian 98* uses the value 17.99916).

Restart Resume a partially-completed calculation from its checkpoint file. When used in combination with **ReadIso**, this option allows for the rapid computation of the energy using different thermochemistry parameters and/or isotope selections.

StartMP2 Assume that the specified checkpoint file contains the results of a Hartree-Fock frequency calculation at the HF/6-31G* optimized structure, and begins the G2 calculation from that point (implies **Geom=AllCheck**).

AVAILABILITY
These methods are available for systems comprised of atoms through chlorine.

EXAMPLES
Calculation Summary Output. After all of the output for the component job steps, *Gaussian 98* prints a table of results for these methods. Here is the output from a G2 calculation:

```
Temperature=         298.150000    Pressure=              1.000000
E(ZPE)=                 .020511    E(Thermal)=             .023346
E(QCISD(T))=         -76.276078    E(Empiric)=            -.024560
DE(Plus)=               -.010827    DE(2DF)=               -.037385
G1(0 K)=             -76.328339    G1 Energy=           -76.325503
G1 Enthalpy=         -76.324559    G1 Free Energy=      -76.303182
E(Delta-G2)=            -.008275    E(G2-Empiric)=          .004560
G2(0 K)=             -76.332054    G2 Energy=           -76.329219
G2 Enthalpy=         -76.328274    G2 Free Energy=      -76.306897
```

The temperature and pressure appear first, followed by the various components used to compute the G2 energy. The output concludes with the G2 energy at 0 K and at the specified temperature (the latter includes a full thermal correction rather than just the zero-point energy correction), and (in the final output line) the G2 theory predictions for the enthalpy and Gibbs free energy (both computed using the thermal-corrected G2 energy). (Note that the same quantities predicted at the G1 level are also printed in this summary section.)

The energy labels thus have the following meanings:

G2 (0 K)	Zero-point-corrected electronic energy: $E_0 = E_{elec} + ZPE$
G2 Energy	Thermal-corrected energy: $E = E_0 + E_{trans} + E_{rot} + E_{vib}$
G2 Enthalpy	Enthalpy computed using the G2 predicted energy: $H = E + RT$
G2 Free Energy	Gibbs Free Energy computed using the G2 predicted energy: $G = H - TS$

Rerunning the Calculation at a Different Temperature. The following two-step job illustrates the method for running a second (very rapid) G2 calculation at a different temperature. This job computes the G2 energy at 298.15 K and then again at 300 K:

```
%Chk=formald
# G2 Test

G2 on formaldehyde

0 1
molecule specification

--Link1--
%Chk=formald
%NoSave
# G2(Restart,ReadIso) Geom=AllCheck Test

300.0 1.0
isotope specifications
```

➤ Gen

DESCRIPTION

A set of "standard" basis sets is stored internally in *Gaussian 98* (see the "Basis Sets" section earlier in this chapter); these basis sets may be specified by including the appropriate keyword within the route section for the calculation. The **Gen** keyword allows a user-specified basis set to be used in a *Gaussian 98* calculation. It is used in the place of a basis set keyword. In this case, the basis set description must be provided as input (in a separate basis set input section).

The **GFPrint** keyword may be used to include the gaussian function table within the output file. The **GFInput** keyword may be used to have the table printed in a form which is suitable for input to **Gen**. The **ExtraBasis** keyword may be used to make additions to standard basis sets.

BASIS FUNCTION OVERVIEW

A single *basis function* is composed of one or more *primitive gaussian functions.* For example, an s-type basis function $\phi_\mu(r)$ is:

$$\phi_\mu(r) = \sum_{i=1}^{N} d_{i\mu} e^{-\alpha_{i\mu} f_\mu^2 r^2}$$

N is the number of primitive functions composing the basis function, and it is called the *degree-of-contraction* of the basis function. The coefficients $d_{i\mu}$ are called *contraction coefficients.* The quantities $\alpha_{i\mu}$ are the *exponents,* and f is the *scale factor* for the basis function. The maximum degree-of-contraction permitted in *Gaussian 98* is 100.

A *shell* is a set of basis functions $\{\phi_\mu\}$ with shared exponents. *Gaussian 98* supports shells of arbitrary angular momentum: s, p, d, f, g, h, and so on. An s-shell contains a single s-type basis function. A p-shell contains the three basis functions p_X, p_Y, and p_Z. An sp-shell contains four basis functions with common gaussian exponents: one s-type function and the three p-functions p_X, p_Y and p_Z.

A d-shell may be defined to contain either the six second-order functions (d_{X^2}, d_{Y^2}, d_{Z^2}, d_{XY}, d_{XZ}, d_{YZ}), or the five "pure d" basis functions ($d_{z^2-r^2}$, $d_{x^2-y^2}$, d_{xy}, d_{xz}, d_{yz}). Likewise, an f-shell may contain either the 10 third-order gaussians or the 7 "pure f" functions. Higher order shells function similarly. Note that the contraction coefficients in a shell must be the same for all functions of a given angular momentum, but that s and p contraction coefficients can be different in an sp-shell. A scale factor is also defined for each shell. It is used to scale all the exponents of primitives in the shell. The program has the ability to convert between pure and Cartesian functions [277].

Consider the series of basis sets STO-3G, 6-31G, and 6-311G(d) for the carbon atom. With the STO-3G, basis there are two shells on a carbon atom. One is an s-shell composed of 3 primitive gaussian functions (which are least-squares fit to a Slater 1s orbital). The other sp-shell is a least-squares fit of 3 gaussians to Slater 2s and 2p orbitals with the constraint that the s and p functions have equal exponents. These expansions are the same for all atoms. Only the scale factors for each shell differ from atom to atom. For carbon atoms, the 1s- and 2sp-shells have scale factors of 5.67 and 1.72, respectively. The 6-31G basis on a first row atom has three shells. One shell is a contraction of six primitive s-type gaussians. The second shell is a combination of three primitive sp-shells. The third shell consists of a single sp-function. These functions were optimized for the atom. Scale factors of 1.00, 1.00, and 1.04, respectively, for each shell for carbon were then determined by molecular calculations. As its name implies, the 6-311G(d) basis has 5 shells: an s-shell with 6 primitives, 3 sp-shells with 3, 1, and 1 primitives, and an uncontracted d-shell. All shells are "unscaled" (have unit scale factor).

BASIS SET INPUT FORMAT

External basis sets are read into *Gaussian 98* by specifying **Gen** (for general basis) in the route section. The keywords **5D**, **6D**, **7F**, and **10F** are used to specify use of Cartesian or pure d and f (and higher) functions; the defaults are **5D** and **7F**. All d-shells in a calculation must have the same number of functions. Similarly, f- and higher shells must either be all Cartesian or all pure.

Defining a shell. External basis input is handled by the routine GenBas in Link 301. The basic unit of information that it reads from the basis set input section is the *shell definition block*. A shell definition block, together with the global specification of pure vs. Cartesian functions, contains all necessary information to define a shell of functions. It consists of a *shell descriptor* line, and one or more *primitive gaussian* lines:

IType NGauss Sc	*Shell descriptor line: shell type, # primitive gaussians, and scale factor.*
α_1 $d_{1\mu}$	*Primitive gaussian specification: exponent and contraction coefficient.*
α_2 $d_{2\mu}$	
...	
α_N $d_{N\mu}$	*There are a total of NGauss primitive gaussian lines.*

IType defines the shell type and shell constraint and may be **S**, **P**, **D**, **SP**, **F**, **G**, ..., for an s-shell, p-shell, d-shell, sp-shell, f-shell, g-shell, and so on. *NGauss* specifies the number of primitive gaussian shells (the degree of contraction) for the shell being defined. The shell scale factor is given by *Sc* (i.e., all primitive exponents are scaled by Sc^2).

The subsequent *NGauss* primitive gaussian lines define the exponents α_k and contraction coefficients, $d_{k\mu}$. Each line provides the exponent for one primitive, followed by its contraction coefficient (or s and p coefficients for an sp-shell).

A second format also exists to specify a shell as a least-squares gaussian expansion of a Slater orbital. This is requested by a shell descriptor line of the form **STO**, *IOrb*, *NGauss*, *Sc*. *IOrb* is one of **1S**, **2S**, **2P**, **2SP**, **3S**, **3P**, **3SP**, **3D**, **4SP**, and specifies which expansion is requested. Note that **2SP** requests the best least-squares fit simultaneously to S and P slater orbitals and is not equivalent to separately specifying the best S and the best P expansions. *NGauss* is the same as above. Gaussian expansions of Slater functions having from 1 to 6 primitives are available. *Sc* is the scale factor and hence the exponent of the slater function being expanded. No primitive gaussian lines are required after a shell descriptor line requesting an STO expansion.

Defining the basis for an atom or atom type. One customarily places at least one, and often several, shells on any given nuclear center ("atom"), via a *center definition block*. A center definition block consists of a *center identifier line*, and one *shell definition block* for each shell desired on the center(s) specified. It is terminated by a line with either asterisks or plus signs in columns 1 through 4:

c_1 c_2 ... **0**	*Center identifier line: specifies applicability for these shells.*
IType NGauss Sc	*First shell definition block.*
α_2 $d_{2\mu}$	
...	
α_N $d_{N\mu}$	
...	*Additional shell definition blocks.*
IType NGauss Sc	*Final shell definition block.*
α_2 $d_{2\mu}$	
...	
α_N $d_{N\mu}$	
****	*Separator: terminates the center definition block.*

The center identifier line specifies a list of centers on which to place the basis functions in the center definition block, terminated by a 0. It can contain one or more integers, which are used to indicate the corresponding atom(s) in the molecule specification; more commonly, it contains a list of atomic symbols to refer to all atoms of a specific type. Center numbers and atomic symbols may be freely intermixed within a single center identifier line.

To help detect input mistakes, if a center definition block specifies an atom that is not present in the molecule, the run is aborted. If the center is preceded by a minus sign (e.g. **–H**), the basis set information is simply skipped if no atom of that type is present in the molecule specification (the terminal zero may also be omitted in this case). The latter syntax is intended for creating basis set include files that specify a standard basis set for many atoms; once built, it can be included in its entirety in the input stream when the basis set is desired, via the include (@) function (as described earlier in this chapter).

A center or atom type may be specified in more than one center definition block. For example, in the *Gaussian 98* basis set directory—$g98root/g98/basis on UNIX systems—there is one file which specifies 6-31G as a general basis set (631.gbs), and another file containing d exponents which would be included as well to specify 6-31G* (631s.gbs). Every atom from H through Cl is specified in both files, and in practice both of them would be included (most often along with additional basis set specifications for those atoms in the molecule for which the 6-31G basis set is not available).

Drawing on Pre-Defined Basis Sets in Gen Input. *Gaussian 98* adds flexibility to general basis set input by allowing them to include pre-defined basis sets within them. Within a center definition block for an atom type (or types), an entire shell definition block may be replaced by a line containing the standard keyword for a pre-defined basis set. In this case, all of the functions within the specified basis set corresponding to the specified atom type(s) will be used for all such atoms within the molecule.

The **SDD**, **SHF**, **SDF**, **MHF**, **MDF**, **MWB** forms may be used to specify Stuttgart/Dresden basis sets/potentials within **Gen** basis input. Note that the number of core electrons must be specified.

EXAMPLES

Here is a portion of the **Gen** input corresponding to the 6-31+G(d) basis set:

```
H  0                                              Applies to all hydrogen atoms.
S      3 1.00
  0.1873113696D+02    0.3349460434D-01
  0.2825394365D+01    0.2347269535D+00
  0.6401216923D+00    0.8137573262D+00
S      1 1.00
  0.1612777588D+00    0.1000000000D+01
 ****
C  0                                              Applies to all carbons.
S      6 1.00                                     6-31G functions.
  0.3047524880D+04    0.1834737130D-02
  0.4573695180D+03    0.1403732280D-01
  0.1039486850D+03    0.6884262220D-01
  0.2921015530D+02    0.2321844430D+00
  0.9286662960D+01    0.4679413480D+00
  0.3163926960D+01    0.3623119850D+00
SP     3 1.00
  0.7868272350D+01  -0.1193324200D+00    0.6899906660D-01
  0.1881288540D+01  -0.1608541520D+00    0.3164239610D+00
  0.5442492580D+00    0.1143456440D+01    0.7443082910D+00
SP     1 1.00
  0.1687144782D+00    0.1000000000D+01    0.1000000000D+01
D      1 1.00
  0.8000000000D+00    0.1000000000D+01                Polarization function.
 ****
C  0                                              Applies to all carbons.
SP     1 1.00                                     Diffuse function.
  0.4380000000D-01    0.1000000000D+01    0.1000000000D+01
 ****
```

The following **Gen** input uses the 6-31G(d,p) basis set for the carbon and hydrogen atoms and the 6-31G†† basis set for the fluorine atoms in the molecule, and places an extra function only on center number 1 (which happens to be the first carbon atom in the molecule specification for 1,1-difluoroethylene):

```
C H 0
6-31G(d,p)
****
F 0
6-31G(d',p')
****
1 0                          Place a diffuse function on just one carbon atom.
SP    1 1.00
  0.4380000000D-01   0.1000000000D+01   0.1000000000D+01
****
```

The following job uses the *Gaussian 98* include file mechanism to specify the basis functions for chromium:

```
# Becke3LYP/Gen Opt Test

HF/6-31G(*) Opt of Cr(CO)6
```

molecule specification

```
C O 0
6-31G(d)
****
@/home/gwtrucks/basis/chrome.gbs/N
```

Note that **.gbs** is the conventional extension for basis set files (for *gaussian basis set*).

RELATED KEYWORDS
ExtraBasis, GFInput, GFPrint; see also the "Basis Sets" section earlier in this chapter.

➤ Geom

DESCRIPTION
The **Geom** keyword specifies the source of the molecule specification input. By default, it is read from the input stream, as described previously. **Geom** may be used to specify an alternate input source. It also controls what geometry-related information is printed and use of internal consistency checks on the Z-matrix. The **Geom** keyword is not meaningful without at least one item selection option.

ITEM SELECTION OPTIONS
Checkpoint   Causes the molecule specification (including variables) to be taken from the checkpoint file. Only the charge and multiplicity are read from the input stream. For

example, **Geom=Checkpoint** may be used by a later job step to retrieve the geometry optimized during an earlier job step from the checkpoint file. This action is safe since *Gaussian 98* will abort the job if an optimization fails, and consequently subsequent job steps which expect to use the optimized geometry will not be executed. May be combined with the **ModRedundant** option if you want to retrieve and alter the molecule specification in a checkpoint file using redundant internal coordinate-style modifications.

AllCheckpoint   Causes the molecule specification (including variables), the charge and multiplicity, and the title section to be taken from the checkpoint file. Thus, only the route section and any input required by keywords within it need be specified when using this option. This option is not valid with **Modify** but may be combined with **ModRed**.

Step=N   Retrieves the structure produced by the Nth step of a failed or partial geometry optimization (it is not valid for a successful optimization). **Step=Original** recovers the initial starting geometry. This option is used for restarting geometry optimization from intermediate points. It must be combined with one of **Checkpoint**, **AllCheck** or **Modify**. Note that not all steps are always present in the checkpoint file; a **Hessian updated** message in the log file means that the corresponding step is available in the checkpoint file.

ModRedundant

Modify the current geometry (regardless of its coordinate system) using redundant internal coordinate modifications before performing the calculation. This option may be used to modify a geometry specified in the input file using these features even when some calculation type other than an optimization is to be performed. It may also be combined with **Step**, **Check** or **AllCheck** to retrieve and modify a geometry from a checkpoint file.

When used with **Check** or **Step**, two input sections will be read: the first contains the charge and multiplicity, and the second contains alterations to the retrieved geometry. When combined with the **AllCheck** option, only the geometry modifications input is needed.

Modification specifications for redundant coordinates have the same format as the input for the **ModRedundant** option of the **Opt** keyword (we summarize these formats only briefly here; see the discussion of the **Opt** keyword for a full description):

$$[Type]\ N1\ [N2\ [N3\ [N4]]]\ [[+=]\ Value]\ [Action\ [Params]]\ [[Min]\ Max]]$$

N1, *N2*, *N3* and *N4* are atom numbers or wildcards. (numbering begins at 1 and any dummy atoms are not counted.) *Value* gives a new value for the specified coordinate, and *+=Value* increments the coordinate by *Value*.

Action is an optional one-character code letter indicating the coordinate modification to be performed, sometimes followed by additional required parameters (the default action is to add the specified coordinate):

B   Add the coordinate and build all related coordinates.

K	Remove the coordinate and kill all related coordinates containing this coordinate.
A	Activate the coordinate for optimization if it has been frozen.
F	Freeze the coordinate in the optimization.
R	Remove the coordinate from the definition list (but not the related coordinates).
S *n stp*	Perform a relaxed potential energy surface scan. Set the initial value to *Value* (or its current value), and increment the coordinate by *stp* a total of *n* times, performing an optimization from each resulting starting geometry.
H *dv*	Change the diagonal element for this coordinate in the initial Hessian to *dv*.
D	Calculate numerical second derivatives for the row and column of the initial Hessian for this coordinate.

An asterisk (*) in the place of an atom number indicates a wildcard. *Min* and *Max* define a range (or maximum value if *Min* is not given) for coordinate specifications containing wildcards. The *Action* is taken only if the value of the coordinate is in the range.

Type can be used to designate a specific coordinate type (by default, the coordinate type is determined automatically from the number of atoms specified):

X	Cartesian coordinates. In this case, *Value, Min* and *Max* are each triples of numbers, specifying the X,Y,Z coordinates.
B	Bond length
A	Valence angle
D	Dihedral angle
L	Linear bend specified by three atoms (or if *N4 is* -1) or by four atoms, where the fourth atom is used to determine the 2 orthogonal directions of the linear bend. In this case, *Value, Min* and *Max* are each pairs of numbers, specifying the two orthogonal bending components.
O	Out-of-plane bending coordinate for a center (*N1*) and three connected atoms.

Modify   Specifies that the geometry is to be taken from the checkpoint file and that modifications will be made to it. A total of two input sections will be read: the first contains the charge and multiplicity, and the second contains alterations to the retrieved geometry. Note that in *Gaussian 98*, **Modi** is the shortest valid abbreviation for this keyword.

Modification specifications for optimizations using redundant coordinates have the same format as the input for the **ModRedundant** option discussed previously.

Modification specifications for geometry optimizations using Z-matrix coordinates have the following form:

> *variable* [*new-value*] [**A**|**F**|**D**]

where *variable* is the name of a variable in the molecule specification, *new-value* is an optional new value to be assigned to it, and the final item is a one-letter code indicating whether the variable is to be active (i.e., optimized) or frozen; the code letter **D** requests numerical differentiation be performed with respect to that variable and activates the variable automatically. If the code letter is omitted, then the variable's status remains the same as it was in the original molecule specification.

Connect   Specify explicit atom bonding data via an additional input section (blank line-terminated) following the geometry specification and any modification to it. This option requires one line of input per atom, ordered the same as in the molecule specification, using the following syntax:

N1 Order1 [*N2 Order2* ...]

where the *N*'s are atoms to which the current atom is bonded, and the *Order*'s are the bond order of the corresponding bond. For example, this input specifies that the current atom is bonded to atoms 4 and 5, with bond orders of 1.0 and 2.0 respectively: 4 1.0 5 2.0

ModConnect   Modify the default connectivity of the atoms in the molecule specification. This option requires an additional input section (blank line-terminated) following the geometry specification and any modification to it. Connectivity modifications use the following syntax:

M N1 Order1 [*N2 Order2* ...]

where *M* is the atom number, the *N*'s are atoms to which that atom is bonded, and the *Order*'s are the bond order of the corresponding bond. A bond order of -1.0 removes a bond. For example, this input specifies that atom 8 is bonded to atoms 4 and 5, with bond orders of 1.0 and 2.0 respectively, and removes any bond to atom 9: 8 4 1.0 5 2.0 9 -1.0

OUTPUT-RELATED OPTIONS

Distance   Requests printing of the atomic distance matrix (which is the default). **NoDistance** suppresses this output.

Angle   Requests printing of the interatomic angles, using the Z-matrix to determine which atoms are bonded. The default is to print unless some atoms are specified by Cartesian coordinates or an optimization in redundant internal coordinates is being performed. **NoAngle** suppresses this output.

CAngle   Requests printing of interatomic angles using distance cutoffs to determine bonded atoms. The default is not to print unless at least one atom is specified using Cartesian coordinates. Only one of **Angle**, **CAngle**, and **NoAngle** may be specified.

Dihedral   Specifies printing of dihedral angles using connectivity information from the Z-matrix to decide which atoms are bonded (the default is not to print). **NoDihedral** suppresses this output.

CDihedral   Requests printing of dihedral angles using distance cutoffs to determine connectivity. Only one of **Dihedral**, **CDihedral**, and **NoDihedral** may be specified

GEOMETRY SPECIFICATION AND CHECKING OPTIONS

KeepConstants   **KeepConstants** retains and **NoKeepConstants** discards information about frozen variables. The default is to retain them in symbolic form for the Berny algorithm, and to discard them for older optimization algorithms (which don't understand them anyway).

KeepDefinition   Retains the definition of the redundant internal coordinates (the default). Its opposite is **NewDefinition**.

NewDefinition   Rebuilds the redundant internal coordinates from the current Cartesian coordinates. If used with **Geom=Modify**, the new modifications are appended to any earlier **Opt=ModRedundant** input before the coordinate system is updated.

Crowd   **Crowd** activates and **NoCrowd** turns off a check which aborts the job if atoms are closer than 0.5 Å. By default, the check is done at the initial point, but not at later points of an optimization.

Independent   **Independent** activates and **NoIndependent** turns off a check on the linear independence of the variables specified in a Z-matrix. This is done by default only if a full optimization is requested using the Berny algorithm (**Opt=Z-matrix**).

MODEL BUILDER OPTIONS

ModelA   These options specify that model builder [345] connectivity information will be read
ModelB   and used to construct a symbolic Z-matrix. This option is implemented only for H through Ne, and in some cases will not generate a symbolic Z-matrix with the correct symmetry-constrained number of variables. If geometry optimization has been requested and this problem occurs, the job will be aborted. The input for the model builder is described in Appendix B.

Print   Turns on additional printing by the model builder facility.

RELATED KEYWORDS
Guess=Read, Opt=ModRedundant

➤ GFInput

DESCRIPTION

The **GFInput** ("Gaussian Function Input") output generation keyword causes the current basis set to be printed in a form suitable for use as general basis set input, and can thus be used in adding to or modifying standard basis sets.

RELATED KEYWORDS
Gen, GFPrint

➤ GFPrint

DESCRIPTION
This output generation keyword prints the current basis set in tabular form.

RELATED KEYWORDS
Gen, GFInput

➤ Guess

DESCRIPTION
This keyword controls the initial guess for the Hartree-Fock wavefunction. **Guess** is not meaningful without an option. By default, an INDO guess is used for first-row systems, CNDO for second-row, and Huckel for third-row and beyond.

OPTIONS

Alter   Indicates that the orbitals selected for occupation in the Hartree-Fock wavefunction should not be those of lowest energy. Normally, the occupied orbitals are selected as those with lowest eigenvalues for the one-electron Hamiltonian used in the initial guess programs. The alteration sections consist of a set of transpositions indicating that one of these occupied orbitals is to be replaced by one of the other (virtual) orbitals. Each such transposition is on a separate line and has two integers N_1 and N_2 (free format, separated by spaces or a comma as usual) indicating that orbital N_1 is to be swapped with orbital N_2. The list of orbital transpositions is terminated by the blank line at the end of the input section.

For UHF calculations, two such orbital alteration sections are required, the first specifying transpositions of α orbitals, and the second specifying transpositions of β orbitals. Both sections are always required. Thus, even if only α transpositions are needed, the β section is required even though it is empty (and vice-versa). The second blank line to indicate an empty β section *must* be included.

Read   Requests that the initial guess be read from the checkpoint file (**Guess=Read** is often specified along with **Geom=Checkpoint**). This option may be combined with **Alter**, in which case the orbitals are read from the checkpoint file, projected onto the current basis set, and then the specified alterations are made. **Checkpoint** is a synonym for **Read**.

Always   Requests that a new initial guess be generated at each point of an optimization. By default, the SCF results from the last point are used for the guess at the next point.

Mix Requests that the HOMO and LUMO be mixed so as to destroy α–β and spatial symmetries. This is useful in producing UHF wavefunctions for singlet states.

LowSymm Requests that irreducible representations of the molecular point group be combined in the symmetry information used in the N^3 steps in the SCF, to allow lowered symmetry of the wavefunction. This enables the orbitals (and possibly but not necessarily the total wavefunction) to have lower symmetry than the full molecular point group. This option is available only for GVB calculations, where it is often necessary for calculations on symmetric systems (see the discussion of the **GVB** keyword below for an example using this option).

The option expects a single line of input (in the format 16I2) giving the *numbers* of the irreducible representations to combine, with the new groups separated by **0**; the list itself must be terminated by a **9**. The numbers correspond to the order in which the representations are listed by Link 301 in the output file (see the examples subsection below).

Since this input section is always exactly one line long, it is not terminated by a blank line. Note that irreducible representations are combined before orbital localization is done and that localized orbitals retain whatever symmetry is kept. **Guess=NoSymm** removes all orbital symmetry constraints without reading any input.

NoSymm Requests that all orbital symmetry constraints be lifted. Synonymous with **SCF=NoSymm** and **Symm=NoSCF**.

Local Requests that orbitals be localized using the Boys method [296]. Occupied and virtual orbitals are localized separately, and the irreducible representations (after possible merging using **LowSymm** or **NoSymm**) are not mixed. Localized orbital analysis of a converged SCF wavefunction may then be done using a second job step, which includes **Guess(Read,Local,Only)** and **Pop=Full** in its route section.

Translate **Translate** requests that the coordinates of the atoms used to produce a guess, which is read in, be translated to the current atomic coordinates. This is the default. It may fail in unusual cases, such as when a wavefunction is used as a guess for a system with a different stoichiometry, in which case **Guess=NoTranslate** should be specified.

Core Requests that the core Hamiltonian be diagonalized to form the initial guess. **Guess=Core** is most commonly used for atomic calculations.

Huckel Requests that a pseudo-extended Huckel guess be generated.

Cards Specifies that after the initial guess is generated, some or all of the orbitals will be replaced with ones read from the input stream. This option can be used to read a complete initial guess from the input stream by replacing every orbital. The replacement orbitals are placed in the input section following the guess alteration commands, if any. For UHF, there are separate α and β replacement orbital input sections.

The replacement orbitals input section (the α replacement orbitals section for UHF) begins with a line specifying the Fortran format with which to read the replacement orbital input, enclosed in parentheses. For example:

(4E20.8)

The remainder of the section contains one or more instances of the following:

IVec	*Orbital to replace (**0** to end, **-1**=replace all orbitals in order).*
(A(I,IVec),I=1,N)	*New orbital in the format specified in the first line.*

The format for the line containing *IVec* is Fortran I5. The β orbital replacement section for UHF calculations differs only in that it omits the initial format specification line.

Only

Guess=Only functions as a calculation type keyword and requests that the calculation terminate once the initial guess is computed and printed. Note that the amount of orbital information that is printed is controlled by the **Pop** keyword. **Guess=Only** may not be used with semi-empirical methods.

This option is useful in preliminary runs to check if configuration alteration is necessary. For example, **Guess=Only** may be specified with **CASSCF** in order to obtain information on the number of CI configurations in the CAS active space (as well as the initial orbitals).

Guess(Only,Read) may also be used to produce population and other post-calculation analyses from the data in a checkpoint file. For example, these options alone will produce a population analysis using the wavefunction in the checkpoint file. **Guess(Only,Read) Prop** will cause electrostatic properties to be calculated using the wavefunction in the checkpoint file.

Save

Save the generated initial guess back into the checkpoint file at the conclusion of a **Guess=Only** run. This option is useful for saving localized orbitals.

These options may be combined in any reasonable combination. Thus **Guess=(Always,Alter)** and **Guess=(Read,Alter)** work as expected (in the former case, alterations are read once and the same interchanges are applied at each geometry). Conversely, **Guess=(Always,Read)** is contradictory and will lead to unpredictable results. Refer to the input sections order table at the beginning of this chapter to determine the ordering of the input sections for combinations of options like **Guess=(Cards,Alter)**.

RESTRICTIONS
Guess=Only may not be used with semi-empirical methods.

RELATED KEYWORDS
Geom, Pop

EXAMPLES

Transposing Orbitals with Guess=Alter. This example finds the UHF/STO-3G structure of the $^2A_1$ excited state of the amino radical. First, a **Guess=Only** calculation is run to determine whether any alter instructions are needed to obtain the desired electronic state. The HF/STO-3G theoretical model is used by default:

```
# Guess=Only Test

Amino radical test of initial guess

0 2
n
h 1 nh
h 1 nh 2 hnh

nh 1.03
hnh 120.0
```

Here is the orbital symmetry summary output from the job, which comes immediately before the population analysis in the output:

```
Initial guess orbital symmetries.
  Alpha Orbitals:
      Occupied (A1) (A1) (B2) (B1) (A1)
      Virtual  (A1) (B2)
  Beta Orbitals:
      Occupied (A1) (A1) (B2) (A1)
      Virtual  (B1) (A1) (B2)
<S**2> of initial guess=  .7544
```

Since a doublet state is involved, α and β orbitals are given separately. From the orbital symmetries, the electron configuration in the initial guess is $a_1^2 a_1^2 b_2^2 a_1^2 b_1$, yielding a $^2B_1$ wavefunction. This is indeed the ground state of NH_2. The expectation value of S^2 for the unrestricted initial guess is printed. In this case, it is close to the pure doublet value of 0.75.

Note that the orbital energies printed in a **Guess=Only** job are simply -1.0 for the occupied orbitals and 0.0 for the virtual orbitals, since no SCF has been performed. If the actual orbital energies are desired, a full semi-empirical energy calculation can be performed specifying the desired method (e.g. INDO).

Returning to our consideration of the amino radical, since we want to model the $^2A_1$ excited state, we will need to alter this initial orbital configuration: a β electron must be moved from orbital 4 to orbital 5 (the electron configuration is then $a_1^2 a_1^2 b_2^2 b_1^2 a_1$). **Guess=Alter** may be used to accomplish this. Here is the input for the geometry optimization

```
# UHF/6-31G(d) Opt Guess=Alter Pop=Reg Test

Amino radical: HF/6-31G(d) structure of 2-A1 state

0 2
n
```

```
h 1 nh
h 1 nh 2 hnh
    Variables:
nh 1.03
hnh 120.0
```

Blank line ends the molecule specification section.
Blank line ends the α section (empty in this case).

`4 5`

Transpose orbitals 4 and 5.
End of the β alteration section.

Note that an extra blank line—line 12—is necessary to indicate an empty α alteration section. The final two lines then constitute the β alteration section.

The initial guess program prints a list of orbitals that were interchanged as a result of the **Alter** option:

```
Projected INDO Guess.
 NO ALPHA ORBITALS SWITCHED.
 PAIRS OF BETA ORBITALS SWITCHED:
    4    5
```

The eigenvalue of S^2 is printed for the UHF wavefunction. The value which results if contamination of the wavefunction from the next possible spin multiplicity (quartets for doublets, quintets for triplets, etc.) is removed is also printed:

```
Annihilation of the first spin contaminant:
S**2 before annihilation   .7534,   after   .7500
```

Although this calculation does in fact converge correctly to $^2A_1$ state, it sometimes happens that the order of orbital symmetries switches during the course of the SCF iterations. If the orbital symmetries of the final wavefunction are different from those in the initial guess (whether or not you are using **Guess=Alter**), we recommend using the direct minimization routine, specified with the **SCF=QC** or **SCF=DM** keywords, which usually holds symmetry from one iteration to the next.

Reading in Orbitals with Guess=Cards. Some or all of the orbitals may be replaced after the initial guess is generated using **Guess=Cards**. Here is some sample input for this option, which replaces orbitals 1 and 4 (note that the format for the third and following lines is specified in line 1):

```
(3E20.8)
    1
    0.5809834509E+00     0.4612416518E+00    -0.6437319952E-04
    0.1724432549E-02     0.1282235396E-14     0.5417658499E-13
    0.1639966912E-02    -0.9146282229E-15    -0.6407549694E-13
   -0.4538843604E-03     0.6038992958E-04    -0.1131035485E-03
    0.6038992969E-04    -0.1131035471E-03
    4
    0.7700779642E-13     0.1240395916E-12    -0.3110890228E-12
   -0.4479190461E-12    -0.1478805861E-13     0.5807753928E+00
    0.6441113412E-12    -0.3119296374E-14     0.1554735923E+00
   -0.1190754528E-11     0.2567325943E+00     0.1459733219E+00
   -0.2567325943E+00    -0.1459733219E+00
    0
```

An orbital number of zero ends the replacement orbital input.

➤ GVB

DESCRIPTION

This method keyword requests a perfect-pairing General Valence Bond (GVB-PP) calculation. GVB requires one parameter: the number of perfect-pairing pairs to split; for example: **GVB(4)**. This parameter may also be specified with the **NPair** option. The natural orbitals for the GVB pairs are taken from occupied and virtual orbitals of the initial guess determinant (described below).

INPUT FOR GVB CALCULATIONS

Normally most of the difficult input for a GVB-PP calculation involves specifying the initial guess. This often includes alteration of orbitals to ensure the correct identification of high-spin, perfect-pairing, and closed-shell orbitals and possible reduction of SCF symmetry to account for the localized orbitals which usually represent the lowest energy solution for GVB-PP.

The GVB program reads the number of orbitals in each GVB pair (in format 40I2). The number of lines read is fixed (and normally 1), so no terminating blank line is needed. For a molecule having spin multiplicity S, N GVB pairs, and $n_1, ... , n_N$ orbitals in each pair, orbitals from the initial guess are used in the following manner by the GVB program:

♦ The S-1 highest occupied orbitals in the initial guess, which would have been singly occupied in an ROHF calculation, become high-spin orbitals.

♦ The next lower N occupied orbitals, which would have been doubly occupied in an ROHF calculation, become the first natural orbitals of the GVB pairs.

♦ Any remaining orbitals occupied in the guess stay closed-shell.

♦ The lowest n_1-1 virtual orbitals become natural orbitals 2 through n_1 of the first GVB pair, then the next n_2-1 orbitals are assigned to pair 2, and so on. The GVB-PP scheme does not allow an orbital to be shared by more than one GVB pair.

♦ Any remaining (virtual) orbitals from the initial guess become virtual orbitals in the GVB calculation.

Generally **Guess=Alter** is required to ensure that guess occupied orbitals, which will be used as first natural orbitals, match up with the correct guess virtual orbitals which will become the corresponding higher natural orbitals. Often it is helpful to start off with **Guess=(Local,Only)**, examine the orbitals to determine alteration requirements, then do **Guess=(Local,Alter)** and **GVB(NPair=N,Freeze)** to allow the higher natural orbitals to become more appropriate. Finally the full calculation can be run with **Guess=Read** and all orbitals optimized in the GVB. If there is any confusion or concern with the orbitals breaking symmetry, the calculation should be done with **Symm=NoSCF** and initially with **Guess=Local**. In fact, this approach is generally recommended except for those very expert users.

If the number of orbitals in a pair is negative, the root of the CI to use for that pair and the pair's initial GVB coefficients are read in format (I2,5D15.8). This is useful if a $^1\Sigma$ or $^1\Delta$ state is being represented as a GVB pair of the form $x^2 \pm y^2$.

OPTIONS

NPair   Gives the number of perfect-pairing pairs. **GVB(N)** is equivalent to **GVB(NPair=N)**. **NPair=0** is acceptable and results in a closed-shell or spin-restricted SCF calculation.

InHam=N   Read in N Hamiltonians (Fock operators, sets of coupling coefficients). This option may be combined with perfect-pairing pairs. Each Hamiltonian is read using the following syntax (format in parentheses):

NO	# of orbitals in current Hamiltonian (I5)
Fj	Occup. # (**1.0**=closed-shell) (D15.8)
(AJ(I), I =1,NHam)	J coefficients (5D15.8)
(AK(I), I =1,NHam)	K coefficients (5D15.8)

Combining several orbitals with the same *AJ* and *AK* coefficients into one "shell" is not currently supported, so *NO* is always 1. The **ham506** utility can be used to generate averaged Hamiltonians for the common case of spherical averaging in atomic calculations. The Hamiltonian coefficients are described in Bobrowicz and Goddard [99]. A good introduction to the qualitative interpretation of GVB wavefunctions can be found in the review article by Goddard and Harding [346].

OSS   Do a two electron, two orthogonal orbital open-shell singlet. This option may be combined with perfect-pairing pairs. **OpenShellSinglet** is a synonym for **OSS**.

Freeze   Freeze closed-shell and open-shell orbitals, and first natural orbitals of GVB pairs, allowing only 2nd and higher orbitals to vary. This option is useful for starting off difficult wavefunctions.

AVAILABILITY
Energies, analytic gradients, and numerical frequencies.

EXAMPLES
Here is a GVB(3/6) calculation performed on singlet methylene:

```
# GVB(3)/6-31G(d) Guess=(Local,LowSym,Alter) Pop=Full Test

GVB(3) on CH2
```

molecule specification

```
 1 4 0 2 3 9                    Guess=LowSym input
2,3                             Guess=Alter input

 2 2 2                          GVB input
```

Each of the 3 valence electron pairs is split into a GVB pair. A preliminary **Guess=Only** calculation was performed to determine the localized orbitals and what alterations would be required.

The perfect pairing GVB method includes the effects of *intra*-pair correlation but not those of *inter*-pair correlation. Consequently, GVB electrons pairs tend to be localized. In the case of singlet methylene, the carbon lone pair is localized even at the Hartree-Fock level. The canonical Hartree-Fock orbitals for the C-H bonds are delocalized into linear combinations ($C-H_1$ + $C-H_2$) and ($C-H_1$ - $C-H_2$) having A_1 and B_2 symmetry, respectively. In order to allow the localization in the guess to produce separate bond pairs, these two irreducible representations must be combined. Similarly, the GVB calculation itself must be told not to impose the full molecular symmetry on the orbitals, which would force them to be delocalized. Combining the A_1 and B_2 representations and combining the A_2 and B_1 representations causes the calculation to impose only C_s symmetry on the individual orbitals, allowing separate GVB pairs for each bond. Since the resulting pairs for each bond will be equivalent, the resulting overall wavefunction and density will still have C_{2v} symmetry.

The **Guess=LowSym** keyword specifies that the irreducible representations of the molecular point group will be combined in the symmetry information used in a GVB calculation. It takes a single line of input consisting of giving the numbers of the irreducible representations to combine, where the numbers correspond to the order in which the representations are listed in the output file (they appear just after the standard orientation). For example, here is the output for a molecule with C_{2v} symmetry:

```
There are    4 symmetry adapted basis functions of A1  symmetry.
There are    0 symmetry adapted basis functions of A2  symmetry.
There are    1 symmetry adapted basis functions of B1  symmetry.
There are    2 symmetry adapted basis functions of B2  symmetry.
```

Thus for C_{2v} symmetry, the order is A1, A2, B1, B2, referred to in the **Guess=LowSym** input as 1 through 4, respectively. A zero separates groups of representations to be combined, and a nine ends the list. Thus, to combine A1 with B2 and A2 with B1, thereby lowering the SCF symmetry to C_s, the appropriate input line is:

```
1 4 0 2 3 9
```

Since this information always requires exactly one line, no blank line terminates this section.

The order of orbitals generated after localization by the initial guess in the first job step was C-1s C-H_1 C-H_2 C-2s for the occupied orbitals, and C-2p C-H_1* C-H_2* for the lowest virtual orbitals. Hence if no orbitals are interchanged, the C-2s lone pair would be correctly paired with the unoccupied p-orbital, but then the next lower occupied, C-H_2, would be paired with the next higher virtual, C-H_1*. So either the two bond occupied orbitals or the two bond virtual orbitals must be exchanged to match up the orbitals properly.

Finally, the one line of input to the GVB code indicates that there are 2 natural orbitals in each of the 3 GVB pairs.

➤ G96

See **DFT Methods** *above*.

➤ HF

DESCRIPTION
This method keyword requests a Hartree-Fock calculation. Unless explicitly specified, **RHF** is used for singlets and **UHF** for higher multiplicities. In the latter case, separate α and β orbitals will be computed [55-57]. **RHF**, **ROHF** or **UHF** can also be specified explicitly.

SCF single point energy calculations involving basis sets which include diffuse functions should use the **SCF=Tight** keyword to request tight SCF convergence criteria.

AVAILABILITY
Energies, analytic gradients, and analytic frequencies for **RHF** and **UHF** and numerical frequencies for **ROHF**.

EXAMPLES
The Hartree-Fock energy appears in the output as follows:

```
SCF Done:   E(RHF) =   -74.9646569691    A.U. after    4 cycles
            Convg  =      .6164D-03           -V/T =  2.0063
            S**2   =      .0000
```

The second and third lines give the SCF convergence limit and the expectation value of S^2.

➤ HFB
➤ HFS

See **DFT Methods** *above*.

➤ INDO

DESCRIPTION
Requests a semi-empirical calculation using the INDO Hamiltonian [40]. No basis set keyword should be specified.

AVAILABILITY
Energies, "analytic" gradients, and numerical frequencies.

EXAMPLES
The INDO energy appears in the output file as follows (followed by the x, y, and z components of the dipole moment):

```
Energy=     -19.034965532835 NIter=   10.
Dipole moment=    .000000    .000000   -.739540
```

The energy is as defined by this semi-empirical model. Note that energy differences computed from the values in semi-empirical calculations are in Hartrees and may be compared directly with energy differences computed from jobs using other methods.

➤ Integral

DESCRIPTION
The **Integral** keyword modifies the method of computation and use of two-electron integrals and their derivatives.

INTEGRATION GRID SELECTION OPTION

Grid=*grid*   Specifies the integration grid to be used for numerical integrations. Note that it is very important to use the *same* grid for all calculations where you intend to compare energies (e.g., computing energy differences, heats of formation, and so on). The parameter to this option is either a grid name keyword or a specific grid specification. If a keyword is chosen, then the option name itself may be optionally omitted (i.e, **Integral(Grid=FineGrid)** and **Integral(FineGrid)** are equivalent).

The default grid is a pruned (75,302) grid, having 75 radial shells and 302 angular points per shell, resulting in about 7000 points per atom [347]; the value **FineGrid** is used to specify this grid.

Grid=UltraFine requests a pruned (99,590) grid. It is recommended for molecules containing lots of tetrahedral centers and for computing very low frequency modes of systems.

Other special values for this parameter are **CoarseGrid**, which requests a pruned version of the (35,110) grid, and **SG1Grid**, a pruned version of (50,194). Note, however, that the **FineGrid** has considerably better numerical accuracy and rotational invariance than these grids, and they are *not* recommended for production calculations [347, 348]. **Pass0Grid** requests the obsolete pruned (35,110) grid once intended for pass 0 of a tight SCF calculation.

Specific grids may be selected by giving an integer value N as the argument to Grid. N may have one of these forms:

♦ A large positive integer of the form *mmmnnn*, which requests a grid with *mmm* radial shells around each atom, and *nnn* angular points in each shell. The total number of integration points per atom is thus *mmm*nnn*. For example, to specify the (99,302) grid, use **Int(Grid=99302)**. The valid numbers of angular points are 38, 50 [349], 72 [350], 86, 110 [349], 146, 194, 302 [351], 434 [352], 590, 770, and 974 [353]. If a larger number of angular points is desired, a spherical product grid can be used.

♦ A large negative integer of the form -*mmmnnn*, which requests *mmm* radial shells around each atom, and a spherical product grid having *nnn* θ points and 2*nnn* φ points in each shell. The total number of integration points per atom is therefore $2*mmm*nnn^2$. This form is used to specify the (96,32,64) grid commonly cited in benchmark calculations: **Int(Grid=−96032)**.

Note, that any value for *nnn* is permitted, although small values are silly (values of *nnn* < 15 produce grids of similar size and inferior performance to the special angular grids requested by the second format above). Large values are expensive. For example, a value of 200100 would use 2*200*100*100 or 4 million points per atom!

INTEGRAL FORMAT OPTION

Raff   **Raff** requests that the Raffenetti format for the two-electron integrals be used. This is the default. **NoRaff** demands that the regular integral format be used. It also suppresses the use of Raffenetti integrals during direct CPHF. This affects conventional SCF and both conventional and direct frequency calculations.

ALGORITHM SELECTION OPTIONS

SSWeights   Use the weighting scheme of Scuseria and Stratman [354] for the numerical integration for DFT calculations. This is the default

BWeights   Use the weighting scheme of Becke for numerical integration.

NoSComp   Turn off symmetry blocking of MO 2-electron integrals. **NoSymmComp** is a synonym for **NoSComp**.

DPRISM   Use the PRISM algorithm [27] for spdf integral derivatives. This is the default.

Rys1E	Evaluate one-electron integrals using the Rys method [355-357], instead of the default method. This is necessary on machines with very limited memory.
Rys2E	If writing two-electron integrals, use Rys method (L314) [152, 355-357]. This is slower than the default method, but may be needed for small memory machines and is chosen by default if regular (non-Rafenetti) integrals are requested (by the **NoRaff** option).
Berny	Use Berny sp integral derivative and second derivative code (L702).
Pass	**Pass** specifies that the integrals be stored in memory via disk, and **NoPass** disables this. Synonymous with **SCF**=[**No**]**Pass**, which is the recommended usage.
Symm	**NoSymm** disables and **Symm** enables the use of symmetry in the evaluation and storage of integrals (**Symm** is the default). Synonymous with the keywords **Symm**=[**No**]**Int**, which is the recommended usage.
NoSP	Do not use the special sp integral program (L311) when writing integrals to disk.

INTEGRAL FILE-RELATED OPTIONS

ReUse	Use an existing integral file. Both the integral file and checkpoint file must have been preserved from a previous calculation. Only allowed for single point calculations and **Polar=Restart**.
WriteD2E	Forces the integral derivative file to be written in HF frequency calculations. Useful only in debugging new derivative code.

BUFFER SIZE OPTIONS

IntBufSize=N	Sets the integral buffer size to N integer words. The default value (which is machine-dependant) is generally adequate.
D2EBufSize=N	Sets the integral derivative buffer size to N words.

RELATED KEYWORDS
SCF

➤ IOp

DESCRIPTION

The **IOp** keyword allows the user to set internal options (variables in system common /IOp/) to specific values. The syntax is:

$$\textbf{IOp}(Ov_1/Op_1=N_1,Ov_2/Op_2=N_2, ...)$$

which sets option number Op_i to the value N_i for every occurrence of overlay Ov_i. Since setting internal options can have arbitrary effects on the calculation, archiving is disabled by use of this keyword.

IOp values explicitly set in the route section are not passed on to the second and subsequent automatically-generated job steps; this applies to keyword combinations like **Opt Freq** and to inherently multi-step methods such as **G2** and the CBS methods. For example, if you want to specify an alternate grid for a DFT optimization+frequency job, you must use an option to the **Int=Grid** keyword rather than an explicit **IOp** value.

The execution of each overlay of *Gaussian 98* is controlled by options (numbered from 1 to 50). Each option may be assigned an integer value, with 0 being the default. The value of an option is held unchanged throughout execution of all of the links in one overlay. Thus the significance of a particular option applies to all the component links in one pass through the overlay. The full list of *Gaussian 98* options is given in the *Gaussian 98 Programmer's Reference*. They are also documented on our web site: www.gaussian.com/iops.htm.

➤ IRC

DESCRIPTION

This method keyword requests that a reaction path be followed [130, 131]. The initial geometry (given in the molecule specification section) is that of the transition state, and the path can be followed in one or both directions from that point. By default, the *forward* direction is defined as the direction the transition vector is pointing when the largest component of the phase is positive; it can be defined explicitly using the **Phase** option.

The geometry is optimized at each point along the reaction path such that the segment of the reaction path between any two adjacent points is described by an arc of a circle, and so that the gradients at the end points of the arc are tangent to the path. The path can be computed in mass-weighted internals, Cartesians or internals coordinates. By default, an IRC calculation steps 6 points in mass-weighted internals in the forward direction and 6 points in the reverse direction, in steps of 0.1 $amu^{1/2}$ bohr along the path.

IRC calculations require initial force constants to proceed. You must provide these to the calculation in some way. The usual method is to save the checkpoint file from the preceding frequency calculation (used to verify that the optimized geometry to be used in the IRC calculation is in fact a transition state), and then specify **IRC=RCFC** in the route section. The other possibilities are providing the force constants in the input stream (**IRC=FCCards**) and computing them at the beginning of the IRC calculation (**IRC=CalcFC**). Note that one of **RCFC**, **CalcFC** and **FCCards** must be specified.

IRC calculations accept Z-matrices or Cartesian coordinates as molecule specifications and uses these coordinates in following the reaction path.

IRC studies are not currently archived.

PATH SELECTION OPTIONS

Phase=(*N1 N2* [*N3* [*N4*]])

Defines the phase for the transition vector such that "forward" motion along the transition vector corresponds to an increase in the specified internal coordinate, designated by up to four atom numbers. If two atom numbers are given, the coordinate is a bond stretch between the two atoms; three atom numbers specify an angle bend, and four atoms define a dihedral angle.

Forward   Follow the path only in the forward direction.

Reverse   Follow the path only in the reverse direction.

Downhill   Follow the reaction path downhill from a starting point that is not a transition state. The gradient for the starting structure must be larger than the optimization convergence threshold. **Downhill** cannot be used with **Forward** or **Reverse**.

ReadVector   Read in the vector to follow. The format is Z-matrix (FFF(I), I=1,NVAR), read as (8F10.6).

MaxPoints=*N*   Number of points along the reaction path to examine (in each direction if both are being considered). The default is 6.

StepSize=*N*   Step size along the reaction path, in units of 0.01 amu$^{-1/2}$-Bohr. The default is 10.

MaxCyc=*N*   Sets the maximum number of steps in each geometry optimization. The default is 20.

Freq   Calculate the projected vibrational frequencies for motion perpendicular to the path, for each optimized point on the path [341]. This option is valid only for reaction paths in mass-weighted internal coordinates.

COORDINATE SYSTEM SELECTION OPTIONS

MassWeighted   Follow the path in mass-weighted internal (Z-matrix) coordinates (which is equivalent to following the path in mass-weighted Cartesian coordinates). **MW** is a synonym for **MassWeighted**. This is the default.

Internal   Follow the path in internal (Z-matrix) coordinates without mass weighting.

Cartesian   Follow the path in Cartesian coordinates without mass weighting.

ISOTOPE SPECIFICATION OPTION

ReadIsotopes   Specify alternate isotopes (the defaults are the most abundant isotopes). This information appears in a separate input section having the format:

isotope mass for atom 1
isotope mass for atom 2

...

isotope mass for atom n

where the lines hold the isotope masses for the various atoms in the molecule, arranged in the same order as they appeared in the molecule specification section. If integers are used to specify the atomic masses, the program will automatically use the corresponding actual exact mass (e.g., 18 specifies O^{18}, and *Gaussian 98* uses the value 17.99916).

OPTIONS FOR GENERATING INITIAL FORCE CONSTANTS

RCFC   Specifies that the computed force constants in Cartesian coordinates from a frequency calculation are to be read from the checkpoint file. **ReadCartesianFC** is a synonym for **RCFC**.

CalcFC   Specifies that the force constants be computed at the first point

CalcAll   Specifies that the force constants be computed at every point.

FCCards   Reads the Cartesian forces and force constants from the input stream after the molecule specifications. This option can be used to read force constants recovered from the Quantum Chemistry Archive using its internal **FCList** command. The format for this input is:

Energy (format D24.16)
Cartesian forces (lines of format 6F12.8)
Force constants (lines of format 6F12.8)

The force constants are in lower triangular form: $((F(J,I),J=1,I),I=1,NAt3)$, where *NAt3* is the number of Cartesian coordinates. If both **FCCards** and **ReadIsotopes** are specified, the masses of the atoms are input before the energy, Cartesian gradients and the Cartesian force constants.

OPTIMIZATION ALGORITHM-RELATED OPTION

VeryTight   Tightens the convergence criteria used in the optimization at each point along the path. This option is necessary if a very small step size along the path is requested.

RESTART OPTION

Restart   Restarts an IRC calculation which did not complete, or restarts an IRC calculation which did complete, but for which additional points along the path are desired.

AVAILABILITY

HF, all DFT methods, CIS, MP2, MP3, MP4(SDQ), CID, CISD, CCD, QCISD, CASSCF, and all semi-empirical methods.

RELATED KEYWORDS
Opt, Scan, IRCMax

EXAMPLES
The output for each step of an IRC calculation is very similar to that from a geometry optimization. Each step is introduced by this banner line (where "IRC" has replaced "Grad"):

```
IRC-IRC-IRC-IRC-IRC-IRC-IRC-IRC-IRC-IRC-IRC-IRC-IRC-IRC-IRC-IRC-IRC
```

As the optimization at each point completes, the optimized structure is displayed:

```
Optimization completed.
   -- Optimized point #   1 Found.
                    ----------------------------
                    !   Optimized Parameters    !
                    ! (Angstroms and Degrees)   !
 --------------------                           --------------------
 !     Name          Value   Derivative information (Atomic Units)
 !
 ------------------------------------------------------------------
 !       CH1         1.3448   -DE/DX =    0.0143                   !
 !       HH          0.8632   -DE/DX =   -0.0047                   !
 !       CH2         1.0827   -DE/DX =    0.0008                   !
 !       HCH       106.207    -DE/DX =   -0.0082                   !
 ------------------------------------------------------------------
   RADIUS OF CURVATURE =      0.39205
   NET REACTION COORDINATE UP TO THIS POINT =      0.09946
```

Once the entire IRC has completed, the program prints a table summarizing the results:

```
 ------------------------------------------------------------------
              SUMMARY OF REACTION PATH FOLLOWING:
              (Int. Coord:  Angstroms, and Degrees)
 ------------------------------------------------------------------
               ENERGY    RX.COORD     CH1       HH       CH2
        1    -40.16837   -0.49759   1.54387   0.73360   1.08145
        2    -40.16542   -0.39764   1.49968   0.74371   1.08164
        3    -40.16235   -0.29820   1.45133   0.76567   1.08193
        4    -40.15914   -0.19914   1.39854   0.80711   1.08232
        5    -40.15640   -0.09946   1.34481   0.86318   1.08274
        6    -40.15552    0.00000   1.30200   0.91500   1.08300
        7    -40.15649    0.09990   1.26036   0.96924   1.08330
        8    -40.15999    0.19985   1.21116   1.03788   1.08349
        9    -40.16486    0.29975   1.16418   1.10833   1.08353
       10    -40.16957    0.39938   1.12245   1.18068   1.08328
       11    -40.17324    0.49831   1.09260   1.25158   1.08276
 ------------------------------------------------------------------
   TOTAL NUMBER OF GRADIENT CALCULATIONS:       28
   TOTAL NUMBER OF POINTS:        10
   AVERAGE NUMBER OF GRADIENT CALCULATIONS:       2.80000
```

The initial geometry appears in the middle of the table (in this case, as point 6). It can be identified quickly by looking for a reaction coordinate value of 0.00000.

➤ IRCMax

DESCRIPTION

Performs an IRCMax calculation using the methods of Petersson and coworkers [142-150]. Taking a transition structure as its input, this calculation type finds the maximum energy along a specified reaction path.

REQUIRED INPUT

IRCMax requires two model chemistries as its options, separated by two slashes: **IRCMax**(*model2*// *model1*). Here is an example route section:

```
# IRCMax(B3LYP/6-31G(d,p)//HF/6-31G(d,p))
```

This calculation will find the point on the HF/6-31G(d,p) reaction path where the B3LYP/6-31G(d,p) energy is at its maximum.

The **Zero** option will produce the data required for zero curvature variational transition state theory (ZC-VTST) [5, 6, 9-12]. Consider the following route:

```
# IRCMax(MP2/6-31G(d)//HF/3-21G(d),Zero,Stepsize=10)
```

This job will start from the HF/3-21G(d) TS and search along the HF/3-21G(d) IRC with a stepsize of 0.1 amu-1/2 bohr until the maximum of the MP2/6-31G(d) energy (including the HF/3-21G(d) ZPE) is bracketed. The position along the HF/3-21G(d) IRC for this MP2/6-31G(d) TS will then be optimized. The output includes all quantities requred for the calculation of reaction rates using the ZC-VTST version of absolute rate theory: TS moments of inertia, all real vibrational frequencies (HF/3-21G(d)), the imaginary frequency for tunneling (fit to MP2/6-31G(d) + ZPE), and the total MP2/6-31G(d) + ZPE energy of the TS.

ZC-VTST OPTIONS

Zero	Include the zero-point energy in the IRCMax computation.

PATH SELECTION OPTIONS

Forward	Follow the path only in the forward direction.
Reverse	Follow the path only in the reverse direction.
ReadVector	Read in the vector to follow. The format is Z-matrix (FFF(I), I=1,NVAR), read as (8F10.6).
MaxPoints=N	Number of points along the reaction path to examine (in each direction if both are being considered). The default is 6.
StepSize=N	Step size along the reaction path, in units of 0.01 amu-1/2-Bohr. The default is 10.
MaxCyc=N	Sets the maximum number of steps in each geometry optimization. The default is 20.

Freq
Calculate the projected vibrational frequencies for motion perpendicular to the path, for each optimized point on the path [13]. This option is valid only for reaction paths in mass-weighted internal coordinates.

COORDINATE SYSTEM SELECTION OPTIONS

MassWeighted
Follow the path in mass-weighted internal (Z-matrix) coordinates (which is equivalent to following the path in mass-weighted Cartesian coordinates). **MW** is a synonym for **MassWeighted**. This is the default.

Internal
Follow the path in internal (Z-matrix) coordinates without mass weighting.

Cartesian
Follow the path in Cartesian coordinates without mass weighting.

ISOTOPE SPECIFICATION OPTION

ReadIsotopes
Specify alternate isotopes (the defaults are the most abundant isotopes). This information appears in a separate input section having the format:

isotope mass for atom 1
isotope mass for atom 2
...
isotope mass for atom n

where the lines hold the isotope masses for the various atoms in the molecule, arranged in the same order as they appeared in the molecule specification section. If integers are used to specify the atomic masses, the program will automatically use the corresponding actual exact mass (e.g., 18 specifies O^{18}, and *Gaussian 98* uses the value 17.99916).

CONVERGENCE-RELATED OPTION

VeryTight
Tightens the convergence criteria used in the optimization at each point along the path. This option is necessary if a very small step size along the path is requested.

OPTIONS FOR GENERATING INITIAL FORCE CONSTANTS

CalcFC
Specifies that the force constants be computed at the first point

CalcAll
Specifies that the force constants be computed at every point.

FCCards
Reads the Cartesian forces and force constants from the input stream after the molecule specifications. This option can be used to read force constants recovered from the Quantum Chemistry Archive using its internal **FCList** command. The format for this input is:

Energy (format D24.16)
Cartesian forces (lines of format 6F12.8)
Force constants (lines of format 6F12.8)

The force constants are in lower triangular form: $((F(J,I),J=1,I),I=1,NАt3)$, where *NАt3* is the number of Cartesian coordinates. If both **FCCards** and **ReadIsotopes** are specified, the masses of the atoms are input before the energy, Cartesian gradients and the Cartesian force constants.

Note that the RCFC option is not supported with **IRCMax**.

RESTART OPTION
Restart   Restarts an IRC calculation which did not complete, or restarts an IRC calculation which did complete, but for which additional points along the path are desired.

AVAILABILITY
Analytic gradients are required for the IRC portion of the calculation (*model1* above). Any non-compound energy method and basis set may be used for *model2*.

RELATED KEYWORDS
IRC, Opt, Freq

➤ LSDA

DESCRIPTION
This method keyword request a Local Spin Density Approximation calculation, using the Slater exchange functional and the VWN correlation functional for the DFT calculation. It is equivalent to **SVWN**. Note that LSDA is not uniquely defined in the literaure. In fact, many differing but related methods are referred to using this term. Other programs offering an LSDA method may use somewhat different functionals. For example, some implement the functional specified by the *Gaussian 98* **SVWN5** keyword, while others use a correlation functional of Perdew. While *Gaussian 98* offers this keyword for convenience, it is probably better practice to specify the exact functional desired; see **DFT Methods** above for full details on specifying and using Density Functional Methods in *Gaussian 98*.

➤ LYP

See **DFT Methods** *above.*

➤ Massage

DESCRIPTION

The **Massage** keyword requests that the molecule specification and basis set data be modified after it is generated. The **Massage** keyword thus makes it possible to add additional uncontracted basis functions to a standard basis set. Common polarization or diffuse functions can be added in this way to standard basis sets for which these functions are not internally defined. For example, diffuse functions could be added to the 3-21G basis set to form 3-21+G. Similarly, polarization functions might be added to 6-311G to form a 6-311G(5d3f) basis, which is larger than the largest internally stored 6-311G-based basis set, 6-311G(3d1f).

The standard basis functions are assigned to atoms before **Massage** alterations take place, while the number of electrons is computed from the atomic numbers after the modifications.

Calculations with massaged basis set data cannot generate archive entries, and do not take advantage of molecular symmetry. Some of this functionality of **Massage** has been superceded by the **ExtraBasis** keyword. Point charges may also be specified for single point energy calculations using **Charge**.

Massage may also be used for counterpoise calculations and BSSE (see the examples).

INPUT

Massage requires one or more lines of input in the following format:

center, func, exp, $[c_X, c_Y, c_Z]$

where *center* is the center number (numbering follows the ordering of the molecule specification section), *func* is a code indicating the type of modification (see below), *exp* is the exponent of Gaussian or new nuclear charge (a value of **0** says to add a ghost atom), and c_X, c_Y, c_Z are the coordinates of the point charge in Angstroms when *func* is **-1** (see below). A blank line terminates this input section.

func can take on these values:

0 *or* **Nuc**	Change the nuclear charge.
1 *or* **SP**	Add an SP shell.
2 *or* **D**	Add a D shell.
3 *or* **P**	Add a P shell.
4 *or* **S**	Add an S shell.
5 *or* **F**	Add an F shell.
-1 *or* **Ch**	Add a point charge.

Note that this keyword is not affected by the setting of the **Units** keyword, and its input is always interpreted as Angstroms.

RELATED KEYWORDS
Charge, ExtraBasis, Gen

EXAMPLES

Adding Point Charges. The following input file adds point charges to a calculation on water using the **Massage** keyword:

```
# RHF/6-31G(d) Massage Test

Water with point charges

0 1
O -0.464  0.177  0.0
H -0.464  1.137  0.0
H  0.441 -0.143  0.0

0 ch 2.0 1.0  1.0 1.0
0 ch 2.5 1.0 -1.0 1.0
```

Adding Basis Functions. The following input adds functions to the D95 basis set (in order to reproduce a calculation from the literature that used a non-standard basis set):

```
# RQCISD(Full)/D95 Freq=Numer Massage Test

H2O Frequencies at QCISD(Full)/DZP

0 1
O
H 1 R
H 1 R 2 A

R=0.961882
A=104.612551

1 D 0.85
2 P 1.0
3 P 1.0
```

Computing Counterpoise Corrections. The following input file performs a portion of a counterpoise calculation, removing the HF molecule but leaving its basis functions. Note that the dummy atom is not included in the numbering of the centers.

```
# HF/6-31G* Massage Test

HF + H2O interaction energy: HF removed

0 1
X
H 1 1.0
F 2 rHF 1 90.0
O 2 rHO 1 90.0 3 180.0
H 4 rOH 2 aHOH 1  90.0
H 4 rOH 2 aHOH 5 180.0

rHF 0.9203
rHO 1.8086
rOH 0.94
```

```
aHOH 126.4442

1 Nuc 0.0
2 Nuc 0.0
```

If a checkpoint file is used with this calculation the structure saved in the checkpoint file will have the ghost atoms rather than the atoms specified in the input so it is best to start from a copy of the checkpoint file to preserve the original data.

➤ MaxDisk

DESCRIPTION

The **MaxDisk** keyword specifies the amount of disk storage available for scratch data, in 8-byte words. The value may optionally be followed by a units designation: **KB**, **MB**, **GB**, **KW**, **MW** or **GB**. Normally, this is set for a site in the site-wide Default.Route file (see chapter 6).

MP3, MP4, QCISD, CCSD, QCISD(T), and CCSD(T) calculations all now look at **MaxDisk**. If the calculation can be done using a full integral transformation while keeping disk usage under **MaxDisk**, this is done; if not, a partial transformation is done and some terms are computed in the AO basis. Since MP2 obeys MaxDisk as much as possible, the **Stingy**, **NoStingy** and **VeryStingy** options are not needed.

Thus, it is *crucial* for a value for MaxDisk to be specified explicitly for these types of jobs, either within the route section or via a system wide setting in the Default.Route file. If **MaxDisk** is left unset, the program now assumes that disk is abundant and performs a full transformation by default, in contrast to *Gaussian 94* where a partial transformation was the default in such cases. If **MaxDisk** is not set and sufficient disk space is not available for a full transformation, the job will fail (where it may have worked in G94).

Not all calculations can dynamically control their disk usage, so the effects of this keyword vary:

♦   SCF energy, gradient, and frequency calculations use a fixed amount of disk. This is quite small (only cubic in the size of the system) and is not usually a limitation.

♦   MP2 energies and gradients obey **MaxDisk**, which must be at least $2ON^2$.

♦   Analytic MP2 frequencies attempt to obey **MaxDisk**, but have minimum disk requirements.

♦   CI-Singles energies and gradients in the MO basis require about $4O^2N^2$ words of disk for a limited set of transformed integrals. Additional scratch space is required during the transformation and this is limited as specified by **MaxDisk**. This disk requirement can be eliminated entirely by performing a direct CI-Singles calculation by using **CIS=Direct**.

♦ CID, CISD, CCD, BD, and QCISD energies also have a fixed storage requirement proportional to O^2N^2, with a large factor, but obey **MaxDisk** in avoiding larger storage requirements.

♦ CID, CISD, CCD, BD, and QCISD densities, and CCSD, CCSD(T), QCISD(T), and BD(T) energies have fixed disk requirements proportional to ON^3.

♦ CID, CISD, CCD, and QCISD gradients have fixed disk requirements of about $N^4/2$ for closed-shell and $3N^4/4$ for open-shell.

♦ Storage of AO integrals is not affected by **MaxDisk**; any calculations which might consume all of the available disk should be run using **SCF=Direct** (the default setting) to avoid consuming limited disk space with AO integrals.

See chapter 4 for a detailed discussion of the efficient use of disk resources in *Gaussian 98* calculations.

➤ MINDO3

DESCRIPTION
This method keyword requests a semi-empirical calculation using the MINDO3 Hamiltonian [41, 42]. No basis set keyword should be specified.

AVAILABILITY
Energies, "analytic" gradients, and numerical frequencies. Restricted open shell (**RO**) wavefunctions are limited to optimizations using the Fletcher-Powell and pseudo-Newton-Raphson methods (**FP** and **EnOnly**, respectively).

EXAMPLES
The MINDO3 energy appears in the output file as follows (followed by the x, y, and z components of the dipole moment):

```
Energy=    -.080309984532 NIter=  10.
Dipole moment=   .000000   .000000  -.739540
```

The energy is as defined by this semi-empirical model. Note that energy differences computed from the values in semi-empirical calculations are in Hartrees and may be compared directly with energy differences computed from jobs using other methods.

➤ MNDO

DESCRIPTION

This method keyword requests a semi-empirical calculation using the MNDO Hamiltonian [41, 43-50, 52]. No basis set keyword should be specified.

AVAILABILITY

Energies, "analytic" gradients, and numerical frequencies. Restricted open shell (**RO**) wavefunctions are limited to optimizations using the Fletcher-Powell and pseudo-Newton-Raphson methods (**FP** and **EnOnly**, respectively).

EXAMPLES

The MNDO energy appears in the output file as follows (followed by the x, y, and z components of the dipole moment):

```
Energy=     -.0908412558735 NIter=  10.
Dipole moment=   .000000   .000000  -.739540
```

The energy is as defined by this semi-empirical model. Note that energy differences computed from the values in semi-empirical calculations are in Hartrees and may be compared directly with energy differences computed from jobs using other methods.

➤ Molecular Mechanics Methods

DESCRIPTION

There are three molecular mechanics methods available in *Gaussian 98*. They are designed for use in ONIOM calculations, but they are also available as independent methods. No basis set keyword should be specified with these keywords.

The following force fields are available:

AMBER. The AMBER force field as described in [35]. The actual parameters (**parm96.dat**) have been updated slightly since the publication of this paper. We use the current version from the AMBER web site (*www.amber.ucsf.edu*).

DREIDING: The DREIDING force field as described in [36].

UFF: The UFF force field as described in [37]. UFF uses charges calculated by the method of charge equilibration [38].

INPUT CONVENTIONS

AMBER calculations require that all atom types be explicitly specified using the usual AMBER notation within the normal molecule specification section:

C-CT	*Specifies an SP3 aliphatic carbon atom.*
C-CT-0.32	*Specifies an SP3 aliphatic carbon atom with a partial charge of 0.32.*
O-O--0.5	*Specifies a carbonyl group oxygen atom with a partial charge of -0.5.*

Consult the AMBER paper for definitions of atom types and their associated keywords.

UFF and DREIDING may also optionally provide atom typing information within the molecule specification, using the type keyword conventions of those methods. If no atom typing information is provided, the program will attempt to determine atom types automatically.

Note: The *GaussView* package specifies correct atom types automatically for all atoms when it sets up a *Gaussian* calculation involving a molecular mechanics method.

AVAILABILITY

Analytic energies and gradients and numerical frequencies.

RELATED KEYWORDS

ONIOM

➤ MP2
➤ MP3
➤ MP4
➤ MP5

DESCRIPTION

These method keywords request a Hartree-Fock calculation (RHF for singlets, UHF for higher multiplicities) followed by a Møller-Plesset correlation energy correction [58], truncated at second-order for **MP2** [20-22, 24, 25, 63], third order for **MP3** [59, 64], fourth-order for **MP4** [60], and fifth-order for **MP5** [62]. Analytic gradients are available for MP2 [21, 22, 118, 119], MP3 and MP4(SDQ) [120, 121], and analytic frequencies are available for MP2 [24, 25].

AVAILABLE ALGORITHMS FOR MP2

There are four basic algorithms for MP2 calculations and for producing transformed (MO) integrals on disk:

♦ *Semi-Direct*, which uses both main memory and external (disk) storage as available [22]. This is the default algorithm.

- *Direct*, which uses no external storage by recomputing the integrals as needed during the transformation.

- *Conventional*, which stores the transformed integrals on disk. This was the only method available in *Gaussian 88*, and the only method for generating MO integrals on disk in *Gaussian 90*. It is seldom a good choice on any but the smallest computer systems.

- *In-core*, in which all the AO integrals are generated and stored in main memory, then used without storing them externally.

The default is to decide between the in-core, direct, and semi-direct algorithms based on available memory and disk. The available disk can be specified via the **MaxDisk** keyword, either in the route section or (preferably) in the **Default.Route** file (see chapter 6).

Note that selection of the direct or semi-direct MP2 and transformation algorithms is separate from selecting direct SCF (which is the default SCF algorithm in *Gaussian 98*). The $E^{(2)}$ calculation or transformation then recomputes integrals as needed in the form required for vectorization.

VARIATIONS OF MP4

MP4(DQ) is specified to use only the space of double and quadruple substitutions, **MP4(SDQ)** for single, double and quadruple substitutions, or **MP4(SDTQ)** for full MP4 with single, double, triple and quadruple substitutions [60, 61]. Just specifying **MP4** defaults to **MP4(SDTQ)**.

LIMITATIONS FOR MP5

The MP5 code has been written for the open shell case only, and so specifying **MP5** defaults to a **UMP5** calculation. This method requires O^3V^3 disk storage and scales as O^4V^4 in cpu time.

FROZEN-CORE OPTIONS (POST-SCF METHODS)

FC   This indicates "frozen-core," and it implies that inner-shells are excluded from the correlation calculation. This is the default calculation mode. Note that **FC**, **Full**, **RW** and **Window** are mutually exclusive.

Full   This implies that all electrons are included in a correlation calculation.

RW   The "read window" option means that specific information about which orbitals are retained in the post-SCF calculation will be given in the input file. The additional input section consists of a line specifying the starting and ending orbitals to be retained, followed by a blank line. A value of zero indicates the first or last orbital, depending on where it is used. If the value for the first orbital is negative (*-m*), then the highest *m* orbitals are retained; if the value for the last orbital is negative (*-n*), then the highest *n* orbitals are frozen. If *m* is positive and *n* is omitted, *n* defaults to 0. If *m* is negative and *n* is omitted, then the highest |*m*| occupied and lowest |*m*| virtual orbitals are retained.

Here are some examples for a calculation on C_4H_4:

0,0	Equivalent to **Full**.
5,0	Freezes the 4 core orbitals and keeps all virtual orbitals (equivalent to **FC** if the basis has a single zeta core).
5,-4	Freezes the four core orbitals and the highest four virtual orbitals. This is the appropriate frozen-core for a basis with a double-zeta core.
6,22	Retains orbitals 6 through 22 in the post-SCF. For example, since C_4H_4 has 28 electrons, if this is a closed shell calculation, there will be 14 occupied orbitals, 5 of which will be frozen, so the post-SCF calculation will involve 9 occupied orbitals (orbitals 6-14) and 8 virtual orbitals (orbitals 15-22).
-6	Retains orbitals 9 through 20.

ReadWindow is a synonym for **RW**.

Window=(*m*[,*n*]) Performs the same function as the **ReadWindow** option, but takes its input as parameters in the route section rather than from the input stream.

Note: **CASSCF MP2** calculations use a different mechanism for specifying the frozen orbitals (see the **NFC** and **NFV** options to the **CASSCF** keyword).

ALGORITHM SELECTION OPTIONS (MP METHODS)

FullDirect Forces the "fully direct" algorithm, which requires no external storage beyond that for the SCF. Requires a minimum of $2OVN$ words of main memory (O=number of occupied orbitals, V=number of virtual orbitals, N=number of basis functions). This is seldom a good choice, except for machines with very large main memory and limited disk.

SemiDirect Forces the semi-direct algorithm.

Direct Requests some sort of direct algorithm. The choice between in-core, fully direct and semidirect is made by the program based on memory and disk limits and the dimensions of the problem.

InCore Forces the in-memory algorithm. This is very fast when it can be used, but requires $N^4/4$ words of memory. It is normally used in conjunction with **SCF=InCore**. **NoInCore** prevents the use of the in-core algorithm.

MP2-SPECIFIC OPTIONS

Stingy Compute MP2 frequencies in Stingy mode, trading CPU time for disk in intermediate results. Up to **MaxDisk** disk is still used, but the number of passes may be reduced (in Link 811). This is the default calculation mode. **NoStingy** says to do the integral transformation once rather than twice, at the expense of additional disk usage.

VeryStingy Compute the MP2 frequencies using the minimum possible disk space. This option is designed *only* for very unusual environments where overall performance on multiple simultaneous *Gaussian* jobs is far more important than the efficiency of the MP2 frequency calculation.

AVAILABILITY

MP2: Energies, analytic gradients, and analytic frequencies.

MP3, MP4(DQ) and **MP4(SDQ):** Energies, analytic gradients, and numerical frequencies.

MP4(SDTQ) and **MP5:** Analytic energies, numerical gradients, and numerical frequencies.

RELATED KEYWORDS

HF, SCF, Transformation, MaxDisk

EXAMPLES

Energies. The MP2 energy appears in the output as follows, labeled as EUMP2:

```
E2=           -.3906492545D-01 EUMP2=            -.75003727493390D+02
```

Energies for higher-order Møller-Plesset methods follow. Here is the output from an MP4(SDTQ) calculation:

```
Time for triples=          .04 seconds.
MP4(T)=       -.55601167D-04
E3=           -.10847902D-01       EUMP3=        -.75014575395D+02
E4(DQ)=       -.32068082D-02       UMP4(DQ)=     -.75017782203D+02
E4(SDQ)=      -.33238377D-02       UMP4(SDQ)=    -.75017899233D+02
E4(SDTQ)=     -.33794389D-02       UMP4(SDTQ)=   -.75017954834D+02
```

The energy labelled EUMP3 is the MP3 energy, and the various MP4-level corrections appear after it, with the MP4(SDTQ) output coming in the final line (labeled UMP4(SDTQ)).

➤ MPW1LYP
➤ MPW1PW91
➤ MPW

See **DFT Methods** *above.*

➤ Name

DESCRIPTION

This keyword specifies the username that is stored in the archive entry for the calculation. It takes the desired username as its parameter (e.g., **Name=RChavez**). This keyword is of most use to *Gaussian 98* users who also use the Browse Quantum Chemistry Database System. On VMS and UNIX systems, the default for the username is the operating system-level login name of the user who runs the job.

RELATED KEYWORDS

Archive, Test, Rearchive

➤ NMR

DESCRIPTION

This properties keyword predicts NMR shielding tensors and magnetic susceptibilities using the Hartree-Fock method, all DFT methods (note, however, that no current functionals include a magnetic field dependence, and so the DFT methods do not provide systematically better NMR results than Hartree-Fock) and the MP2 method [358].

NMR shielding tensors may be computed with the Continuous Set of Gauge Transformations (CSGT) method [170-172] and the Gauge-Independant Atomic Orbital (GIAO) method [173-177]. Magnetic susceptibilities may be computed with the CSGT method. *Gaussian 98* also supports the IGAIM method [171, 172] (a slight variation on the CSGT method) and the Single Origin method, for both shielding tensor and magnetic susceptibilities.

Structures used for NMR calculations should have been optimized at a good level of theory. Note that CSGT calculations require large basis sets to achieve accurate results.

OPTIONS

CSGT   Compute NMR properties using the CSGT method only.

GIAO   Compute NMR properties using the GIAO method only. This is the default.

IGAIM   Use atomic centers as gauge origins.

SingleOrigin Use a single gauge origin. This method is provided for comparison purposes but is not generally recommended.

All   Compute properties with **SingleOrigin**, **IGAIM**, and **CSGT** methods.

Use **IOp33(10=1)** to request that the eigenvectors for the shielding tensor be included in the output.

AVAILABILITY

SCF, DFT and MP2 methods. **NMR** may not be combined with **SCRF**.

EXAMPLES

Here is an example of the default output from **NMR**:

```
Magnetic properties (GIAO method)

Magnetic shielding (ppm):
   1   C    Isotropic =     57.7345   Anisotropy =     194.4092
      XX=     48.4143   YX=        .0000   ZX=        .0000
      XY=       .0000   YY=     -62.5514   ZY=        .0000
      XZ=       .0000   YZ=        .0000   ZZ=     187.3406
   2   H    Isotropic =     23.9397   Anisotropy =       5.2745
      XX=     27.3287   YX=        .0000   ZX=        .0000
      XY=       .0000   YY=     24.0670   ZY=        .0000
      XZ=       .0000   YZ=        .0000   ZZ=     20.4233
```

For this molecular system, the values for all of the atoms of a given type are equal, so we have truncated the output after the first two atoms.

➤ ONIOM

DESCRIPTION
This keyword requests a two- or three-layer ONIOM [132-137]. In this procedure, the molecular system being studied is divided into two or three layers which are treated with different model chemistries. The results are then automatically combined into the final predicted results.

The layers are conventionally known as the Low, Medium and High layers. By default, atoms are placed into the High layer. (From a certain point of view, a normal calculation can be viewed as a one-layer ONIOM.) Layer assignments are specified as part of the molecule specification (see below).

REQUIRED INPUT
The two or three desired model chemistries are specified as the options to the **ONIOM** keyword, in the order High, Medium, Low (the final one may obviously be omitted). The distinct models are separated by colons. For example, this route section specifies a three-layer ONIOM calculation, using AMBER for the Low layer, AM1 for the Medium layer, and HF for the High layer:

```
# ONIOM(HF/6-31G(d):AM1:UFF)
```

Atom layer assignment is done as part of the molecule specification, via some additional parameters on each line according to the following syntax:

atom coordinate-spec layer [*replace-atom* [*link-atom* [*distance*]]]

where *atom* and *coordinate-spec* represent the normal molecule specification input for the atom. *Layer* is a keyword indicating the layer assignment for the atom, one of **High**, **Medium** and **Low**. The other optional parameters specify how the atoms located at a layer boundary are to be treated. By default, atoms in a lower layer bound to an atom in a higher layer are replaced by hydrogen atoms during the higher-level part of the ONIOM calculation. You can use *replace-atom* to specify a different atom type with which to replace the atom. Similarly, *link-atom* and *distance* can be used to specify which atom the current atom is to be bonded to during the higher-level calculation portion as well as the bond distance between them.

AVAILABILITY
Energies, gradients and frequencies. Note that if *any* of the specified models require numerical frequencies, then numerical frequencies will be computed for *all* models, even when analytic frequencies are available.

EXAMPLES
Here is a simple ONIOM input file:

```
# ONIOM(B3LYP/6-31G(d,p):AM1:UFF) Opt Test

3-layer ONIOM optimization

0 1
C
O,1,B1
```

```
H,1,B2,2,A1
C,1,B3,2,A2,3,180.0,0     M    H
C,4,B4,1,A3,2,180.0,0     L         H
H,4,B5,1,A4,5,D1,0        M
H,4,B5,1,A4,5,-D1,0       M
H,5,B6,4,A5,1,180.0,0     L
H,5,B7,4,A6,8,D2,0        L
H,5,B7,4,A6,8,-D2,0       L
```

variable definitions

The High layer consists of the first three atoms (placed there by default). The other atoms are explicitly placed into the Medium and Low layers. Note that the Z-matrix specification *must* include the final 0 code indicating the Z-matrix format when ONIOM input is included.

➤ Opt

DESCRIPTION

This keyword requests that a geometry optimization be performed. The geometry will be adjusted until a stationary point on the potential surface is found. Gradients will be used if available. For the Hartree-Fock, CIS, MP2, MP3, MP4(SDQ), CID, CISD, CCD, QCISD, CASSCF, and all DFT and semi-empirical methods, the default algorithm for both minimizations (optimizations to a local minimum) and optimizations to transition states and higher-order saddle points is the Berny algorithm using redundant internal coordinates [128, 129] (specified by the **Redundant** option). The default algorithm in *Gaussian* 92 was the Berny algorithm using internal coordinates (**Opt=Z-matrix**) [115, 127, 359]. The default algorithm for all methods lacking analytic gradients is the eigenvalue-following algorithm (**Opt=EF**).

The remainder of this quite lengthy section discusses various aspects of geometry optimizations, and it includes these subsections:

- ◆ Options to the **Opt** keyword.
- ◆ Overview of geometry optimizations in *Gaussian 98*.
- ◆ Ways of generating initial force constants.
- ◆ Optimizing to transition states and higher-order saddle points.
- ◆ Summary of the Berny optimization algorithm.
- ◆ Notes on optimizing in redundant internal coordinates, including examples of **Opt** input and output and using the **ModRedundant** option.
- ◆ Examples for **Opt=Z-matrix**.

Users should consult those subsection(s) that apply to their interests and needs.

Basic information as well as techniques and pitfalls related to geometry optimizations are discussed in detail in chapter 3 of *Exploring Chemistry with Electronic Structure Methods* [210]. See also Appendix B if you are interested in details about setting up Z-matrices for various types of molecules.

GENERAL PROCEDURAL OPTIONS

MaxCycle=N Sets the maximum number of optimization steps to N. The default is the maximum of 20 and twice the number of redundant internal coordinates in use (for the default procedure) or twice the number of variables to be optimized (for other procedures).

StepSize=N Sets the maximum size for an optimization step to $0.01N$ Bohr or radians. The default value for N is 30.

TS Requests optimization to a transition state rather than a local minimum.

Saddle=N Requests optimization to a saddle point of order N.

QST2 Search for a transition structure using the STQN method. This option requires the reactant and product structures as input, specified in two consecutive groups of title and molecule specification sections. Note that the atoms must be specified in the same order in the two structures. **TS** should *not* be specified with **QST2**.

QST3 Search for a transition structure using the STQN method. This option requires the reactant, product, and initial TS structures as input, specified in three consecutive groups of title and molecule specification sections. Note that the atoms must be specified in the same order within the three structures. **TS** should *not* be specified with **QST3**.

Path=M In combination with either the **QST2** or the **QST3** option, requests the simultaneous optimization of a transition state and an M-point reaction path in redundant internal coordinates [138]. No coordinate may be frozen during this type of calculation.

If **QST2** is specified, the title and molecule specification sections for both reactant and product structures are required as input as usual. The remaining M-2 points on the path are then generated by linear interpolation between the reactant and product input structures. The highest energy structure becomes the initial guess for the transition structure. At each step in the path relaxation, the highest point at each step is optimized toward the transition structure.

If **QST3** is specified, a third set of title and molecule specification sections must be included in the input as a guess for the transition state as usual. The remaining M-3 points on the path are generated by two successive linear interpolations, first between the reactant and transition structure and then between the transition structure and product. By default, the central point is optimized to the transition structure, regardless of the ordering of the energies. In this case, M must be an odd number so that the points on the path may be distributed evenly between the two sides of the transition structure.

In the output for a simultaneous optimization calculation, the predicted geometry for the optimized transition structure is followed by a list of all M converged reaction path structures.

The treatment of the input reactant and product structures is controlled by other options: **OptReactant**, **OptProduct**, **BiMolecularReactant** and **BiMolecularProduct**.

Note that the SCF wavefunction for structures in the reactant valley may be quite different from that of structures in the product valley. **Guess=Always** can be used to prevent the wavefunction of a reactant-like structure from being used as a guess for the wavefunction of a product-like structure.

OptReactant   Specifies that the input structure for the reactant in a simultaneous optimization calculation should be optimized to a local minimum. The default is **NoOptReactant**, which retains the input structure as a point that is already on the reaction path (which generally means that it should have been previously optimized to a minimum). **OptReactant** may not be combined with **BiMolecularReactant**.

BiMolecularReactant
                   Specifies that the reactants are bimolecular and that the input reactant structure will be used as an anchor point. This anchor point will not appear as one of the M points on the path. Instead, it will be used instead to control how far the reactant side spreads out from the transition state. By default, this option is off.

OptProduct   Specifies that the input structure for the product in a simultaneous optimization calculation should be optimized to a local minimum. The default is **NoOptProduct**, which retains the input structure as a point that is already on the reaction path (which generally means that it should have been previously optimized to a minimum). **Optproduct** may not be combined with **BiMolecularProduct**.

BiMolecularProduct
                   Specifies that the products are bimolecular and that the input product structure will be used as an anchor point. This anchor point will not appear as one of the M points on the path. Instead, it will be used instead to control how far the product side spreads out from the transition state. By default, this option is off.

Conical   Search for a conical intersection or avoided crossing using the state-averaged CASSCF method. See the discussion of the **CASSCF** keyword for details and examples. **Avoided** is a synonym for **Conical**. Note that **CASSCF=SlaterDet** is needed in order to locate a conical intersection between a singlet state and a triplet state.

Restart   Restarts a geometry optimization from the checkpoint file. In this case, the entire route section will consist of the **Opt** keyword and the same options to it as specified for the original job (along with **Restart**). No other input is needed (see the examples).

NoFreeze   Activates (unfreezes) all variables (normally used with **Geom=Check**).

ModRedundant   Add, delete or modify redundant internal coordinate definitions (including scan and constraint information). This option requires a separate input section following the geometry specification. When used in conjunction with **QST2** or **QST3**, a **ModRedundant** input section must follow *each* geometry specification. **AddRedundant** is synonymous with **ModRedundant**.

                   Lines in a **ModRedundant** input section use the following syntax:

[*Type*] *N1* [*N2* [*N3* [*N4*]]] [[+=]*value*] [A | F] [[*min*] *max*]]
[*Type*] *N1* [*N2* [*N3* [*N4*]]] [[+=]*value*] B [[*min*] *max*]]
[*Type*] *N1* [*N2* [*N3* [*N4*]]] K | R [[*min*] *max*]]
[*Type*] *N1* [*N2* [*N3* [*N4*]]] [[+=]*value*] D [[*min*] *max*]]
[*Type*] *N1* [*N2* [*N3* [*N4*]]] [[+=]*value*] H *diag-elem* [[*min*] *max*]]
[*Type*] *N1* [*N2* [*N3* [*N4*]]] [[+=]*value*] S *nsteps stepsize* [[*min*] *max*]]

N1, *N2*, *N3* and *N4* are atom numbers or wildcards (discussed below). Atom numbering begins at 1, and any dummy atoms are not counted. *Value* specifies a new value for the specified coordinate, and +=*value* increments the coordinate by *value*.

The atom numbers and coordinate value are followed by a one-character code letter indicating the coordinate modification to be performed; the action code is sometimes followed by additional required parameters as indicated above. If no action code is included, the default action is to add the specified coordinate. These are the available action codes:

A   Activate the coordinate for optimization if it has been frozen.
F   Freeze the coordinate in the optimization.
B   Add the coordinate and build all related coordinates.
K   Remove the coordinate and kill all related coordinates containing this coordinate.
R   Remove the coordinate from the definition list (but not the related coordinates).
D   Calculate numerical second derivatives for the row and column of the initial Hessian for this coordinate.
H   Change the diagonal element for this coordinate in the initial Hessian to *diag-elem*.
S   Perform a relaxed potential energy surface scan. Set the initial value of this coordinate to *value* (or its current value), and increment the coordinate by *stepsize* a total of *nsteps* times, performing an optimization from each resulting starting geometry.

An asterisk (*) in the place of an atom number indicates a wildcard. *Min* and *max* then define a range (or maximum value if *min* is not given) for coordinate specifications containing wildcards. The action specified by the action code is taken only if the value of the coordinate is in the range.

Here are some examples of wildcard use:

*   All atoms specified by Cartesian coordinates
* *   All defined bonds
3 *   All defined bonds with atom 3
* * *   All defined valence angles
* 4 *   All defined valence angles around atom 4
* * * *   All defined dihedral angles
* 3 4 *   All defined dihedral angles around the bond connecting atoms 3 and 4

When the action codes **K** and **B** are used with one or two atoms, the meaning of a wildcard is extended to include *all* applicable atoms, not just those involving defined coordinates.

By default, the coordinate type is determined from the number of atoms specified: Cartesian coordinates for 1 atom, bond stretch for 2 atoms, valence angle for 3 atoms and dihedral angle for 4 atoms. Optionally, *Type* can be used to designate these and additional coordinate types:

X   Cartesian coordinates. In this case, *value*, *min* and *max* are each triples of numbers, specifying the X,Y,Z coordinates.
B   Bond length
A   Valence angle
D   Dihedral angle
L   Linear bend specified by three atoms (or if *N4 is* **-1**) or by four atoms, where the fourth atom is used to determine the 2 orthogonal directions of the linear bend. In this case, *value*, *min* and *max* are each pairs of numbers, specifying the two orthogonal bending components.
O   Out-of-plane bending coordinate for a center (*N1*) and three connected atoms.

See the examples later in this section for illustrations of the use of this keyword.

HBond   Specifies how hydrogen bonds are generated as defined redundant internal coordinates. **HBond** says to generate hydrogen bonds but not to build extra bond angles and dihedral angles for them, and it is the default. **NoHBond** turns off the hydrogen bond generation, and **AllHBond** defines all hydrogen bonds and all related bond angles and dihedral angles involving those bonds. These options are valid only for optimizations in redundant internal coordinates.

HindRot   Requests the identification of internal rotation modes for the optimized structure during the vibrational frequency analysis at the end of an **Opt=CalcAll** optimization [342]. If any normal modes are identified as internal rotation, hindered or free, the thermodynamic functions are corrected. **HindRot** is valid only for optimizations perfomed in redundant internal coordinates and must be combined with the **CalcAll** option.

COORDINATE SYSTEM SELECTION OPTIONS

Redundant   Perform the optimization using the Berny algorithm in redundant internal coordinates. This is the default for methods for which analytic gradients are available.

Z-matrix   Perform the optimization in internal coordinates. In this case, the keyword **FOpt** rather than **Opt** requests that the program verify that a full optimization is being done (i.e., that the variables including inactive variables are linearly independent and span the degrees of freedom allowed by the molecular symmetry). The **POpt** form requests a partial optimization in internal coordinates. It also suppresses the frequency analysis at the end of optimizations which include second derivatives at every point (via the **CalcAll** option).

Cartesian   Requests that the optimization be performed in Cartesian coordinates, using the Berny algorithm. Note that the initial structure may be input using any coordinate system. No partial optimization or freezing of variables can be done with purely Cartesian optimizations; the mixed optimization format with all atoms specified via Cartesian lines in the Z-matrix can be used along with **Opt=Z-matrix** if these features are needed (see Appendix B for details and examples).

When a Z-matrix without any variables is used for the molecule specification, and **Opt=Z-matrix** is specified, then the optimization will actually be performed in Cartesian coordinates.

Note that a variety of other coordinate systems, such as distance matrix coordinates, can be constructed using the **ModRedundant** option.

OPTIONS RELATED TO INITIAL FORCE CONSTANTS

EstmFC   Estimate the force constants using the old diagonal guesses. Only available for the Berny algorithm.

NewEstmFC   Estimate the force constants using a valence force field. This is the default.

ReadFC   Extract force constants from a checkpoint file. These will typically be the final approximate force constants from an optimization at a lower level, or the force constants computed correctly by a lower-level frequency calculation (the latter are greatly preferable to the former).

FCCards   Reads the Cartesian forces and force constants from the input stream after the molecule specifications. This can be used to read force constants recovered from the Quantum Chemistry Archive using its internal **FCList** command. The format for this input is:

Energy (format D24.16)
Cartesian forces (lines of format 6F12.8)
Force constants (lines of format 6F12.8)

The force constants are in lower triangular form—$((F(J,I),J=1,I),I=1,NAt3)$, where $NAt3$ is the number of Cartesian coordinates.

RCFC   Specifies that the computed force constants in Cartesian coordinates from a frequency calculation are to be read from the checkpoint file. This is used when the definitions of variables are changed, making previous internal coordinate force constants useless. **ReadCartesianFC** is a synonym for **RCFC**.

CalcHFFC   Specifies that the analytic HF force constants are to be computed at the first point. Note that this option is equivalent to **CalcFC** for DFT methods.

CalcFC   Specifies that the force constants be computed at the first point using the current method (available for the HF, MP2, CASSCF, DFT, and semi-empirical methods only).

CalcAll   Specifies that the force constants are to be computed at every point using the current method (available for the HF, MP2, CASSCF, DFT, and semi-empirical methods only). Note that vibrational frequency analysis is automatically done at the converged structure and the results of the calculation are archived as a frequency job.

VCD   Calculate VCD intensities at each point of an **Opt=CalcAll** optimization.

NoRaman   Specifies that Raman intensities are not to be calculated at each point of an **Opt=CalcAll** job (since it includes a frequency analysis using the results of the final point of the optimization). The Raman intensities add 10-20% to the cost of each intermediate second derivative point.

CONVERGENCE-RELATED OPTIONS
These options are available for the Berny algorithm only.

Tight   This option tightens the cutoffs on forces and step size that are used to determine convergence. An optimization with **Opt=Tight** will take several more steps than with the default cutoffs. For molecular systems with very small force constants (low frequency vibrational modes), this may be necessary to ensure adequate convergence and reliability of frequencies computed in a subsequent job step. This option can only be used with Berny optimizations.

VeryTight   Extremely tight optimization convergence criteria. **VTight** is a synonym for **VeryTight**.

EigenTest   **EigenTest** requests and **NoEigenTest** suppresses testing the curvature in Berny optimizations. The test is on by default only for transition states in internal (Z-matrix) or Cartesian coordinates, for which it is recommended. Occasionally, transition state optimizations converge even if the test is not passed, but **NoEigenTest** is only recommended for those with large computing budgets.

Expert   Relaxes various limits on maximum and minimum force constants and step sizes enforced by the Berny program. This option can lead to faster convergence but is quite dangerous. It is used by experts in cases where the forces and force constants are very different from typical molecules and Z-matrices, and sometimes in conjunction with **Opt=CalcFC** or **Opt=CalcAll**. **NoExpert** enforces the default limits and is the default.

Loose   Sets the optimization convergence criteria to a maximum step size of 0.01 au and an RMS force of 0.0017 au. These values are consistent with the **Int(Grid=SG1)** keyword, and may be appropriate for initial optimizations of large molecules using DFT methods which are intended to be followed by a full convergence optimization using the default (**Fine**) grid. It is *not* recommended for use by itself.

ALGORITHM-RELATED OPTIONS
Big   Requests the optimization to be done using the fast equation solving methods [360] for the coordinate transformations and the Newton-Raphson or RFO step. This option is default for semiempirical calculations. The use of **Opt=Big** is recommended for optimization of very large systems when the energy and gradient is calculated by

O(N) scaled methods. This option can be turned off using **Opt=Small**. **Large** is a synonym for **Big**.

This method avoids the matrix diagonalizations. Consequently, the eigenvector following methods (**Opt=TS**) cannot be used in conjunction with it. **QST2** and **QST3** calculations are guided using an associated surface approximation, but this may not be as effective as the normal method involving eigenvector following.

Micro The use of microiterations in geometry optimizations is the default for MM optimizations and ONIOM optimizations with an MM component. Use the **Opt=NoMicro** option to turn off microiterations.

CheckCoordinates
Rebuild the connectivity matrix before each optimization step. If there is any change in it, rebuild the redundant internal coordinate system. This option is off by default.

Linear **Linear** requests and **NoLinear** suppresses the linear search in Berny optimizations. The default is to use the linear search whenever possible.

TrustUpdate **TrustUpdate** requests and **NoTrustUpdate** suppresses dynamic update of the trust radius in Berny optimizations. The default is to update for minima.

RFO Requests the Rational Function Optimization [361] step during Berny optimizations. It is the default.

GDIIS Specifies the use of the modified GDIIS algorithm [362-364]. Recommended for use with large systems, tight optimizations and molecules with flat potential energy surfaces. It is the default for semiempirical calculations. This option is turned off by the **RFO** and **Newton** options.

Newton Requests the Newton-Raphson step rather than the RFO step during Berny optimizations.

NRScale **NRScale** requests that if the step size in the Newton-Raphson step in Berny optimizations exceeds the maximum, then it is be scaled back. **NoNRScale** causes a minimization on the surface of the sphere of maximum step size [365]. Scaling is the default for transition state optimizations and minimizing on the sphere is the default for minimizations.

EF Requests an eigenvalue-following algorithm [361, 366, 367]. Available for both minima and transition states, with second, first, or no analytic derivatives as indicated by **CalcAll**, **CalcFC**, the defaults, or **EnOnly**. **EigFollow**, **EigenFollow**, and **EigenvalueFollow** are all synonyms for **EF**. Note that when analytic gradients are available and the lowest eigenvector is being followed, then the default Berny algorithm has all of the features of the eigenvalue-following algorithm.

TVector=N Follow the eigenvector with N^{th} eigenvalue of the actual Hessian. The use of **Opt=CalcFC** in conjunction with this option is highly recommended. **TVector** cannot be used in conjunction of **Opt=Big**.

Steep   Requests steepest descent instead of Newton-Raphson steps during Berny optimizations. This is only compatible with Berny local minimum optimizations. It may be useful when starting far from the minimum, but is unlikely to reach full convergence.

OPTIONS FOR INTERPRETING NUMERICAL ERROR

HFError   Assume that numerical errors in the energy and forces are those appropriate for HF and PSCF calculations (1.0D-07 and 1.0D-07, respectively). This is the default for optimizations using those methods.

FineGridError   Assume that numerical errors in the energy and forces are those appropriate for DFT calculations using the default grid (1.0D-07 and 1.0D-06, respectively). This is the default for optimizations using a DFT method and using the default grid (or specifying **Int=FineGrid**). **SEError** is a synonym for this option, as these values are also appropriate for semi-empirical calculations (for which it is also the default).

SG1Error   Assume that numerical errors in the energy and forces are those appropriate for DFT calculations using the SG-1 grid (1.0D-07 and 1.0D-05, respectively). This is the default for optimizations using a DFT method and **Int(Grid=SG1Grid)**.

ReadError   Read in the accuracy to assume for the energy and forces, in format 2F10.6 (there is no terminating blank line for this input section since it is always a single line).

OVERVIEW OF GEOMETRY OPTIMIZATIONS IN *GAUSSIAN 98*

By default, *Gaussian 98* performs the optimization in redundant internal coordinates. This is a change from previous versions of the program. There has been substantial controversy in recent years concerning the optimal coordinate system for optimizations. For example, Cartesian coordinates were shown to be preferable to internal coordinates (Z-matrices) for some cyclic molecules [368]. Similarly, mixed internal and Cartesian coordinates were shown to have some advantages for some cases [369] (among them, ease of use in specifying certain types of molecules).

Pulay has demonstrated [370-372], however, that redundant internal coordinates are the best choice for optimizing polycyclic molecules, and Baker reached a similar conclusion when he compared redundant internal coordinates to Cartesian coordinates [373]. By default, *Gaussian 98* performs optimizations via the Berny algorithm in redundant internal coordinates; these new procedures are also the work of H. B. Schlegel and coworkers [128].

In addition to employing a new coordinate system, this optimization procedure operates somewhat differently from those traditionally employed in the program:

♦   The choice of coordinate system for the starting molecular structure is, quite literally, irrelevant, and it has no effect on the way the optimization proceeds. All of the efficiency factors in the various coordinate systems are of no consequence, since all structures are converted internally to redundant internal coordinates.

♦   All optimizations in redundant internal coordinates are full optimizations unless variables are explicitly frozen using the **ModRedundant** option. Including a separate contants variable section in the molecule specification does *not* result in any frozen variables. Similarly, the requirement that all variables in the Z-matrix be linearly independent does not apply to these optimizations.

Optimizations in redundant internal coordinates *do* make use of geometry constraint information and numerical differentiation specifications. See the examples subsection for details.

Optimizations in internal coordinates, which was the default procedure in *Gaussian 92*, is still available, via the **Opt=Z-Matrix** option.

WAYS OF GENERATING INITIAL FORCE CONSTANTS

Unless you specify otherwise, a Berny geometry optimization starts with an initial guess for the second derivative matrix—also known as the Hessian—which is determined using connectivity determined from atomic radii and a simple valence force field [128, 374]. The approximate matrix is improved at each point using the computed first derivatives.

This scheme usually works fine, but for some cases, such as Z-matrices with unusual arrangements of dummy atoms, the initial guess may be so poor that the optimization fails to start off properly or spends many early steps improving the Hessian without nearing the optimized structure. In addition, for optimizations to transition states (see also below), some knowledge of the curvature around the saddle point is essential, and the default approximate Hessian must always be improved.

In these cases, there are several methods for providing improved force constants:

♦ **Use force constants from a lower-level calculation:** The force constants can be read from the checkpoint file (**Opt=ReadFC**). These will typically be the final approximate force constants from an optimization at a lower level or (much better) the force constants computed correctly at a lower level during a frequency calculation.

♦ **Extract Cartesian force constants from a checkpoint file:** The Cartesian (as opposed to internal) force constants can be read from the checkpoint file. Normally it is preferable to pick up the force constants already converted to internal coordinates as described above. However, a frequency calculation occasionally reveals that a molecule needs to distort to lower symmetry. Usually this means that a new Z-matrix with fewer symmetry constraints must be specified to optimize to the lower energy structure. In this case the computed force constants in terms of the old Z-matrix variables cannot be used, and instead the command **Opt=RCFC** is used to read the Cartesian force constants and transform them to the current Z-matrix variables.

Note that Cartesian force constants are only available on the checkpoint file after a frequency calculation. You cannot use this option after an optimization dies because of a wrong number of negative eigenvalues in the approximate second derivative matrix. In that case, you may want to start from the most recent geometry and compute some derivatives numerically.

♦ **Calculate initial force constants at the HF level:** You can also request that the analytic Hartree-Fock second derivatives be calculated at the first point of the optimization. This can be used with HF, DFT or post-SCF gradient optimizations. This is done by specifying **Opt=CalcHFFC**. Note that this option is equivalent to **CalcFC** for DFT methods.

♦ **Calculate initial force constants at the current level of theory:** You can request that the second derivatives of the method being used in the optimization be computed at the first point by specifying **Opt=CalcFC**. This is only possible for HF, DFT, MP2, and semi-empirical methods.

♦ **Calculate new force constants at every point:** Normally after the initial force constants have been decided upon, they are updated at each point using the gradient information available from the points done in the optimization. For a Hartree-Fock, MP2, or semi-empirical optimization, you can specify **Opt=CalcAll**, which requests that second derivatives be computed at every point in the optimization. Needless to say, this is very expensive.

♦ **Input new guesses:** The default approximate matrix can be used, but with new guesses read in for some or all of the diagonal elements of the Hessian. This is specified in the **ModRedundant** input or on the variable definition lines in the Z-matrix. For example:

```
Redundant Internals              Z-matrix
1 2 3 104.5                      A 104.5
1 2 1.0 H 0.55                   R 1.0 H 0.55
```

The first line specifies that the angle formed by atoms 1, 2 and 3 (the variable *A* in the Z-matrix) is to start at the value 104.5, and the second line sets the initial value of the bond between atoms 1 and 2 (the variable *R* in the Z-matrix) to 0.55 Angstroms. The letter **H** on the second line indicates that a diagonal force constant is being specified for this coordinate and that its value is 0.55 hartree/au^2. Note that the units here are Hartrees and Bohrs or radians.

This option is valid only with the Berny algorithm.

♦ **Compute some or all of the Hessian numerically:** You can ask the optimization program to compute part of the second derivative matrix numerically. In this case each specified variable will be stepped in only one direction, not both up and down as would be required for an accurate determination of force constants. The resulting second-derivatives are not as good as those determined by a frequency calculation but are fine for starting an optimization. Of course, this requires that the program do an extra gradient calculation for each specified variable. This procedure is requested by a flag (**D**) on the variable definition lines:

```
Redundant Internals              Z-matrix
1 2 1.0 D                        R1 1.0 D
2 3 1.5                          R2 1.5
1 2 3 104.5 D                    A1 104.5 D
2 3 4 110.0                      A2 110.0
```

This input tells the program to do three points before taking the first optimization step: the usual first point, a geometry with the bond between atoms 1 and 2 (*R1*) incremented slightly, and a geometry with the angle between atoms 1, 2 and 3 (*A1*) incremented slightly. The program will use the default diagonal force constants for the other two coordinates and will estimate all force constants (on and off diagonal) for bond(1,2)/*R1* and angle(1,2,3)/*A1* from the three points. This option is only available with the Berny and EF algorithms.

OPTIMIZING TO A TRANSITION STATE OR HIGHER-ORDER SADDLE POINT

Transition State Optimizations Using Synchronous Transit-Guided Quasi-Newton (STQN) Methods. *Gaussian 98* includes a new method for locating transition structures. This STQN method, implemented by H. B. Schlegel and coworkers [128, 129], uses a quadratic synchronous transit approach to get closer to the quadratic region of the transition state and then uses a quasi-Newton or eigenvector-following algorithm to complete the optimization. Like the default algorithm for minimizations, it performs optimizations by default in redundant internal coordinates. This method will converge efficiently when provided with an empirical estimate of the Hessian and suitable starting structures.

This method is requested with the **QST2** and **QST3** options. **QST2** requires two molecule specifications, for the reactants and products, as its input, while **QST3** requires three molecule specifications: the reactants, the products, and an initial structure for the transition state, in that order. *The order of the atoms must be identical within all molecule specifications.* See the examples for sample input for and output from this method.

Despite the superficial similarity, this method is very different from the Linear Synchronous Transit method for locating transition structures requested with the now-deprecated LST keyword. **Opt=QST2** generates a guess for the transition structure that is midway between the reactants and products in terms of redundant internal coordinates, and it then goes on to optimize that starting structure to a first-order saddle point automatically. The Linear Synchronous Transit method merely locates a maximum along a path connecting two structures which may be used as a starting structure for a subsequent manually-initiated transition state optimization; *LST does not locate a proper stationary point.* In contrast, **QST2** and **QST3** do locate proper transition states.

Traditional Transition State Optimizations Using the Berny Algorithm. The Berny optimization program can also optimize to a saddle point using internal coordinates, if it is coaxed along properly. The options to request this procedure are **Opt=TS** for a transition state (saddle point of order 1) or **Opt(Saddle=**N**)** for a saddle point which is a maximum in N directions.

When searching for a local minimum, the Berny algorithm uses a combination of rational function optimization (RFO) and linear search steps to achieve speed and reliability (as described below). This linear search step cannot be applied when searching for a transition state. Consequently, transition state optimizations are much more sensitive to the curvature of the surface. A transition state optimization should always be started using one of the options described above for specifying curvature information. Without a full second derivative matrix the initial step is dependent on the choice of coordinate system, so it is best to try to make the reaction coordinate (direction of negative curvature) correspond to one or two redundant internal coordinates or Z-matrix variables (see the examples below).

In the extreme case in which the optimization begins in a region known to have the correct curvature (e.g., starting with **Opt=CalcFC**) and steps into a region of undesirable curvature, the **Opt=CalcAll** option may be useful. This is quite expensive, but the full optimization procedure with correct second derivatives at every point will usually reach a stationary point of correct curvature if started in the desired region. For suggestions on locating transition structures, refer to the literature [127].

An eigenvalue-following (mode walking) optimization method [125, 126] can be requested by **Opt=EF**. This was sometimes superior to the Berny method in *Gaussian 88*, but since the RFO step [361] has now been incorporated into the Berny algorithm, EF is seldom preferable unless its ability to follow a particular mode is needed, or gradients are not available (in which case Berny can't be used anyway). This algorithm has a dimensioning limit of 50 active variables. By default, the lowest mode is followed.

This is correct when already in a region of correct curvature and when the softest mode is to be followed uphill. This default can be overridden in two ways:

♦ The mode having the largest magnitude component for a specific Z-matrix variable can be requested by placing a **4** on the variable definition line:

```
Ang1 104.5 4
```

♦ The Nth mode in order of increasing Hessian eigenvalue can be requested by placing a **10** after the Nth variable definition line, as in this input file:

```
# Opt=(EF,TS)

HCN --> HNC transition state search
This job deliberately follows the wrong (second) mode!

0,1
N
C,1,CN
H,1,CH,2,HCN

CN 1.3
CH 1.20 10          Requests the second mode.
HCN 60.0
```

By default, the Berny optimization program checks the curvature (number of negative eigenvalues) of its approximate second derivative matrix at each step of a transition state optimization. If the number is not correct (1 for a transition state), the job is aborted. A search for a minimum will often succeed in spite of bad real or approximate curvature, because the steepest descent and RFO parts of the algorithm will keep the optimization moving downward, although it may also indicate that the optimization has moved away from the desired minimum and is headed through a transition state and on to a different minimum. On the other hand, a transition state optimization has less chance of success if the curvature is wrong at the current point. However, the test can be suppressed with the **NoEigenTest** option. If **NoEigenTest** is used, it is best to **MaxCycle** to a small value (e.g. 5) and check the structure after a few iterations.

THE BERNY OPTIMIZATION ALGORITHM

The Berny geometry optimization algorithm in *Gaussian 98* is based on an earlier program written by H. B. Schlegel which implemented his published algorithm [115]. The program has been considerably enhanced since this earlier version using techniques either taken from other algorithms or never published, and consequently it is appropriate to summarize the current status of the Berny algorithm here.

At each step of a Berny optimization the following actions are taken:

♦ The Hessian is updated[†] unless an analytic Hessian has been computed or it is the first step, in which case an estimate of the Hessian is made. By default, this is derived from a valence force field [374], but upon request either a unit matrix or a diagonal Hessian can also be generated as estimates.

♦ The trust radius (maximum allowed Newton-Raphson step) is updated if a minimum is sought, using the method of Fletcher [375-377].

♦ Any components of the gradient vector corresponding to frozen variables are set to zero or projected out, thereby eliminating their direct contribution to the next optimization step.

If a minimum is sought, perform a linear search between the latest point and the best previous point (the previous point having lowest energy). If second derivatives are available at both points and a minimum is sought, a quintic polynomial fit is attempted first; if it does not have a minimum in the acceptable range (see below) or if second derivatives are not available, a constrained quartic fit is attempted. This fits a quartic polynomial to the energy and first derivative (along the connecting line) at the two points with the constraint that the second derivative of the polynomial just reach zero at its minimum, thereby ensuring that the polynomial itself has exactly one minimum. If this fit fails or if the resulting step is unacceptable, a simple cubic is fit is done

Any quintic or quartic step is considered acceptable if the latest point is the best so far but if the newest point is not the best, the linear search must return a point in between the most recent and the best step to be acceptable. Cubic steps are never accepted unless they are in between the two points or no larger than the previous step. Finally, if all fits fail and the most recent step is the best so far, no linear step is taken. If all fits fail and the most recent step is not the best, the linear step is taken to the midpoint of the line connecting the most recent and the best previous points.

♦ If the latest point is the best so far or if a transition state is sought, a quadratic step is determined using the current (possibly approximate) second derivatives. If a linear search was done, the quadratic step is taken from the point extrapolated using the linear search and uses forces at that point estimated by interpolating between the forces at the two points used in the linear search. By default, this step uses the Rational Function Optimization (RFO) approach [125, 126, 361, 367]. The RFO step behaves better than the Newton-Raphson method used in earlier versions of *Gaussian* when the curvature at the current point is not that desired. The old Newton-Raphson step is available as an option.

♦ Any components of the step vector resulting from the quadratic step corresponding to frozen variables are set to zero or projected out.

♦ If the quadratic step exceeds the trust radius and a minimum is sought, the step is reduced in length to the trust radius by searching for a minimum of the quadratic function on the sphere having the trust radius, as discussed by Jorgensen [365]. If a transition state is sought or if **NRScale** was requested, the quadratic step is simply scaled down to the trust radius.

[†] By default, the update is done using an iterated BFGS for minima and an iterated Bofill for transition states in redundant internal coordinates, and using a modification of the original Schlegel update procedure for optimizations in internal coordinates.

♦ Finally, convergence is tested against criteria for the maximum force component, root-mean-square force, maximum step component, and root-mean-square step. The step is the change between the most recent point and the next to be computed (the sum of the linear and quadratic steps).

CHANGE IN TRADITIONAL CONVERGENCE CRITERIA

There has been one small but significant change in the criteria for determining when a geometry has converged. When the forces are two orders of magnitude smaller than the cutoff value (i.e., 1/100th of the limiting value), then the geometry is considered converged even if the displacement is larger than the cutoff value. This test was introduced to facilitate optimizations of large molecules which may have a very flat potential energy surface around the minimum.

AVAILABILITY

Analytic gradients are available for the HF, all DFT methods, CIS, MP2, MP3, MP4(SDQ), CID, CISD, CCD, QCISD, CASSCF, and all semi-empirical methods.

The **Tight**, **VeryTight**, **Expert**, **Eigentest** and **EstmFC** options are available for the Berny algorithm only.

RELATED KEYWORDS

IRC, Scan

EXAMPLES ILLUSTRATING OPTIMIZATIONS IN REDUNDANT INTERNAL COORDINATES

The examples in the subsection will focus on optimization procedures new to *Gaussian 98*. However, at the end of the subsection, examples illustrating traditional, Z-matrix-based optimizations using the Berny algorithm will also be given.

Basic Optimization Input. Traditionally, geometry optimizations required a Z-matrix specifying both the starting geometry and the variables to be optimized. For example, the input file in the left column below could be used for a such an optimization on water:

```
# HF/6-31G(d) Opt Test          # HF/6-31G(d) Opt Test

Water opt                        Water opt

0  1                             0  1
O1                               O   0.00  0.00   0.00
H1 O1 R                          H   0.00  0.00   1.00
H2 O1 R H1 A                     H   0.97  0.00  -0.25
   Variables:
R=1.0
A=104.5
```

This Z-matrix specifies the starting configuration of the nuclei in the water molecule. It also specifies that the optimization should determine the values of R and A which minimize the energy. Since the OH bond distance is specified using the same variable for both hydrogen atoms, this Z-matrix also imposes (appropriate) symmetry constraints on the molecule.

The Cartesian coordinate input in the right column is equivalent to the Z-matrix in the left column. In earlier versions of *Gaussian*, such input would lead to an optimization performed in Cartesian coordinates; in *Gaussian 92*, Z-matrix input could be used for optimizations in either coordinate system.

By contrast, in *Gaussian 98* these two input files are *exactly equivalent*. They both will result in a Berny optimization in redundant internal coordinates, giving identical final output.

Output from Optimization Jobs. The string GradGradGrad... delimits the output from the Berny optimization procedures. On the first, initialization pass, the program prints a table giving the initial values of the variables to be optimized. For optimizations in redundant internal coordinates, *all* coordinates in use are displayed in the table (not merely those present in the molecule specification section):

```
GradGradGradGradGradGradGradGradGradGradGradGradGradGradGradGradGrad
Berny optimization.    The opt. algorithm is identified by the header format & this line.
Initialization pass.
                     ----------------------------
                     !     Initial Parameters     !
                     ! (Angstroms and Degrees)    !
----------------------                             --------------------
! Name   Definition                Value          Derivative Info.      !
----------------------------------------------------------------------
! R1     R(2,1)                     1.             estimate D2E/DX2      !
! R2     R(3,1)                     1.             estimate D2E/DX2      !
! A1     A(2,1,3)                   104.5          estimate D2E/DX2      !
----------------------------------------------------------------------
```

The manner in which the initial second derivative are provided is indicated under the heading Derivative Info. In this case the second derivatives will be estimated.

Each subsequent step of the optimization is delimited by lines like these:

```
GradGradGradGradGradGradGradGradGradGradGradGradGradGradGradGradGrad
Berny optimization.
Search for a local minimum.
Step number   4 out of a maximum of   20
```

Once the optimization completes, the final structure is displayed:

```
Optimization completed.
   -- Stationary point found.
                     ----------------------------
                     !    Optimized Parameters    !
                     ! (Angstroms and Degrees)    !
----------------------                             --------------------
! Name   Definition                Value          Derivative Info.      !
----------------------------------------------------------------------
! R1     R(2,1)                     0.9892         -DE/DX =    0.0002    !
! R2     R(3,1)                     0.9892         -DE/DX =    0.0002    !
! A1     A(2,1,3)                   100.004        -DE/DX =    0.0001    !
----------------------------------------------------------------------
```

The redundant internal coordinate definitions are given in the second column of the table. The numbers in parentheses refer to the atoms within the molecule specification. For example, the variable R1, defined as R(2,1), specifies the bond length between atoms 1 and 2.

When a Z-matrix was used for the initial molecule specification, this output will be followed by an expression of the optimized structure in that format, whenever possible.

The energy for the optimized structure will be found in the output from the final optimization step, which *precedes* this table in the output file.

Compound Jobs. Optimizations are commonly followed by frequency calculations at the optimized structure. To facilitate this procedure, the **Opt** keyword may be combined with **Freq** in the route section of an input file, and this combination will automatically generate a two-step job.

It is also common to follow an optimization with a single point energy calculation at a higher level of theory. The following route section automatically performs an HF/6-31G(d,p) optimization followed by an MP4/6-31G(d,p) single point energy calculation :

```
# MP4/6-31G(d,p)//HF/6-31G(d,p) Test
```

Note that the **Opt** keyword is not required in this case. However, it may be included if setting any of its options is desired.

Specifying Redundant Internal Coordinates. The following input file illustrates the method for specifying redundant internal coordinates within an input file:

```
# HF/6-31G(d) Opt=ModRedun Test

Opt job

0,1
C1  0.000   0.000   0.000
C2  0.000   0.000   1.505
O3  1.047   0.000  -0.651
H4 -1.000  -0.006  -0.484
H5 -0.735   0.755   1.898
H6 -0.295  -1.024   1.866
O7  1.242   0.364   2.065
H8  1.938  -0.001   1.499

3   8
2   1   3
```

This structure is acetaldehyde with an OH substituted for one of the hydrogens in the methyl group; the first input line for **ModRedundant** creates a hydrogen bond between that hydrogen atom and the oxygen atom in the carbonyl group. Note that this line adds *only* the bond between these two atoms. The associated angles and dihedral angles would need to be added as well if they were desired.

Displaying the Value of a Desired Coordinate. The second input line for **ModRedundant** specifies the C-C=O bond angle, ensuring that its value will be displayed in the summary structure table for each optimization step.

Using Wildcards in Redundant Internal Coordinates. A distance matrix coordinate system can be activated using the following input:

```
*  *  B                          Define all bonds between pairs of atoms
*  *  *  K                       Remove all other redundant internal coordinates
```

The following input defines partial distance matrix coordinates to connect only the closest layers of atoms:

```
*  *  B  1.1                     Define all bonds between atoms within 1.1 Å
*  *  *  K                       Remove all other redundant internal coordinates
```

The following input sets up an optimization in redundant internal coordinates in which atoms **N1** through **Nn** are frozen. Note that the lines containing the **B** action code will generate Cartesian coordinates for all of the coordinates involving the specified atom since only one atom number is specified:

```
N1  B                            Generate Cartesian coordinates involving atom N1
...
Nn  B                            Generate Cartesian coordinates involving atom Nn
*  F                             Freeze all Cartesian coordinates
```

The following input defines special "spherical" internal coordinate appropriate for molecules like C_{60} [378] by removing all dihedral angles from the redundant internal coordinates:

```
*  *  *  *  R                    Remove all dihedral angles
```

The following input rotates the group about the N2-N3 bond by 10 degrees:

```
*  N2  N3  *   +=10.0            Add 10.0 to the values to dihedrals involving N2-N3 bond
```

Additional examples are found in the section on relaxed PES scans below.

Performing Partial Optimizations in _Gaussian 98._ The following job illustrates the method for freezing variables during a redundant internal coordinate optimization:

```
# HF/6-31G* Opt=ModRedundant Test

Partial optimization

1 1
C
H 1 R1
H 1 R1 2 A1
O 1 R2 2 A2 3 120.0
H 4 R3 3 A3 2 180.0
```

```
A1=120.0
. . .
R3=1.1

4 5          1.3 F
5 4 3 2          F
```

The structure is specified as a traditional Z-matrix, with its variables defined in a separate section. The final input section gives the values for the **ModRedundant** option. This input fixes the O-H bond and the dihedral angle for the final hydrogen atom. Note that any value specified in this manner need not be the same as the one listed in the preceding Z-matrix (as is the case for the O-H bond length); the structure is adjusted to enforce this constraint. The constrained value is optional. For example, in this case the value of second modified redundant internal coordinate defaults to the value from the Z-matrix (180.0).

Modifying Optimized Structures (Why You Don't Need a Z-matrix). Use the Cartesian coordinates version of the optimized structure as your starting point. It can be generated by a route like this one:

```
# Guess=Only Geom=Check
```

(It can also be extracted from an archive entry.) Once you have the structure in Cartesian coordinates, you can use it in a variety of ways:

♦   *Add and/or remove atoms from it.* Additional atoms may be specified in either Cartesian or internal coordinates.

♦   *Modify it by substituting atoms or groups:* For example, you could change a hydrogen to a methyl group by editing the structure, replacing the desired hydrogen with a carbon atoms, and then adding three additional hydrogen atoms bonded to that carbon. The latter could be given in internal coordinates:

```
H6 1.2 2.3 1.1          H6 1.2 2.3 1.1
H7 1.2 0.0 -.9          C7 1.2 0.0 -.9
H8 0.0 -.9 0.0          H8 0.0 -.9 0.0
                        H9  C7 R H5 A C2 180.0
                        H10 C7 R H6 A C2 180.0
                        H11 C7 R H8 A C2 -180.0

                        R=1.0
                        A=120.0

                        7 2 1.5
```

The new structure on the right also uses an additional redundant internal coordinate (specifying **Opt=ModRedundant** on the final job) to alter the bond distance for the new carbon atom which is replacing the hydrogen (bonded to atom 2).

If all you want to do is change the value or activate/frozen status of one or more variables, then you can use **Geom=ModRedundant** rather than this approach.

Restarting an Optimization. A failed optimization may be restarted from its checkpoint file by simply repeating the route section of the original job, adding the **Restart** option to the **Opt** keyword. For example, this route section restarts a Berny optimization to a second-order saddle point:

```
# RHF/6-31G(d) Opt=(Saddle=2,Restart,MaxCyc=50) Test
```

Reading a Structure from the Checkpoint File. Redundant internal coordinate structures may be retrieved from the checkpoint file with **Geom=Checkpoint** as usual. The read-in structure may be altered by specifying **Geom=ModRedundant** as well; modifications have a form identical to the input for **Opt=ModRedundant**:

[*Type*] *N1* [*N2* [*N3* [*N4*]]] [[+=]*Value*] [*Action* [*Params*]] [[*Min*] *Max*]]

Locating a Transition Structure with the STQN Method. The **QST2** option initiates a search for a transition structure connecting specific reactants and products. The input for this option has this general structure:

# HF/6-31G(d) Opt=QST2 Test	# HF/6-31G(d) (Opt=QST2,ModRedun) Test
First title section	*First title section*
Molecule specification for the reactants	*Molecule specification for the reactants*
Second title section	*ModRedundant input for the reactants*
Molecule specification for the products	*Second title section*
	Molecule specification for the products
	ModRedundant input for the products

Note that each molecule specification is preceded by its own title section (and separating blank line). If the **ModRedundant** option is specified, than each molecule specification is followed by any desired modifications to the redundant internal coordinates.

Gaussian 98 will automatically generate a starting structure for the transition structure midway between the reactant and product structures, and then perform an optimization to a first-order saddle point.

The **QST3** option allows you to specify a better initial structure for the transition state. It requires the two title and molecule specification sections for the reactants and products as for **QST2** and also additional, third title and molecule specification sections for the initial transition state geometry (along with the usual blank line separators), as well as three corresponding modifications to the redundant internal coordinates if the **ModRedundant** option is specified. The program will then locate the transition structure connecting the reactants and products closest to the specified initial geometry.

The optimized structure found by **QST2** or **QST3** appears in the output in a format similar to that for other types of geometry optimizations:

```
                   --------------------------------
                   !   Optimized Parameters    !
                   !   (Angstroms and Degrees) !
------------------------------------        -------------------------------
! Name   Definition      Value      Reactant  Product   Derivative Info.  !
------------------------------------------------------------------------
! R1      R(2,1)         1.0836      1.083    1.084     -DE/DX =     0.    !
! R2      R(3,1)         1.4233      1.4047   1.4426    -DE/DX =    -0.    !
! R3      R(4,1)         1.4154      1.4347   1.3952    -DE/DX =    -0.    !
! R4      R(5,3)         1.3989      1.3989   1.3984    -DE/DX =     0.    !
! R5      R(6,3)         1.1009      1.0985   1.0995    -DE/DX =     0.    !
! ...                                                                        !
------------------------------------------------------------------------
```

In addition to listing the optimized values, the table includes those for the reactants and products.

Performing a Relaxed Potential Energy Surface Scan. The **Opt=Z-matrix** and **Opt=ModRedundant** keywords may also be used to perform a relaxed potential energy surface (PES) scan. Like the scan facility provided by previous versions of *Gaussian*, a relaxed PES scan steps over a rectangular grid on the PES involving selected internal coordinates. It differs from the operation of the **Scan** keyword in that a constrained geometry optimization is performed at each point.

Relaxed PES scans are available only for the Berny algorithm. If any scanning variable breaks symmetry during the calculation, then you must include **NoSymm** in the route section of the job, or it will fail with an error.

Redundant internal coordinates specified with the **Opt=ModRedundant** option may be scanned using the **S** code letter: *N1 N2 [N3 [N4]] [[+=]value]* **S** *steps step-size*. For example, this input adds a bond between atoms 2 and 3, setting its initial value to 1.0 Å, and specifying three scan steps of 0.05 Å each:

```
2 3 1.0 S 3 0.05
```

Wildcards in the **ModRedundant** input may also be useful in setting up relaxed PES scans. For example, the following input is appropriate for a potential energy surface scan involving the N1-N2-N3-N4 dihedral angle. Note that all other dihedrals around the bond should be removed:

```
* N2 N3 * R          Remove all dihedrals involving the N2-N3 bond
N1 N2 N3 N4 S 20 2.0  Specify a relaxed PES scan of 20 steps in 2° increments
```

EXAMPLES FOR OPTIMIZATIONS IN INTERNAL (Z-MATRIX) COORDINATES

Full vs. Partial Optimizations. When it is performed in internal (Z-matrix) coordinates, the Berny optimization algorithm makes a distinction between full and partial optimizations. Full optimizations optimize all specified variables in order to find the lowest energy structure,[†] while partial optimizations optimize only a specified subset of the variables.

Those variables whose values should be held fixed are specified in a separate input section, separated by the usual variables section by a blank line or a line containing a space in the first column and the string

---

[†] Note that the **Fopt** keyword form is used to request that the optimization variables be tested for linear independance prior to beginning the optimization.

Constants:. For example, the following input file will optimize only the bond distance R, but not the angle A, which will be held fixed at 105.4 degrees throughout the optimization:

```
# HF/6-31G(d) Opt=Z-matrix Test

Partial optimization for water

0 1
O
H1 O R
H2 O R H1 A
   Variables:
R 1.0
   Constants:
A 105.4
```

Freezing and Unfreezing Optimization Variables. When a geometry is retrieved from a checkpoint file, the active/frozen status as well as the values of variables may be changed for a subsequent optimization by using the **Geom=Modify** keyword. Consider the following input file, which performs a partial optimization on methanol, optimizing only the dihedral angles:

```
%Chk=methanol
# HF/6-31G(d) Opt=Z-matrix Test

Methanol--optimize just dihedral angles

0,1
C
C 1 CO
H 2 CH 1 COH
H 1 CHA 2 OCHA 3   180.0
H 1 CHB 2 OCHB 3   HOCH
H 1 CHB 2 OCHB 3 -HCCH
   Variables:
HOCH=65.0
   Constants:
CC=1.4
CH=1.0
remaining variables ...
```

The geometry from the checkpoint file created by the previous job may be used for another optimization, using the following input file, which optimizes the bond angles and dihedral angles within the molecule:

```
%Chk=methanol
# HF/6-31G(d) Opt(ReadFC,Z-matrix) Geom=Modify Guess=Read Test

Methanol--optimize just bond and dihedral angles,
changing the values of CC, CH, and COH

0,1

CC=1.45
CH=0.95
```

```
COH=105.0 A
OCHA A
OCHB A
```

The final input section contains modifications to the geometry retrieved from the checkpoint file. The **A** code letter indicates that a variable is to be made active (i.e., optimized); the code letter **F** freezes a variable's value. If no code letter is specified, the variable's status remains the same as it was in the original job. Variables of either type may also be assigned new values (as illustrated).

The following input file illustrates the method for activating all variables in a subsequent optimization, using the **NoFreeze** option to the **Opt** keyword:

```
%Chk=methanol
# HF/6-31G(d) Opt(Z-matrix,NoFreeze,ReadFC)
# Geom=Check Guess=Read Test

Methanol--optimize everything

0,1
```

Note that **NoFreeze** is not needed for a subsequent Berny optimization using redundant internal coordinates, as this procedure ignores the distinction between active and frozen variables.

Breaking Symmetry During an Optimization in Internal Coordinates. Below are two geometry specifications for water. The one on the left has been constrained to C_{2v} symmetry; since the same variable is used for both bond lengths, their values will always be the same:

```
O                              O
H  1 R1                        H  1 R1
H  1 R1  2 A                   H  2 R2  2 A

R1=0.9                         R1=0.9
A=105.4                        R2=1.1
                               A=105.4
```

By contrast, the Z-matrix on the right is unconstrained since the two bond lengths are specified by different variables having different initial values. Note that an optimization in redundant internal coordinates which begins from a C_{2v} structure will retain that symmetry throughout the optimization.

Relaxed PES Scans. For **Opt=Z-matrix**, a relaxed PES scan is requested simply by tagging the Z-matrix variables whose values are to be incremented with the **S** code letter and the number of steps and the increment size. For example, the following input file requests a relaxed PES scan for the given molecule:

```
# HF/6-31G(d) Opt=Z-matrix Test

Relaxed PES scan

0 1
O
H 1 R1
C 1 R2 2 A2
...
```

```
    Variables:
R1 0.9 S 5 0.05
R2 1.1
A2 115.4 S 2 1.0
...
```

This causes the variable R1 to be incremented five times, by 0.05 Å each time, and the variable A2 to be incremented twice, by 1 degree each time, resulting in a total of 18 geometry optimizations (the initial values for each variable also constitute a point within the scan).

Transition State Optimizations Using Internal Coordinates. We'll conclude the examples of geometry optimizations by considering traditional ways of approaching transition state optimizations (using the **Opt=TS**). Here is a simple example input file for determining the transition state for the 1,2-hydrogen shift which converts HCN into HNC:

```
# HF/6-31G(d) Opt(TS,Z-matrix) Test

HCN --> HNC TS Opt

0 1
C
N 1 NC
X 2 QN 1 90.0
H 3 HQ 2 90.0 1 0.0

NC=1.18
HQ=0.8 D
QN=1.15
```

This Z-matrix uses a dummy atom so that the shift of the hydrogen is largely given by a single coordinate (HQ). The force constants for this variable are estimated numerically giving (hopefully) one negative eigenvalue for the force constant matrix. This is noted in the output in the table labeled Initial Parameters:

```
 !    HQ        0.8       calc D2E/DXDY, stepsize =    0.0026        !
```

The first point of the optimization proceeds as usual. At the start of the second point, Link 103 notes that the second derivatives are being estimated numerically:

```
GradGradGradGradGradGradGradGradGradGradGradGradGradGradGradGradGradGrad
Berny optimization.
Numerically estimating second derivatives.
```

The first step is taken once this estimation is complete. The output for that point includes the eigenvector corresponding to the negative eigenvector of the Hessian matrix (i.e., the approximate reaction coordinate):

```
The second derivative matrix:
                        NC        HQ        QN
          NC         1.15446
          HQ          .07430   -.05078
          QN          .00000   -.02113    .28679
```

```
      Eigenvalues ---    -.05664    .28808   1.15902
 Eigenvectors required to have negative eigenvalues:
                        NC         HQ        QN
           1         -.06112    .99625    .06129
```

This output can be helpful in determining whether an optimization is proceeding toward the desired transition state.

The following input file is a two-step job illustrating a useful technique for locating transition state structures. It locates the 1,2-hydrogen shift transition structure for hydrogen cyanide:

```
%Chk=hcn_ts
# HF/6-31G(d) Opt=Z-matrix Test

HCN --> CNH Initial partial opt

0 1
C
N 1 CN
H 1 CH 2 A

CN 1.3
CH 1.2

A 70.0
```

In the first step, the bond angle has been guessed to be about 70 degrees. The corresponding variable is held fixed while the energy is minimized with respect to the two bond lengths. The transition state is located in a second job step, starting from this partially-optimized structure:

```
--Link1--
%Chk=hcn_ts
%NoSave
# HF/6-31G(d) Opt(TS,Z-matrix,ReadFC) Geom=Modify Guess=Read Test

CN --> CNH Final TS opt

0 1

A D
```

The single line in the geometry modification input section specifies numerical differentiation with respect to the variable A be performed before proceeding with the optimization. Note that requesting numerical differentiation with the **D** code letter automatically activates the variable. Since no new value is given for A, it initially has the same value as was retrieved from the checkpoint file (70 degrees). Since the angle contributes significantly to the reaction coordinate, differentiating with respect to it ensures that the initial Hessian in the second job step will have the correct curvature (one negative eigenvalue).

➤ Output

DESCRIPTION
The **Output** keyword requests output of Fortran unformatted files. Its options control the contents of the created file.

OPTIONS

PolyAtom   This requests output of an integral file in one variant of the format originated for the **PolyAtom** integrals program. The format produced by default is that used by the Caltech MQM programs, but the code in Link 9999 is easily modified to produce other variations on the same theme.

Trans   Write an MO coefficient file in Caltech (**Tran2P5**) format. This is only of interest to users of the Caltech programs.

WFN   Write a PROAIMS wavefunction (.wfn) file. The name for the created file is read from the input stream. **PSI** is a synonym for **WFN**.

RELATED KEYWORDS
Punch

➤ ROVGF
➤ UOVGF

DESCRIPTION
These method keywords request an Outer Valence Green's Function (propagator) calculation of correlated electron affinities and ionization potentials [184-190, 379]. Either **R** or **U** must be specified with **OVGF**. The unrestricted code requires a two-electron integral file as well as <ia||bc> transformed integrals.

ROVGF calculations default to storage of <ia||bc> integrals, but can be run **Tran=Full** to save CPU time at the expense of disk usage, or with **Tran=IJAB** to save on disk space at the expense of CPU time. In the latter case, electron affinities are not computed.

Use **IOp(9/11=100)** to specify the starting and ending orbitals to refine as input (in a separate input section with a terminal blank line). By default, all orbitals are used.

OPTIONS

FC   This indicates "frozen-core," and it implies that inner-shells are excluded from the correlation calculation. This is the default calculation mode. **Full** specifies the inclusion of all electrons, and **RW** and **Window** allow you to input specific information about which orbitals to retain in the post-SCF calculation (see the discussion of the **MP*n*** keywords for an example).

AVAILABILITY

Single point energy calculations only.

EXAMPLES

For **ROVGF** calculations, the results for each orbital appear as follows:

```
Method    Orbital   HF-eigenvalue 3rd-order  Polestrength
  A:         6        19.59832      17.47750     .86138
  B:         6        19.59832      17.51817     .86527
  C:         6        19.59832      17.56548     .86406
Renormalization of interaction,  recommended value
Orbital   HF-eigenvalue 3rd-order  Polestrength
   6        19.59832      17.47750  .86138
```

The first part of the output gives the results from the three OVGF methods [186]. The third-order column in the final line gives the etimate of ionization potential/electron affinity (which property is given depends on whether the orbital is occupied or not, respectively) for the specified orbital. The pole strength is a measure of how easy it is to make this excitation, with 1.0 as the maximum value. Note that orbitals are listed in the output in order of symmetry (and not necessarily in numerical order).

For **UOVGF** calculations, the equivalent results appear in the output like this:

```
Summary of results for alpha spin-orbital    6:
...
Outer Valence Approximation:  .64377D+00 au    17.518 eV
```

These results are the same as for method B from the **ROVGF** calculation.

➤ **PL**
➤ **P86**
➤ **PW91**

See **DFT Methods** *above.*

➤ PM3
➤ PM3MM

DESCRIPTION
The method keywords request a semi-empirical calculation using the PM3 Hamiltonian [53, 54]. **PM3MM** specifies the PM3 model including the optional molecular mechanics correction for HCON linkages. No basis set keyword should be specified with either of these keywords.

AVAILABILITY
Energies, "analytic" gradients, and numerical frequencies.

EXAMPLES
The PM3 energy appears in the output file as follows (followed by the x, y, and z components of the dipole moment):

```
Energy=    -.080731473251 NIter=  10.
Dipole moment=    .000000    .000000  -.739540
```

The energy is as defined by the PM3 semi-empirical model. Note that energy differences computed from the values in semi-empirical calculations are in Hartrees and may be compared directly with energy differences computed from jobs using other methods.

➤ Polar

DESCRIPTION
This method keyword requests that the dipole electric field polarizabilities (and hyperpolarizabilities, if possible) be computed. No geometry change or derivatives are implied, but this keyword may be combined in the same job with numerical differentiation of forces by specifying both **Freq** and **Polar** in the route section. **Freq** and **Polar** may *not* be combined for methods lacking analytic gradients (MP4(SDTQ), QCISD(T), CCSD(T), BD, and so on). Note that **Polar** is done by default when second derivatives are computed analytically.

OPTIONS
Step=N Specifies the step size in the electric field to be $0.0001N$ atomic units.

Analytic   Compute polarizability and hyperpolarizability analytically. This is possible for RHF and UHF for which it is the default. The polarizability is always computed during analytic frequency calculations.

Numerical   Computes the polarizability as a numerical derivative of the dipole moment (itself the analytic derivative of the energy, of course, not the expectation value in the case of

MP2 or CI energies). The default for methods for which only analytic first derivatives are available.

EnOnly   Requests double numerical differentiation of energies to produce polarizabilities. **EnergyOnly**, a synonym for **EnOnly**, is a misnomer, since analytic first derivatives will also be differentiated twice, to produce hyperpolarizabilities, when they are available.

Restart   Restarts a *numerical* polarizability calculation from the checkpoint file. A failed **Polar** calculation may be restarted from its checkpoint file by simply repeating the route section of the original job, adding the **Restart** option to the **Polar** keyword. No other input is required.

Dipole   Compute the dipole polarizabilities (this is the default).

AVAILABILITY
Polarizabilities and hyperpolarizabilities will be automatically computed for HF, all DFT methods, and MP2. **Polar** will compute polarizabilities only, and **Polar=EnOnly** will produce both polarizabilities and hyperpolarizabilities for CIS, MP2, MP3, MP4(SDQ), CID, CISD, CCD, QCISD, and CASSCF. **Polar** will produce only polarizabilities for all other methods (for which no analytic derivatives are available, making **EnOnly** the default). Note that **Polar** is not available for any semi-empirical method.

RELATED KEYWORDS
Freq

➤ Population

DESCRIPTION
This properties keyword controls printing of molecular orbitals and several types of population analysis and atomic charge assignments. The default is to print just the total atomic charges and orbital energies, except for **Guess=Only** jobs, for which the default is **Pop=Full** (see below). Populations are done once for single-point calculations and at the first and last points of geometry optimizations.

The density that is used for the population analysis is controlled by the **Density** keyword. Note that only one density and method of charge fitting can be used in a job step. If several combinations are of interest, additional jobs steps can be added which specify **Guess=Only Density=Check**, to avoid repeating any costly calculations.

Population analysis results are given in the standard orientation.

Output controlled by the **Pop** keyword includes:

♦ Molecular orbitals and orbital energies
♦ Atomic charge distribution

♦ Multipole moments (dipole through hexadecapole)

By default, *Gaussian 98* prints molecular orbitals and performs population analyses regarding the MO coefficients from a semi-empirical calculation as coefficients of orthogonalized atomic orbitals (OAO's). There are important theoretical reasons for preferring this interpretation, but some other semi-empirical programs interpret these coefficients as referring to raw atomic orbitals. Use **IOp(4/24=3)** to compare orbitals from *Gaussian 98* semi-empirical calculations to the results of such other programs.

Note that the **AIM** keyword computes Atoms in Molecules-based atomic charges and performs other related analyses.

OPTIONS CONTROLLING OUTPUT FILE CONTENTS

None   No orbitals are printed, and no population analysis is done.

Minimal   Total atomic charges and orbital energies are printed. This is the default for all job types except **Guess=Only**.

Regular   The five highest occupied and five lowest virtual orbitals are printed, along with the density matrices and a full (orbital by orbital and atom by atom) Mulliken population analysis. Since the size of the output depends on the square of the size of the molecule, it can become quite substantial for larger molecules.

Full   Same as the **Regular** population analysis, except that *all* orbitals are printed.

BONDING ANALYSIS OPTION

Bonding   Do a bonding population analysis in addition to the standard analysis. This is a Mulliken population analysis in which only density terms involving pairs of basis functions on different centers are retained. The other options control how much is printed.

NATURAL ORBITAL-RELATED OPTIONS

NaturalOrbitals Do a natural orbital analysis of the total density. **NO** is a synonym for **NaturalOrbitals**.

NOAB   Do separate natural orbital analyses for the α and β densities. **NaturalSpinOrbitals** is a synonym for **NOAB**.

AlphaNatural Do separate natural orbital analyses for the α and β densities, but store only the α densities for use in a .wfn file (see **Output=WFN**). **NOA** is a synonym for **AlphaNatural**.

BetaNatural   Do separate natural orbital analyses for the α and β densities, but store only the β densities for use in a .wfn file (see **Output=WFN**). **NOB** is a synonym for **BetaNatural**.

SpinNatural   Generate natural orbitals for the spin density (with α considered positive).

By default, natural orbitals are not included in the checkpoint file. Use a second job step of this form to place the natural orbitals into the checkpoint file:

```
--Link1--
%Chk=name
# IOP(4/5=8,4/38=-1) Guess=(Read,Save,Only) Geom=AllCheck
```

Run the **formchk** utility on the resulting checkpoint file to prepare the orbitals for visualization.

OPTIONS FOR GENERATING ELECTROSTATIC POTENTIAL-DERIVED CHARGES

MK
Produce charges fit to the electrostatic potential at points selected according to the Merz-Singh-Kollman scheme [166, 167]. **ESP** and **MerzKollman** are synonyms for **MK**.

CHelp
Produce charges fit to the electrostatic potential at points selected according to the CHelp scheme [168].

CHelpG
Produce charges fit to the electrostatic potential at points selected according to the CHelpG scheme [169].

Dipole
When fitting charges to the potential, constrain them to reproduce the dipole moment. **ESPDipole** is a synonym for **Dipole**.

AtomDipole
When fitting charges to the potential, also fit a point dipole at each atomic center.

ReadRadii
Read in alternative radii (in Angstroms) for each element for use in fitting potentials. These are read as pairs of atomic symbol and radius, terminated by a blank line.

ReadAtRadii
Read in alternative radii (in Angstroms) for each atom for use in fitting potentials. These are read as pairs of atom number and radius, terminated by a blank line.

NBO-RELATED OPTIONS

NBO
Requests a full Natural Bond Orbital analysis [11-18]. (Contact Gaussian, Inc. to obtain the NBO manual.)

NPA
Requests just the Natural Population Analysis phase of NBO.

NBORead
Requests a full NBO analysis, with input controlling the analysis read from the input stream. Refer to the NBO documentation for details on this input.

NBODel
Requests NBO analysis of the effects of deletion of some interactions. Only possible at the Hartree-Fock level. Implies that NBO input will be read; refer to the NBO documentation for details. Note that NBO input starts in column 2 so that the UNIX shell does not interpret the initial $.

RELATED KEYWORDS
AIM, Density, Output=WFN

➤ Prop

DESCRIPTION

This properties keyword tells *Gaussian 98* to compute electrostatic properties [274, 380-382]. By default, the potential, electric field, and electric field gradient at each nucleus are computed. The density used for the electrostatic analysis is controlled by the **Density** keyword.

PROPERTY SELECTION OPTIONS

EFG   Specifies that potential, field and field gradient are to be computed. This is the default.

Potential   Specifies that the potential but not the field or field gradient are to be computed. **NoPotential** suppresses computation of the electric potential and higher properties.

Field   Specifies that the potential and field, but not the field gradient, are to be computed.

EPR   Compute the anisotropic hyperfine coupling constants [274, 381, 382].

INPUT SOURCE-RELATED OPTIONS

If both **Read** and **Opt** are specified, the order of the input sections is fixed points (**Read**), then optimized points (**Opt**).

Read   Causes the program to read a list of additional centers at which properties will be computed from the input stream. The Cartesian coordinates of each center in angstroms are read in free field, with one center per line, in the standard orientation.

Opt   Causes the program to read a list of centers as in **Prop=Read**, but then to locate the minimum in the electric potential closest to each specified point.

FitCharge   Fit atomic charges to the electrostatic potential at the Van der Waals surface.

Dipole   Constrain fitted charges to the dipole moment.

Grid   Specifies that the potential is to be calculated at one or more grids of points and written to an external file (generally superseded by **Cube=Potential**). This option requests mapping of the electric potential over a 2D grid of points. The points can be specified as a uniform rectangular grid, as an arbitrary collection read from an auxiliary file (both described below), or via the input format used by **Cube=Potential** (documented earlier in this chapter).

Three additional input lines are required for a uniform grid:

KTape,XO,YO,ZO   The Fortran unit to which to write the map, and the coordinates of the map's lower left corner.

N1,X1,Y1,Z1   The number of rows in the grid, and the vertical step size.

N2,X2,Y2,Z2	The number of columns in the grid, and the horizontal step size.

For points read from an auxiliary file, a single line of input supplies all of the necessary information:

N,NEFG,LTape,KTape

The coordinates of N points in Angstroms will be read from unit *LTape,* in format 3F20.12. *LTape* defaults to 52. The potential (*NEFG*=3), potential and field (*NEFG*=2), or potential, field, and field gradient (*NEFG*=1) will be computed and written to unit *KTape.* For example, the following input indicates that 19,696 points for the electrostatic potential (code 3) will be read from Fortran unit 10, with output written to Fortran unit 11:

```
19696,3,10,11
```

AVAILABILITY
HF, all DFT methods, CIS, MP2, MP3, MP4(SDQ), CID, CISD, CCD, and QCISD.

RELATED KEYWORDS
Density, Cube

➤ Pseudo

DESCRIPTION
This keyword requests that a model potential be substituted for the core electrons. The **Cards** option is by far its most-used mode. *Gaussian 98* supports a new effective core potential (ECP) input format (similar to that used by **ExtraBasis**) which is described below. When reading-in pseudopotentials, do not give them the same names as any internally-stored pseudopotentials: **CEP, CHF, LANL1, LANL2, LP-31, SDD** and **SHC**.

OPTIONS

Read   Read pseudo-potential data from the input stream. Input is described in the next subsection below. **Cards** is a synonym for **Read**.

Old   Read pseudo-potential data using the old format (used by *Gaussian 92* and earlier versions).

CHF   Requests the Coreless Hartree-Fock potentials. This option is normally used with the LP-31G basis sets.

SHC   Requests the SHC potentials.

LANL1   Requests the LANL1 potentials.

LANL2   Requests the LANL2 potentials.

FULL ECP INPUT FORMAT

Effective Core Potential operators are sums of products of polynomial radial functions, Gaussian radial functions and angular momentum projection operators. ECP input therefore specifies which potential to use on each atomic center, and then includes a collection of triplets of:

(coefficient, power of R, exponent)

for each potential for each term in each angular momentum of the ECP. Since only the first few angular momentum components have different terms, the potential is expressed as (1) terms for the general case, typically d or f and higher projection, and (2) the extra terms for each special angular momentum. Thus for an LP-31G potential, which includes special s and p projected terms, the input includes the general (d and higher) term, the s-d term (i.e., what to add to the general term to make the s component) and the p-d term.

ECP input has changed somewhat with *Gaussian* 98 to allow ECPs in internally-stored basis sets to be referenced.

All ECP input is free-format. Each block is introduced by a line containing the center numbers (from the molecule specification) and/or atomic symbols, specifying the atoms and/or atoms types to which it applies (just as for general basis set input—see the discussion of the **Gen** keyword). The list ends with a value of 0.

The pseudo-potential for those centers/atoms follows:

Name,Max,ICore   Name of the potential, maximum angular momentum of the potential (i.e., 2 if there are special s and p projections, 3 if there are s, p, and d projections), and number of core electrons replaced by the potential. If *Name* matches the name of a previous potential, that potential is reused and no further input other than the terminator line (see below) is required.

For each component (*I*=1 to *Max*) of the current potential, a group of terms is read, containing the following information:

Title   A description of the block, not otherwise used.

NTerm   Number of terms in the block.

NPower,Expon,Coef   Power of R, exponent, and coefficient for each of the *NTerm* terms. *NPower* includes the R^2 Jacobian factor.

An example of an input file which includes a nonstandard ECP with its associated basis set is given below.

SIMPLIFIED ECP INPUT FORMAT
Gaussian 98 adds flexibility to ECP input by allowing it to include pre-defined basis sets names. An ECP definition may be replaced by a line containing the standard keyword for a pre-defined basis set. In this case, the ECPs within the specified basis set corresponding to the specified atom type(s) will be used for that atom (see the examples).

KEYWORDS FOR STUTTGART/DRESDEN ECP INPUT
In **Pseudo** input, keywords for these ECP's are of the form **ECP*n*XY** where *n* is the number of core electrons which are replaced by the pseudopotential and *X* denotes the reference system used for generating the pseudopotential (**S** for a single-valence-electron ion or **M** for a neutral atom).

Y specifies the theoretical level of the reference data: **HF** for Hartree-Fock, **WB** for Wood-Boring quasi-relativistic and **DF** for Dirac-Fock relativistic. For one- or two-valence electron atoms **SDF** is a good choice; otherwise **MWB** or **MDF** is recommended (although for small atoms or for the consideration of relativistic effects, the corresponding **SHF** and **MHF** pseudopotentials may be useful).

RELATED KEYWORDS
ChkBasis, ExtraBasis, Gen

EXAMPLES
Specifying an ECP. This input file runs an RHF/LP-31G calculation on hydrogen peroxide, with the basis set and ECP data read from the input file:

```
# HF/Gen Pseudo=Read Test

Hydrogen peroxide

0,1
O
H,1,R2
O,1,R3,2,A3
H,3,R2,1,A3,2,180.,0

R2=0.96
R3=1.48
A3=109.47
```

General basis set input
****

O 0			*ECPs for the oxygen atoms.*
OLP 2 2			*ECP name=OLP, applies to d & higher, replaces 2 electrons.*
D component			*Description for the general terms.*
3			*Number of terms to follow.*
1 80.0000000	-1.60000000		
1 30.0000000	-0.40000000		
2 1.0953760	-0.06623814		
S-D projection			*Corrections for projected terms (lowest angular momentum).*
3			
0 0.9212952	0.39552179		
0 28.6481971	2.51654843		

```
2  9.3033500  17.04478500
P-D                                    Corrections for projected terms (highest angular momentum).
2
2 52.3427019  27.97790770
2 30.7220233 -16.49630500
                                       Blank line indicates end of the ECP block for oxygen.
```

Using Standard Basis Set Keywords to Specify ECPs. The following input file illustrates the use of the simplified ECP input format:

```
# Becke3LYP/Gen Pseudo=Read Opt Test

HF/6-31G(*) Opt of Cr(CO)6

0 1
Cr 0.0  0.0  0.0
molecule specification continues ...

C O O
6-31G(d)
****
Cr 0
LANL2DZ
****

Cr 0                                   ECP for chromium atom.
LANL2DZ                                Use the ECP in this basis set.
```

➤ Punch

DESCRIPTION

This output specification keyword allows the user to "punch"—in more modern parlance, send to a separate output file—useful information at various points in the calculation. The output is disposed of in whatever manner is usual for Fortran alternate-unit output under the appropriate operating system (for example, unit 7 is sent to the file FOR007.DAT on VMS systems and to fort.7 under UNIX.) Options are used to specify what information should be output. All of these options can be combined, except that only one of **MO** and **NaturalOrbitals** can be requested. Note, however, that they are distinct and non-interacting. For example, Punch(MO, Gamess) sends both the molecular orbital and Gamess input information to the file; it does *not* format the MO information in Gamess input format.

OPTIONS

Archive   Requests that a summary of the important results of the calculation be punched. This output is in the same format used by the Browse Quantum Chemistry Database System. Refer to its documentation for details.

Title   Punches the title section.

Coord	Punches the atomic numbers and Cartesian coordinates in a form which could be read back into *Gaussian 98*.
Derivatives	Punches the energy, Cartesian nuclear coordinate derivatives, and second derivatives in format 6F12.8, suitable for later use with **Opt=FCCards**.
MO	Punches the orbitals in a format suitable for **Guess=Cards** input.
NaturalOrbitals	Punches natural orbitals (for the density selected with the **Density** keyword).
HondoInput	Punches an input deck for one version of Hondo, which is probably easily modified to fit most others.
GAMESSInput	Punches an input deck for GAMESS.
All	Punches everything except natural orbitals.

RELATED KEYWORDS
Output

➤ QCISD

DESCRIPTION
This method keyword requests a Quadratic CI calculation [70], including single and double substitutions. Note that this keyword requests only QCISD and does not include the triples correction [383-385] by default.

OPTIONS

T	Requests a Quadratic CI calculation including single and double substitutions with a triples contribution to the energy added [70].
E4T	Requests a Quadratic CI calculation including single and double substitutions with a triples contribution to the energy and also an evaluation of MP4 triples. Must be specified with the **T** option.
TQ	Requests a Quadratic CI calculation including single and double substitutions with an energy contribution from triples and quadruples [62] added.
T1Diag	Computes the Q1 diagnostic of T. J. Lee and coworkers [298, 386]. Note that Q1 is analogous to the T1 diagnostic for CCSD when it is computed using QCISD instead of the Coupled Cluster method.

FC   This indicates "frozen-core," and it implies that inner-shells are excluded from the correlation calculation. This is the default calculation mode. **Full** specifies the inclusion of all electrons, and **RW** and **Window** allow you to input specific information about which orbitals to retain in the post-SCF calculation (see the discussion of the **MP**n keywords for an example).

Conver=N   Sets the convergence calculations to 10^{-N} on the energy and $10^{-(N+2)}$ on the wavefunction. The default is $N=7$ for single points and $N=8$ for gradients.

MaxCyc=n   Specifies the maximum number of cycles.

RELATED KEYWORDS
CCSD

EXAMPLES
The predicted energy from a QCISD calculation appears in the output in the final QCISD iteration:

DE(CORR)= -.54999890D-01   E(CORR)= -.7501966245dD+02

When **QCISD(T)** is specified, the preceding output is followed by the energy including the non-iterative triples contribution:

QCISD(T)= -.75019725718D+02

➤ ReArchive

DESCRIPTION
This calculation type keyword requests that the information on the checkpoint file be used to generate an archive entry. In this case, no new calculation is performed.

RELATED KEYWORDS
Archive, Test

➤ SP

DESCRIPTION
This calculation type keyword requests a single-point energy calculation. It is the default when no calculation type keyword is specified.

AVAILABILITY
All methods.

EXAMPLES
See the discussion of the methods keywords for examples of their energy output formats.

➤ Sparse

DESCRIPTION
Use sparse matrix storage for performance enhancement of large calculations (above around 400 atoms) [34]. The keyword's option allows you to specify the cutoff value for considering matrix elements to be zero.

OPTIONS

Loose   Sets the cutoff to $5 * 10^{-5}$.

Medium   Sets the cutoff to $5 * 10^{-7}$. This is the default for semi-empirical methods.

Tight   Sets the cutoff to $1 * 10^{-10}$. This is the default for DFT methods.

N   Sets the cutoff to $1 * 10^{-N}$.

AVAILABILITY
Energies and gradients for AM1, PM3, MNDO and DFT methods.

RELATED KEYWORDS
FMM

➤ Scan

DESCRIPTION

This calculation type keyword requests that a potential energy surface (PES) scan be done. A *rigid* PES scan is performed, which consists of single point energy evaluations over a rectangular grid involving selected internal coordinates. The molecular structure must be defined using Z-matrix coordinates. The number of steps and step size for each variable are specified on the variable definition lines, following the variable's initial value. For example:

```
R1 1.41   3 0.05
A1 104.5 2 1.0
A2 120.0
```

This input causes variable R1 to be stepped 3 times by 0.05. Thus four, R1 values (1.41, 1.46, 1.51, and 1.56) will be done for each combination of other variables. Similarly, 3 values for A1 will be used, and A2 will be held fixed at 2.2. All in all, a total of 12 energy evaluations will be performed. Any number of variables can be stepped. The units of the step-sizes are controlled by the **Units** keyword and default to Angstroms and degrees.

A *relaxed* PES scan (with geometry optimization at each point) is requested with the **Opt** keyword.

If any scanning variable breaks symmetry during the calculation, then you must include **NoSymm** in the route section of the job, or the job will fail with an error.

OPTIONS

Restart   Restarts a PES scan calculation. A failed **Scan** calculation may be restarted from its checkpoint file by simply repeating the route section of the original job, adding the **Restart** option to the **Scan** keyword. No other input is required.

RELATED KEYWORDS
Opt

EXAMPLES
Output files from PES scans conclude with a table summarizing the results for the job:

```
Scan completed.

Summary of the potential surface scan:
  N       R          A          HF
 ----  ---------  ---------  -----------
   1     0.9600    104.5000    -38.39041
   2     1.0100    104.5000    -38.41306
   3     1.0600    104.5000    -38.42336
   4     0.9600    105.5000    -38.39172
   5     1.0100    105.5000    -38.41430
   6     1.0600    105.5000    -38.42453
   7     0.9600    106.5000    -38.39296
   8     1.0100    106.5000    -38.41547
```

```
    9      1.0600     106.5000     -38.42564
   10      0.9600     107.5000     -38.39412
   11      1.0100     107.5000     -38.41657
   12      1.0600     107.5000     -38.42668
 ----    ---------   ---------   -----------
```

Chapter 8 of *Exploring Chemistry with Electronic Structure Methods* [210] provides a detailed discussion of potential energy surface scans.

➤ SCF

DESCRIPTION

This keyword controls the functioning of the SCF procedure. Options are used to specify the desired behavior, alternate algorithms, and so on. See chapter 4 for more information on maximizing performance in the SCF for different problems.

Single point direct SCF calculations are run with modest convergence criteria automatically in the interest of speed. The default for this case is sufficient for 0.1 kcal mole^{-1} accuracy in the SCF energy and 3 decimal places in the density matrix—sufficient for population analysis, electrostatic potential derived charges, and the like. **SCF=Tight** requests full convergence for this case.

SCF and DFT single point energy calculations involving basis sets which include diffuse functions should always use the **SCF=Tight** keyword to request tight SCF convergence criteria.

At the other extreme, sometimes it is useful to start off optimizations with less accurate integral, SCF, and CPHF cutoffs and convergence criteria and then to enable the more accurate and expensive limits only when the geometry has stabilized. The **Sleazy** option reduces all of these cutoff values. It also turns off archiving.

See reference [387] for a discussion of SCF convergence and stability.

ALGORITHM SELECTION OPTIONS

Direct   Requests a direct SCF calculation, in which the two-electron integrals are recomputed as needed. This is the default SCF procedure in *Gaussian 98*. This is possible for all available methods, except for MCSCF second derivatives and anything using complex orbitals. Note that for single-point direct SCF calculations, a loose convergence criterion (10^{-4}) is used in the interest of speed.

InCore   Insists that the SCF be performed storing the full integral list in memory. This is done automatically in a direct SCF calculation if sufficient memory is available. **SCF=InCore** is available to force in-core storage or abort the job.

QC   Calls for the use of a quadratically convergent SCF procedure [388]. By default this involves linear searches when far from convergence and Newton-Raphson steps when close (unless the energy goes up). This method is slower than regular SCF with DIIS extrapolation but is more reliable. It is available only for RHF closed shell and UHF open shell calculations.

DIIS   **DIIS** calls for and **NoDIIS** prohibits use of Pulay's Direct Inversion in the Iterative Subspace extrapolation method [389] with Hartree-Fock and DFT methods. **DIIS** may be used to enable it for the MINDO3, MNDO, and AM1 methods.

SD   Does steepest descent SCF.

SSD   Does scaled steepest descent SCF.

DM   Calls for use of the direct minimization SCF program [390]. It is usually inferior to **SCF=QC** and retained for backwards compatibility and as a last resort. Available only for RHF closed shell and UHF open shell calculations.

Conventional   The two-electron integrals are stored on disk and read-in each SCF iteration. **NoDirect** is a synonym for **Conventional**.

PROCEDURE-RELATED OPTIONS
FON   Start the SCF calculation by doing a superposition of states (simulated annealing). This procedure partially occupies virtual orbitals in the first few iterations in order to help get to the ground state wavefunction. It is the default. The **NoDIIS** option disables this procedure.

VShift[=N]   Shift orbital energies by $N*0.001$ (i.e., N millihartrees); N defaults to 100. This option disables automatic archiving.

MaxCycle=N   Changes the maximum number of SCF cycles permitted to N; the default is 64 (or 512 for **SCF=DM** and **SCF=QC**). Note that with DIIS turned on, memory requirements increase with increasing maximum number of cycles.

FullLinear   Specifies that L508 (**SCF=QC**, **SD**, or **SSD**) should do full linear searches at each iteration. By default, a full minimization is done only if the initial microiteration caused the energy to go up.

MaxRot=N   Set the maximum rotation gradient for a Newton-Raphson step in **SCF=QC** to 10^{-N}. Above this, scaled steepest descent is used, above 100 times this, steepest descent is used. The default value for N is 2.

FinalIteration   **FinalIteration** performs and **NoFinalIteration** prevents a final non-extrapolated, non-incremental iteration after an SCF using DIIS or a direct SCF has converged. The default is **NoFinalIteration**.

IncFock   Forces use of incremental Fock matrix formation. This is the default for direct SCF. **NoIncFock** prevents the use of incremental Fock matrix formation, and it is the default for conventional SCF.

Pass For in-core calculations, saves the integrals on disk as well, to avoid recomputing them in Link 1002. Only useful for frequency jobs in conjunction with **SCF=InCore**. **NoPass** forces integrals to be recomputed during each in-core phase.

TightLinEq Use tight convergence in linear equation solution throughout **SCF=QC**. By default, the convergence criterion is tightened up as the rotation gradient is reduced.

VeryTightLinEq Use even tighter convergence in the linear equation solutions (microiterations) throughout the QCSCF. This option is sometimes needed for nearly lineraly-dependant cases. **VTL** is a synonym for **VeryTightLinEq**.

OPTIONS RELATED TO CONVERGENCE AND CUTOFFS

Conver=N Sets the SCF convergence criterion to 10^{-N}. This is a density-based convergence criterion except for GVB and CASSCF, for which it is in terms of the orbital change and energy change, respectively.

VarAcc Use modest integral accuracy early in direct SCF, switching to full accuracy later on. The default for direct SCF, can be turned off via **NoVarAcc**. **VarInt** is a synonym for **VarAcc**, and **NoVarInt** is a synonym for **NoVarAcc**.

Tight Use normal, tight convergence in the SCF. The default for everything except CASSCF and direct SCF single points. Synonymous with **NoSinglePoint**, **NoSP**, **NoSleazy** and **TightIntegrals**.

SinglePoint Requests the loose SCF convergence criteria appropriate for single points. The default for single point CASSCF or direct SCF. Can be abbreviated **SP**. **NoSinglePoint** and **NoSP** are synonymous with **Tight**.

Sleazy Reduce cutoffs for integrals, SCF, and CPHF (also disables automatic archiving). Not recommended for production-quality energies. **NoSleazy** is synonymous with **Tight**.

SYMMETRY-RELATED OPTIONS

IDSymm Symmetrize the density matrix at the first iteration to match the symmetry of the molecule ("initial density symmetrize"). **NoIDSymm** is the default.

DSymm Symmetrize the density matrix at every SCF iteration to match the symmetry of the molecule ("density symmetrize"). **NoDSymm** is the default. **DSymm** implies **IDSymm**.

NoSymm Requests that all orbital symmetry constraints be lifted. It is synonymous with **Guess=NoSymm** and **Symm=NoSCF**.

Symm Retain all symmetry constraints: make the number of occupied orbitals of each symmetry type (abelian irreducible representation) match that of the initial guess. Use this option to retain a specific state of the wavefunction throughout the calculation. It is the default only for GVB calculations.

IntRep	Calls for the SCF procedure to account for integral symmetry by replicating the integrals using the symmetry operations. Allows use of a short integral list even if the wavefunction does not have the full molecular symmetry. Available for L502 (the default for RHF, ROHF and UHF) and L508 (**SCF=QC**).

FockSymm	Calls for the SCF procedure to account for integral symmetry (use of the "petite" integral list) by symmetrizing the Fock matrices. This is the default. **FSymm** is a synonym for **FockSymm**.

RESTART-RELATED OPTIONS

Save	Save the wavefunction on the checkpoint file every iteration, so the SCF can be restarted. This is the default for direct SCF. **NoSave** suppresses saving the wavefunction.

Restart	Restart the SCF from the checkpoint file. **SCF=DM** cannot be restarted.

➤ SCRF

DESCRIPTION

This keyword requests that a calculation be performed in the presence of a solvent, using an Onsager model [196-199, 391, 392], the Polarized Continuum (overlapping spheres) model (PCM) of Tomasi and coworkers [200-208], a (static) isodensity surface polarized continuum model (IPCM) [209], or a Self-Consistent Isodensity PCM (SCI-PCM) model [209].

REQUIRED INPUT: ONSAGER MODEL

For the Onsager model (**SCRF=Dipole**), the solute radius in Angstroms and the dielectric constant of the solvent are read as two free-format real numbers on one line from the input stream. A suitable solute radius is computed by a gas-phase molecular volume calculation (in a separate job step); see the discussion of the **Volume** keyword below.

REQUIRED INPUT: IPCM AND SCI-PCM MODELS

For the IPCM and SCI-PCM models, the input consists of a line specifying the dielectric constant of the solvent and an optional isodensity value (the default for the latter is 0.0004).

REQUIRED AND OPTIONAL INPUT: PCM MODELS

Keywords and options specifying details for a PCM calculation (**SCRF=PCM, DPCM, CPCM** or **IEFPCM**) may be specified in an additional blank-line terminated input section provided that the **Read** option is also specified. Keywords within this section follow general *Gaussian* input rules. The available keywords are listed at the end of the manual section for the **SCRF** keyword.

OPTION FOR SPECIFYING THE SOLVENT

Solvent=_item_ Selects the solvent in which the calculation is to be performed. Note that the solvent may also be specified in the input stream in various ways for the different SCRF methods. If unspecified, the solvent defaults to water. _Item_ may be either a solvent name or solvent ID number chosen from the following list:

Solvent	ID	ε	Solvent	ID	ε
Water H2O	1	78.39	ChloroBenzene	11	5.621
DiMethylSulfoxide DMSO	2	46.7	Chloroform CHCl3	12	4.9
NitroMethane	3	38.2	Ether DiEthylEther	13	4.335
Methanol CH3OH	4	32.63	Toluene	14	2.379
Ethanol CH3CH2OH	5	24.55	Benzene	15	2.247
Acetone CH3COCH3	6	20.7	CarbonTetrachloride CCl4	16	2.228
DiChloroEthane CH3ClCH3Cl	7	10.36	CycloHexane	17	2.023
DiChloroMethane CH2Cl2	8	8.93	Heptane	18	1.92
TetraHydroFuran THF	9	7.58	Acetonitrile	19	36.64
Aniline	10	6.89			

METHOD SELECTION OPTIONS

Dipole Perform an Onsager model reaction field calculation. This is the default.

PCM Perform a PCM reaction field calculation using the polarizable dielectric model [200-202]. **DPCM**, **Tomasi** and **Pisa** are synonyms for this option.

CPCM Perform a PCM calculation using the polarizable conductor calculation model [207]. **Cosmo** is a synonym for this option.

IEFPCM Perform a PCM calculation using the integral equation formalism model [203, 205, 208].

IPCM Perform an IPCM model reaction field calculation. **Isodensity** is a synonym for **IPCM**.

SCIPCM Perform an SCI-PCM model reaction field calculation: perform an SCRF calculation using a cavity determined self-consistently from an isodensity surface. This is the default for single point energy calculations and optimizations.

DIPOLE MODEL OPTIONS

A0=*val*   Sets the value for the solute radius in the route section (rather than reading it from the input stream). If this option is included, then **Solvent** or **Dielectric** must also be included.

Dielectric=*val*   Sets the value for the dielectric constant of the solvent. This option overrides **Solvent** if both are specified.

PCM MODELS OPTION

Read   Indicates that a separate section of keywords and options providing calculation parameters should be read from the input stream (as described above).

IPCM MODEL OPTIONS

GradVne   Use Vne basins for the numerical integration.

GradRho   Use density basins for the numerical integration. The job may fail if non-nuclear attractors are present.

SCI-PCM MODEL OPTIONS

UseDensity   Force the use of the density matrix in evaluating the density.

UseMOs   Force the use of MOs in evaluating the density.

GasCavity   Use the gas phase isodensity surface to define the cavity rather than solving for the surface self-consistently. This is mainly a debugging option.

NoScale   Turn off scaling (designed to account for charge outside the cavity) for the SCI-PCM calculation. Scaling is performed by default. **NoScale** reproduces the behavior of SCI-PCM in *Gaussian 94*.

NUMERICAL SCRF OPTIONS

Numer   Force numerical SCRF rather than analytic. This keyword is required for multiple orders beyond **Dipole**.

Dipole   The options **Dipole, Quadrupole, Octopole,** and **Hexadecapole** specify the order of multipole to use in the SCRF calculation. All but **Dipole** require that the **Numer** option be specified as well.

Checkpoint Begin the numerical SCRF with a previously computed reaction field from the checkpoint file. This is synonymous with **Field=EChk**.

Cards   Begin the numerical SCRF with a previously computed reaction field read from the input stream, immediately after the line specifying the dielectric constant and radius (three free-format reals).

AVAILABILITY AND RESTRICTIONS

The Onsager model is available for HF, DFT, MP2, MP3, MP4(SDQ), QCISD, CCD, CID, and CISD energies, and for HF and DFT optimizations and frequency calculations.

The PCM models are available for HF, DFT, MP2, MP3, MP4(SDQ), QCISD, CCD, CID, and CISD energies and and Hartree-Fock and DFT gradients.

The IPCM model is available for HF, DFT, MP2, MP3, MP4(SDQ), QCISD, CCD, CID, and CISD energies only.

The SCI-PCM model is available for HF and DFT energies and optimizations and numerical frequencies.

The **Opt Freq** keyword combination may not be used in **SCRF** calculations.

SCRF=PCM and **SCRF=IPCM** jobs can be restarted from the checkpoint file by using the **Restart** keyword in the job's route section. **SCRF=SCIPCM** calculations which fail during the SCF iterations should be restarted via the **SCF=Restart** keyword.

RELATED KEYWORDS
Volume, Restart, SCF

EXAMPLES

The energy computed by an Onsager SCRF calculation appears in the output file as follows:

```
Total energy (include solvent energy) =   -74.95061789532
```

Energy output from the other SCRF models appears in the normal way within the output file, followed by additional information about the calculation. For example, here is the section of the output file containing the predicted energy from a PCM calculation:

```
IN VACUO Dipole moment (Debye):
   X=  0.0000  Y=  0.0000  Z= -2.0683  Tot=  2.0683
IN SOLUTION Dipole moment (Debye):
   X=  0.0000  Y=  0.0000  Z= -2.1876  Tot=  2.1876
SCF Done:  E(RHF) =  -100.029187240      A.U. after      5 cycles
              Convg  =    0.4249D-05              -V/T =   2.0033
              S**2   =    0.0000
-------------------------------------------------------------
------------- VARIATIONAL  PCM  RESULTS -------------
-------------------------------------------------------------
   <Psi(0)| H |Psi(0)>         (a.u.) =   -100.024068
   <Psi(0)|H+V(0)/2|Psi(0)>    (a.u.) =   -100.028947
   <Psi(0)|H+V(f)/2|Psi(0)>    (a.u.) =   -100.029186
   <Psi(f)| H |Psi(f)>         (a.u.) =   -100.023819
   <Psi(f)|H+V(f)/2|Psi(f)>    (a.u.) =   -100.029187
   Total free energy in sol.
   (with non electrost.terms) (a.u.) =   -100.028994
-------------------------------------------------------------
```

```
(Unpol.Solute)-Solvent (kcal/mol) =     -3.06
(Polar.Solute)-Solvent (kcal/mol) =     -3.37
Solute Polarization    (kcal/mol) =      0.16
Total Electrostatic    (kcal/mol) =     -3.21
-------------------------------------------------------
Cavitation energy      (kcal/mol) =      3.20
Dispersion energy      (kcal/mol) =     -4.12
Repulsion energy       (kcal/mol) =      1.04
Total non electr.      (kcal/mol) =      0.12
-------------------------------------------------------
DeltaG (solv)          (kcal/mol) =     -3.09
-------------------------------------------------------
```

Note that the PCM results also include the dipole moment in the gas phase and in solution, the various components of the predicted SCRF energy and $\Delta G^{solvation}$.

For all iterative SCRF methods, note that the energy to use is the one preceding the **Convergence achieved** message (i.e., the one from the final iteration of the SCRF method).

INPUT SYNTAX AND KEYWORDS FOR PCM CALCULATIONS
The following keywords are available for controlling PCM calculations (arranged in groups of related items):

SPECIFYING THE SOLVENT
The solvent for the PCM calculation may be specified using the normal **Solvent** option to the **SCRF** keyword. The solvent name keyword or ID number may also be placed within the PCM input section. Alternatively, the **EPS** and **RSOLV** keywords may be used in the PCM input section to define a solvent explicitly:

EPS=*e*   Dielectric constant of the solvent.

RSOLV=*radius*   Solvent radius in Angstroms.

EPSINF=*val*   Optional value for the dielectric constant at infinite frequency.

CALCULATION METHOD VARIATIONS
NODIS   Skip the calculation of dispersion-repulsion solute solvent interaction.

NOCAV   Skip the calculation of cavitation energy.

DUMP   Provide verbose output as the calculation progresses.

NOSCFVAC   Skip the gas phase calculation before that in solution. While this saves some computation time, it prevents the calculation of $\Delta G^{solvation}$, the variation of the dipole moment in solution, and so on.

FIXCAV   Compute the electrostatic energy gradients neglecting the geometrical contributions (i.e., at "fixed cavity"). Be aware that the geometrical contributions are always included in the calculation of non-electrostatic energy gradients (the latter gradients can be skipped with **NOCAV** and **NODIS**).

ACCPCM=*val*   Accuracy threshold for the calculation of electric potential on the cavity. The default value is 10^{-6}.

TABS=*temp*   Temperature in Kelvin. The default value is 298.15. Note that you must also specify the correct value of the dielectric constant (episilon) at that temperature using the **EPS** keyword.

CHARGE NORMALIZATION

ICOMP=*N*   Specifies the method used to normalize the polarization charge to get the value predicted by Gauss' law. *N* can take on the following values:

1   The difference between the calculated and the theoretical (Gauss) polarization charge is distributed on each tessera proportionally to its area.
2   The calculated charge on each tessera is scaled by a constant factor.
3   The charge difference is distributed according to the solute electronic density on each tessera.
4   The effect of outlying charge is accounted for by means of an additional effective charge, distributed according to the solute electronic density.

Normally, the default is **4** for single point calculations and **2** for geometry optimizations (this one being the only method allowing the calculation of gradients). For **CPCM** (which is less affected by the outlying charge effects), the default is always **2**.

SPECIFYING CHARACTERISTICS OF THE CAVITY

By default, the program builds up the cavity by putting a sphere around each solute heavy atom; hydrogen atoms are always enclosed in the sphere of the atom to which they are bonded; the radius of the atom is increased by a constant amount for each bonded hydrogen atom, up to a maximum of 3 (the increase is 0.9 for second-row atoms, 0.13 for third-row atoms, and 0.15 for atoms in higher rows). Explicit hydrogen atoms can be added by specifying the UFF atom type within the molecule specification, as in this example:

```
H-H 3 1.5 2 110.0 1 180.0
```

The atoms C, N, O, F, P, S, Cl, Br and I use UAHF radii, and all other atoms use UFF radii. Both use scaling factors of 1.0 for acidic hydrogens and 1.2 for all the other elements.

RADII=UAHF   Use the United Atom Topological Model [204] to build the cavity, automatically set by the program according to the molecular topology, hybridization, formal charge, etc. Note that hydrogens don't have individual spheres defined and that these radii were optimized for the HF/6-31G(d) level of theory.

RADII=UFF   Use atomic radii from the UFF force field.

RADII=BONDI   Use Bondi's atomic radii.

RADII=PAULING Use Pauling's (actually Merz-Kollman) atomic radii.

ALPHA=*scale* Specify the scaling factor (for all the elements but acidic hydrogens) for the definition of solvent accessible surfaces. In other words, the radius of each atomic sphere is determined by multiplying the van der Waals radius by *scale*. The default value is 1.2.

ALPHAH=*hscale* Specify the scaling factor for acidic hydrogens (automatically recognized by the program as those bonded to N, O, P or S halogens). The default value is 1.0.

RET=*len* Sets the minimum radius (in Angstroms) of the "added spheres." Increasing this parameter causes the number of added spheres to decrease (for example, to inhibit the creation of added spheres, use **RET=100**). The default value is 0.2.

NSFE=*n* Sets the number of initial spheres (useful if this number is not equal to the number of solute atoms, e.g. if a methyl group is enclosed in one sphere, and so on). When included, the program looks for the positions and the radii of the *n* spheres in an additional input section following the PCM input (this section is also blank-terminated).

The spheres can be defined using lines in either of the following formats:

N1 [*radius* [*scale hscale*]]
X Y Z [*radius* [*scale hscale*]]

In the first case, the line specifies an atom number and (optionally) the sphere radius and one or both scaling factors for that atom. In the second case, used to define arbitrary spheres, the Cartesian coordinates of the center of the sphere are again optionally followed by its radius and scaling factors. If parameters are omitted, then the standard values are used automatically. Note that lines of different formats can be freely intermixed in this input section as the program will automatically determine the syntax based on the number and types of parameter specified on any given line.

SELECTING THE POLYDEDRON FOR THE SURFACE TESSERAE

In standard calculations the surface of each sphere is subdivided in 60 triangular tesserae, by projecting the faces of an inscribed pentakisdodecahedron. Other polyhedra with a different number of faces can be used, to get rougher or finer descriptions of the surface, by using one of these keywords:

TSNUM=*N* Sets the number of tesserae on each sphere (60 is the default for the usual pentakisdodecahedron). The program automatically selects the polyhedron with the closest number of faces to the specified value of *N*.

TSARE=*area* Specifies the area of the tesserae, in units of $\mathrm{\AA}^2$ (0.4 is a typical value). The program automatically determines the best polyhedron for each sphere.

EXAMPLE PCM INPUT

The following *Gaussian* job performs a PCM energy calculation on the molecule HF using the solvent cyclohexane. The calculation is performed at a temperature of 300 K using a scaling factor for all atoms except acidic hydrogens of 1.21 and a value of 70 tesserae per sphere:

```
# HF/6-31++G(d,p) SCF=Tight SCRF=(PCM,Read,Solvent=Cyclohexane) Test

PCM SP calculation on hydrogen fluoride

0,1
H
F 1 R

R=0.9161

TABS=300.0
ALPHA=1.21
TSNUM=70
```

The final input section ends as usual with a blank line.

➤ Stable

DESCRIPTION
This calculation type method requests that the stability of the Hartree-Fock or DFT wavefunction be tested. *Gaussian 98* has the ability to test the stability of a single-determinant wavefunction with respect to relaxing various constraints [100, 101] (see also [387]). These include:

- ◆ Allowing an RHF determinant to become UHF.
- ◆ Allowing orbitals to become complex.
- ◆ Reducing the symmetry of the orbitals.

The default is to test for all instabilities but not to re-optimize the wavefunction. If **Stable=Opt** is specified, by default the wavefunction is allowed to be unrestricted if necessary. In examining the results prior to a frequency calculation, it suffices to see if any singlet instabilities exist for restricted wavefunctions or if any instabilities (singlet or triplet) exist for unrestricted wavefunctions. In examining the results prior to a Møller-Plesset calculation, an internal instability only affects the validity of the results if the pairs of orbitals mixed are of the same spatial symmetry. The validity of restricted Møller-Plesset energies based on wavefunctions which are unstable with respect to becoming UHF is also questionable [393].

The **Stable** keyword causes the program to compute a wavefunction as usual and then to determine if the resulting determinant is a local minimum with the specified degrees of freedom taken into consideration. Note that analytic frequency calculations are only valid if the wavefunction has no internal instabilities, and Møller-Plesset calculations are only valid if the wavefunction has no internal instabilities within the constrained symmetry. By default, only real instabilities (i.e., not complex) are sought. The code which checks for a complex stability (Link 902) is older and less reliable and should not be used unless complex orbitals are of interest.

GENERAL OPTIONS

RExt   Test for external real instability as well as internal instability (the default).

Int   Test for internal instability (a lower determinant with the same constraints) only.

Symm   Retain symmetry restrictions. **NoSymm** relaxes symmetry restrictions and is the default.

RRHF   Constrain the wavefunction testing or reoptimization to be real, spin-restricted. Synonymous with **Singlet**.

RUHF   Constrain the wavefunction testing or reoptimization to be real, spin-unrestricted. Synonymous with **Triplet**.

CRHF   Allow testing for real to complex instabilities in spin-restricted wavefunctions.

CUHF   Allow testing for real to complex instabilities in spin-unrestricted wavefunctions.

WAVEFUNCTION REOPTIMIZATION OPTIONS

Opt   If an instability is found, reoptimize the wavefunction with the appropriate reduction in constraints, repeating stability tests and reoptimizations until a stable wavefunction is found. **RepOpt** is a synonym for **Opt**. **NoOpt** prevents reoptimization and is the default.

1Opt   Redo the SCF once if an instability is detected.

ALGORITHM-RELATED OPTIONS

Direct   Forces a direct calculation (the default).

MO   Forces a stability calculation using transformed two-electron integrals (i.e., in the MO basis).

AO   Forces a calculation using the AO integrals (written to disk), avoiding an integral transformation. The AO basis is seldom an optimal choice, except for small molecules on systems having very limited disk. It is the default when **SCF=Conven** is also specified.

InCore   Forces an in-core algorithm.

ICDiag   Forces in-core full diagonalization of the matrix formed in memory from transformed integrals. It implies the use of MO integrals.

AVAILABILITY

HF and DFT methods.

RELATED KEYWORDS
SCF

➤ SVWN
➤ SVWN5

See **DFT Methods** *above.*

➤ Symmetry

DESCRIPTION
This keyword specifies the uses of molecular symmetry within the calculation. If symmetry is in use, the molecule may be rotated to a different coordinate system, called the *standard orientation*, before the calculation is performed. Derivatives are then rotated back to the original (*Z-matrix*) orientation. Orbitals are printed in the standard orientation, and input for properties and background charge distributions is required in the standard orientation.

The **NoSymmetry** keyword prevents the reorientation and causes all computations to be performed in the Z-matrix orientation. By default, symmetry is used wherever possible to reduce CPU, disk storage, and I/O requirements. Symmetry use can be completely disabled by **NoSymm**, or modified by the **Symm** keyword and one or more of the following options:

OPTIONS

Int   **Int** enables and **NoInt** disables use of integral symmetry (use of the "petite list"). Synonymous with **Int**=[No]Symm.

Grad   **NoGrad** Disables and **Grad** enables use of symmetry in integral derivative evaluation.

SCF   **NoSCF** disables and **SCF** enables use of N^3 symmetry in SCF, which is used by default only for GVB calculations. **SCF=NoSCF** is equivalent to **Guess=LowSym** and combining all irreducible representations together.

Loose   Tells the program to use looser cutoffs in determining symmetry at the first point. It is designed for use with suboptimal input geometries.

RELATED KEYWORDS
Int, SCF

➤ TD

DESCRIPTION
This method keyword requests an excited state energy calculation using the time-dependent Hartree-Fock or DFT method [103-105].

TD jobs will also usually include the **Density** keyword; without options, this keyword causes the population analysis to use the current density rather than its default of the Hartree-Fock density.

The output from an TD calculation is very similar to that of a CIS calculation as described previously.

OPTIONS

Singlets   Solve only for singlet excited states. Only effective for closed-shell systems, for which it is the default.

Triplets   Solve only for triplet excited states. Only effective for closed-shell systems.

50-50   Solve for half triplet and half singlet states. Only effective for closed-shell systems.

Root=N   Specifies the "state of interest" to be optimized in geometry optimizations, for which the generalized density is to be computed. The default is the first excited state ($N=1$).

NStates=M   Solve for M states (the default is 3). If **50-50** is requested, **NStates** gives the number of each type of state for which to solve (i.e., the default is 3 singlets *and* 3 triplets).

Add=N   Read converged states off the checkpoint file and solve for an additional N states.

AVAILABILITY
Energies using an SCF or DFT method.

RELATED KEYWORDS
CIS, ZINDO, Density

➤ Test

DESCRIPTION
This keyword suppresses the automatic creation of an archive entry for the Browse Quantum Chemistry Database System. Its antonym is **Archive**, which is the default. Note that archive entries may be extracted from *Gaussian 98* log files after the fact. Refer to the Browse Quantum Chemistry Database System documentation for information on making use of the archive entries.

RELATED KEYWORDS
Archive, Rearchive

➤ TestMO

DESCRIPTION
The cutoffs used in computing and storing integrals and the convergence criteria applied in SCF and CPHF calculations are appropriate for most molecules and basis sets. However, if a nearly linearly dependent basis set is used, very large MO coefficients may occur and in combination with the finite accuracy of other terms lead to substantial numerical errors. By default CPHF and post-SCF calculations are aborted if any MO coefficient is larger than 1000. (Note that this corresponds to a coefficient of 10^{12} for the contribution of an AO integral to an MO integral involving four virtual orbitals.) The **NoTestMO** keyword suppresses this check. It should be used only after careful thought. **TestMO** is the default.

➤ TrackIO

DESCRIPTION
This keyword requests routine-by-routine statistics of I/O and CPU usage

RELATED KEYWORDS
#P

➤ Trajectory

DESCRIPTION
This keyword requests a direct dynamics trajectory calculation. The classical equations of motion are integrated using analytical second derivatives [151]. The selection of the initial conditions using quasi-classical fixed normal mode sampling and the final product analysis are carried out in the same manner as in the classical trajectory program VENUS [394]. Alternatively, initial Cartesian coordinates and velocities may be read in directly from the input.

REQUIRED INPUT
Trajectory reads the following information from the input stream:

NPath	*Number of dissociation paths*
IFrag(1), . . . IFrag(NAtoms)	*Fragmentation information*
...	*Repeated NPath times*
R1, R2, R3, R4, G5, ITest, IAtom, JAtom, R6	*Stopping criteria*
...	*Repeated NPath times*

Mode-num, VibEng(Mode-num)	*Normal mode energies*
...	
	Terminate subsection with a blank line
Initial-Velocity	*If the* **ReadVel** *option is specified*
Atom1, Atom2, E0, Len, De, Be	*Morse parameters for each diatomic product*
...	
	Terminate subsection with a blank line
Isotopes ...	*If the* **ReadIso** *option is specified*
	Terminate **Trajectory** *input with a blank line*

NPath is the number of dissociation paths for which stopping criteria are specified (the maximum value is 20). For *NPath* = 0, the trajectory is integrated for a fixed number of steps as specified by the **Steps** option. For *NPath* > 0, the fragment information and stopping criteria for each path are read next.

IFrag defines the fragmentation information for each path. *IFrag(I)* specifies that the Ith atom belongs to that fragment. Note that each specification must begin on a new line, but a specification may be continued over as many lines as necessary.

Up to six stopping criteria may be specified for each path. A trajectory is terminated when all of the active criteria are satisfied. A value of zero for any parameter turns off testing for the corresponding stopping criteria. Note that all distances in this section of the input are specified in Bohr. The criteria are tested as follows:

◆ Test if the minimum distance between the centers of mass of each pair of fragments exceeds *R1*.

◆ Test if the minimum distance between atoms located in different fragments exceeds *R2*.

◆ Test if the maximum distance between the center of mass and the atoms located in the same fragment is less than *R3*.

◆ Test if the maximum distance between atoms located in the same fragment is less than *R4*.

◆ Test if the interfragment gradient is less than *G5* (**Hartrees/Bohr**).

◆ If *ITest*=1, test if the distance between atoms *IAtom* and *JAtom* exceeds *R6*. Otherwise, test if the distance between them is less than *R6*.

The next part of the input specifies how much energy is in each normal mode. For mode 1—the transition vector—*VibEng* is the translational energy in kcal/mol in the forward direction along the transition vector. If *VibEng*(1) < 0, then the initial velocity is in the reverse direction (where the forward direction may be specified using the **Phase** option). For all other modes, *VibEng* is the number of vibrational quanta. Input in this subsection is terminated by a blank line.

The initial velocity is specified as a Cartesian velocity in atomic units.

The Morse parameter data is used to determine the vibrational excitation of diatomic fragments using the EBK quantization rules. It consists of the atomic symbols for the two atoms, the bond length between them (*Len,* in Angstrons), the energy at **that distance** (E_0 in Hartrees) and the Morse curve parameters D_e (Hartrees) and B_e (Angstroms^{-1}). Input in this subsection is terminated by a blank line.

Finally, the desired isotope of each atom is listed in the same order as it appears in the molecule specification section. If integers are used to specify the atomic masses, the program will automatically use the corresponding actual exact isotopic mass. Input is terminated by a blank line.

OPTIONS

NTraj=N   Specifies that N trajectories will be propagated (the default is 50). Note that if a trajectory job is restarted, the number of trajectories will default to the number specified in the original calculation.

Steps=N   Specifies the maximum number of steps that may be taken in each trajectory (the default is 50). If a trajectory job is restarted, the maximum number of steps will default to the number specified in the original calculation.

Phase=(N1 N2 [N3 [N4]])

Defines the phase for the transition vector such that forward motion along the transition vector corresponds to an increase in the specified internal coordinate. If two atom numbers are given, the coordinate is a bond stretch between the two atoms; three atom numbers specify an angle bend and four atoms define a dihedral angle.

ReadIsotopes Read in a list of atomic isotopic masses from the input stream. If not specified, the most abundant isotope of each element is used.

ReadVelocity Read in initial Cartesian velocities from the input stream. Note that the velocities must have the same symmetry orientation as the molecule.

RTemp=N   Specifies the rotational temperature. The default is to choose the initial rotational energy from a thermal distribution assuming a symmetric top (defaults to 0 K).

CASSCF METHOD-SPECIFIC OPTIONS

Adiabatic   Perform only the adiabatic hop test (the default is to perform both tests).

NonAdiabatic Perform only the nonadiabatic hop test (the default is to perform both tests).

AVAILABILITY

All semi-empirical, SCF, CASSCF, MP2 and DFT methods.

EXAMPLES

The following input will calculate 10 trajectories for H_2CO dissociating to H_2 + CO, starting at the transition state. A maximum of 100 steps of 0.3 amu$^{1/2}$ bohr will be taken for each trajectory. There is only one fragmentation pathway: C and O belong to fragment 1, and the two hydrogens belong to fragment 2.

A trajectory will be stopped if the distance between the centers of mass of H_2 and CO exceed 13 bohr, the closest distance between H_2 and CO exceeds 11 bohr, all atoms in a fragment are less than 1.3 bohr from the center of mass of the fragment, any atom in the fragment is less than 2.5 bohr from all other atoms in the fragment, the gradient for the separation of the fragments is less than 0.0000005 hartree/bohr, and the distance between atoms 1 and 3 is greater than 13 bohr.

The initial kinetic energy along the transition vector is 5.145 kcal/mol, in the direction of the products. The Morse parameters for H_2 and CO are specified to determine the vibrational excitation of the product diatomics; they were computed in a previous calculation. The calculation will be carried out at 300 K using standard isotopes for all atoms.

```
# HF/3-21G Traj(NTraj=10,Steps=100,Phase=(1,3),RTemp=300) Geom=Crowd

HF/3-21G dissociation of H2CO --> H2 + CO

0 1
C
O 1 r1
H 1 r2 2 a
H 1 r3 3 b 2 180.

r1 1.15275608
r2 1.74415774
r3 1.09413376
a 114.81897892
b 49.08562961

1
1 1 2 2
13.0 11.0 1.3 2.5 0.0000005 1 1 3 13.0
1 5.145

C O -112.09329898 1.12895435 0.49458169 2.24078955
H H -1.12295984 0.73482237 0.19500473 1.94603924
```

Note that all six stopping criteria are used here only for illustrative purposes. In most cases, one or two stopping criteria are sufficient.

➤ Transformation

DESCRIPTION
This keyword controls the algorithm used for integral transformation, as well as the types of transformed integrals produced.

INTEGRAL TRANSFORMATION ALGORITHM OPTIONS

Direct   Requests that the direct transformation routines be used. Equivalent to **L804**. Link 804 will select between the in-core, fully direct, and semi-direct methods automatically. This is the default.

InCore   Forces use of the in-core algorithm in Link 804.

FullDirect   Forces use of the fully direct (MO integrals in core) method in Link 804.

SemiDirect   Forces use of the semi-direct algorithm in Link 804.

Conventional   Requests that the original transformation method based on externally stored integrals be used. This was the only choice in *Gaussian 90* and earlier versions. **NoDirect** is a synonym for **Conventional**.

Old2PDM   Forces the old-fashioned process of the 2PDM in post-SCF gradients (sorted in L1111 and then processed in L702 and L703). This is slow, but it reduces memory requirements. This option cannot be used for frozen-core calculations.

New2PDM   Causes the 2PDM to be generated, used, and discarded by L1111 in post-SCF gradient calculations. This is the default and fastest method, and it must be used for frozen-core calculations.

INTEGRAL SELECTION OPTIONS

Full   Forces a transformation over all orbitals (i.e., including transformed integrals involving all virtuals). **ABCD** is a synonym for **Full**.

IJAB   Produce only <IJ||AB> integrals.

IAJB   Produce <IJ||AB> and <IA||JB> integrals.

IJKL   Produce <IJ||AB>, <IA||JB>, and <IJ||KL> integrals.

IJKA   Produce <IJ||AB>, <IA||JB>, <IJ||KL>, and <IJ||KA> integrals.

IABC   Produce <IJ||AB>, <IA||JB>, <IJ||KL>, <IJ||KA>, and <IA||BC> integrals.

➤ UFF

See **Molecular Mechanics Methods** *above.*

➤ Units

DESCRIPTION
The **Units** keyword controls the units used in the Z-matrix for distances and angles and related values, such as step-sizes in numerical differentiation. The defaults are Angstroms and degrees.

OPTIONS
Ang   Distances are in Angstroms (this is the default).

AU   Distances are in atomic units (Bohrs).

Deg   Angles are in degrees (the default).

Rad   Angles are in radians.

RESTRICTIONS
The **Cube** and **Massage** keywords are not affected by the setting of the **Units** keyword, and their input is always interpreted in units of Angstroms and degrees.

➤ Volume

DESCRIPTION
This keyword requests that the molecular volume be computed, defined as the volume inside a contour of 0.001 electrons/bohr^3 density. The density to be used can be specified with the **Density** keyword. Since a Monte-Carlo integration is done, the computed volume is only accurate to about two significant figures, but this is sufficient to estimate a radius for use with the Onsager solvent reaction field model. The recommended radius (which is 0.5Å larger than the radius corresponding to the computed volume) is printed in the output.

Since other, more accurate solvent models are available in *Gaussian 98*, this keyword has applicability only in preparation for frequency calculations using **SCRF=Dipole**.

OPTIONS
Tight   Requests an increased density of points for more accurate integration. By default, the volume is computed to an accuracy of about 10%. Use of this option is recommended if the computed molecular volume is needed more quantitatively.

AVAILABILITY
HF, all DFT methods, CIS, MP2, MP3, MP4(SDQ), CID, CISD, CCD, and QCISD.

RELATED KEYWORDS
SCRF=Dipole

➤ **VWN**
➤ **VWN5**
➤ **XA**
➤ **XAlpha**

See **DFT Methods** *above.*

➤ **ZINDO**

DESCRIPTION
This method keyword requests an excited state energy calculation using the ZINDO-1 method [106-114]. Note that ZINDO calculations must not specify a basis set keyword.

By default, a ZINDO calculation is performed using the ten highest occupied orbitals and the ten lowest virtual orbitals. Use the **Window** option to define a different orbital set.

ZINDO jobs will also usually include the **Density** keyword; without options, this keyword causes the population analysis to use the current density rather than its default of the Hartree-Fock density.

The output from a ZINDO calculation is very similar to that of a CIS calculation as described previously.

OPTIONS

Singlets   Solve only for singlet excited states. Only effective for closed-shell systems, for which it is the default.

Triplets   Solve only for triplet excited states. Only effective for closed-shell systems.

50-50   Solve for half triplet and half singlet states. Only effective for closed-shell systems.

Root=N Specifies the "state of interest" to be optimized in geometry optimizations, for which the generalized density is to be computed. The default is the first excited state ($N=1$).

NStates=M Solve for M states (the default is 3). If **50-50** is requested, **NStates** gives the number of each type of state for which to solve (i.e., the default is 3 singlets *and* 3 triplets).

Add=N Read converged states off the checkpoint file and solve for an additional N states.

Window=$(m[,n])$ The two values specify the starting and ending orbitals to be used. A value of zero indicates the first or last orbital, depending on where it is used. If the value for the first orbital is negative (-m), then the highest m orbitals are retained; the value for the last orbital is negative (-n), then the highest n orbitals are frozen. If m is positive and n

is omitted, n defaults to 0. If m is negative and n is omitted, then the highest $|m|$ occupied and lowest $|m|$ virtual orbitals are retained. (See the discussion of the **MP2** keyword for examples.)

AVAILABILITY
Energies only for systems containing H through Cd.

The **Density** keyword is ignored for ZINDO calculations.

RELATED KEYWORDS
CIS, TD, Density

Link 0 Commands Summary

This section lists all Link 0 commands, which are optional and precede the route section if present. See chapter 2 for a more detailed discussion of the scratch file naming commands.

%Mem=N Sets the amount of dynamic memory used to N words ($8N$ bytes). The default is 6MW. N may be optionally followed by a units designation: **KB, MB, GB, KW, MB** or **GW**.

%Chk=*file*   Locates and names the checkpoint file.

%RWF=*file*   Locates and names a single, unified Read-Write file (old-style syntax).

%RWF=*loc1,size1,loc2,size2*, ...
An alternate syntax is provided for splitting the Read-Write file among two or more disks (or file systems). Each location is followed by a maximum size for the file segment at that location. The default units for each *size* is words; the value may be optionally followed by **KB, MB, GB, KW, MW** or **GW** (with no intervening spaces) to indicate units. A value of **-1** for any size parameter indicates that any and all available space may be used, and a value of **0** indicates that an existing segment should retain its current size. The locations may be either directory locations, or full pathnames. Note that directory specifications *must* include terminal slashes (on UNIX systems).

%Int=*spec*   Locates and names the two-electron integral file(s). *spec* may take on either of the forms used for the Read-Write file (described above).

%D2E=*spec*   Locates and names the two-electron integral derivative file(s). *spec* may take on either of the forms used for the Read-Write file (described above).

%KJob LN [M]   Tells the program to stop the run after the Mth occurrence of Link N. For example, **%KJob L502 2** will cause the run to terminate after Link 502 has been run for the second time. M may be omitted; it defaults to 1.

%NProc=N   Requests that the job use up to N processors. This capability is only available on some computer systems, and *Gaussian 98* must have been built with parallel processing enabled. On parallel machines, the number of processors to use in production runs is usually set in the **Default.Route** file, and the **%NProc** Link 0 command is used to override this local default (e.g., to run debug jobs on a single processor even if the default is to use 4 processors). If **%NProc** is not used, and no default is provided in the **Default.Route** file, then one processor is used.

%Save   Causes Link 0 to save scratch files at the end of the run. By default, all non-specified scratch files are deleted and all named scratch files are saved when the run completes successfully.

%NoSave   Causes Link 0 to delete scratch files at the end of a run, including any files that were named explicitly *following* this directive. In other words, if a file is named before **%NoSave** is encountered, it will not be saved. However, if the % directive naming the file appears after the **%NoSave** directive, the file will be retained.

For example, these commands specify a name for the checkpoint file, and an alternate name and directory location for the read-write file, and cause only the checkpoint file to be saved at the conclusion of the *Gaussian 98* job:

```
%RWF=/chem/scratch2/water          Files to be deleted go here.
%NoSave
%Chk=water                         Files to be saved go here.
```

If both **%Save** and **%NoSave** are specified, then the one appearing latest in the input file takes precedence.

%Subst LN *dir*   Tells Link 0 to take the executable (.exe file) for a link from an alternate directory. For example **%SUBST L913 /user/chem** will cause /user/chem/l913.exe to be run instead of the default executable (in $g98root). The directory specification should be in the usual format for the machine involved. Only the directory can be specified; the file name must have the standard form of l*nnnn*.exe, where *nnnn* is the Link number.

Specifying Non-Standard Routes

DESCRIPTION

If a combination of options or links is required which is drastically different than a standard route, then a complete sequence of overlays and links with associated options can be read in. The job-type input section begins with the line:

```
# NonStd
```

This is followed by one line for each desired overlay, in execution order, giving the overlay number, a slash, the desired options, another slash, the list of links to be executed, and finally a semicolon:

Ov/*Opt*=*val*,*Opt*=*val*,.../*Link*,*Link*,...;

For example:

```
7/5=3,7=4/2,3,16;
```

specifies a run through the links 702, 703, and 716 (in this order), with option 5 set equal to 3 and option 7 equal to 4 in each of the links. If all options have their default value, the line would be

```
7//2,3,16;
```

A further feature of the route specification is the *jump number*. This is given in parentheses at the end of the link list, just before the semicolon. It indicates which overlay line is executed after completion of the current overlay. If it is omitted, the default value is **+0**, indicating that the program will proceed to the next line in the list (skipping no lines). If the jump number is set to **-4**, on the other hand, as in

```
7//2,3,16(-4);
```

then execution will continue with the overlay specified four route lines back (not counting the current line).

This feature permits loops to be built into the route and is useful for optimization runs. An argument to the program chaining routine can override the jump. This is used during geometry optimizations to loop over a sequence of overlay lines until the optimization has been completed, at which point the line following the end of the loop is executed.

Note that non-standard routes are not generally created from scratch but rather are built by printing out and modifying the sequence produced by the standard route most similar to that desired. This can be accomplished most easily with the **testrt** utility (described in chapter 5).

EXAMPLES
A Simple Route. The standard route:

```
#  RHF/STO-3G
```

causes the following non-standard route to be generated:

```
1/29=10000/1;
2/10=1,12=2/2;
3/11=1,25=14,30=1/1,2,3,11,14;
4/7=1/1;
5//2;
6/7=2,8=2,9=2,10=2,19=1,28=1/1;
99/5=1,9=1/99;
```

The resulting sequence of programs is illustrated below:

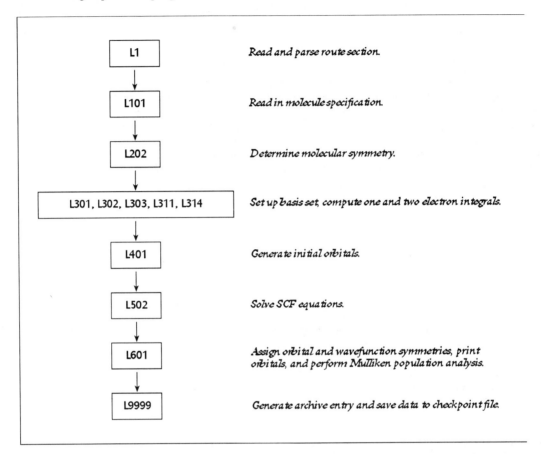

The basic sequence of program execution is identical to that found in any ab initio program, except that Link 1 (reading and interpreting the route section) precedes the actual calculation, and that Link 9999 (generating an archive entry) follows it. An AM1 single-point would be similar, except that only Link 301 (set up of basis set) would be included from overlay 3 and that Link 402 (code excerpted from the MOPAC program) would replace Link 502. Similarly, an MP4 single point has integral transformation (links 801 and 802) and the MP calculation (links 901, 909, 910, 911, 912, and 913) inserted after the population analysis and before Link 9999. Link 9999 automatically terminates the job step when it completes.

A Route Involving Loops. The standard route:

```
# RHF/STO-3G Opt
```

produces the following non-standard route:

```
1/10=7,29=10000/1,3;
2/10=1,12=2/2;
3/11=1,25=14,30=1/1,2,3,11,14;
```

```
4/7=1/1;
5//2;
6/7=2,8=2,9=2,10=2,28=1/1;
7/25=1,27=1,29=1/1,2,3,16;
1/10=7/3(1);
99//99;
2//2;
3/11=1,25=14,30=1/1,2,3,11,14;
4/5=5,7=1,16=2/1;
5//2;
7/27=1/1,2,3,16;
1//3(-5);
3/11=1,30=1,39=1/1,3;
6/7=2,8=2,9=2,10=2,28=1/1;
99/9=1/99;
```

The resulting sequence of program execution is illustrated on the next page.

Several considerations complicate this route:

♦ The first point of the optimization must be handled separately from later steps, since several actions must be performed only once. These include reading the initial Z-matrix and generating the initial orbitals.

♦ There must be a loop over geometries, with the optimization program (in this case the Berny optimizer, Link 103) deciding whether another geometry was required or the structure has been optimized.

♦ If a converged geometry is supplied, the program should calculate the gradients once, recognize that the structure is optimized, and quit.

♦ Population analysis and orbital printing should be done only at the first and last points, not at the relatively uninteresting intermediate geometries.

The first point has been dealt with by having two basic sequences of integrals, guess, SCF, and integral derivatives in the route. The first sequence includes Link 101 (to read the initial geometry), Link 103 (which does its own initialization), and has options set to tell Link 401 to generate an initial guess. The second sequence uses geometries produced in Link 103 in the course of the optimization, and has options set to tell Link 401 to retrieve the wavefunction from the previous geometry as the initial guess for the next.

The forward jump on the eighth line has the effect that if Link 103 exits normally (without taking any special action) the following line (invoking Link 9999) is skipped. Normally, in this second invocation of Link 103 the initial gradient will be examined and a new structure chosen. The next link to be executed will be Link 202, which processes the new Z-matrix, followed by the rest of the second energy+gradient sequence, which constitutes the main optimization loop. If the second invocation of Link 103 finds that the geometry is converged, it exits with a flag which suppresses the jump, causing Link 9999 to be invoked by the following line and the job to complete.

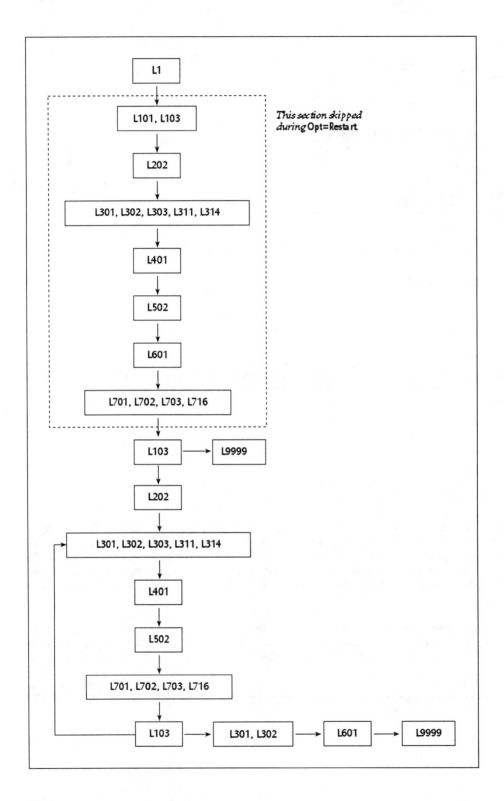

Lines 10-15 form the main optimization loop. This evaluates the integrals, wavefunction, and gradient for the second and subsequent points in the optimization. It concludes with Link 103. If the geometry is still not converged, Link 103 chooses a new geometry and exits normally, causing the backward jump on line 15 to be executed, and the next line processed to be line 10, beginning a new cycle. If Link 103 finds that the geometry has converged, it exits and suppresses the jump, causing the concluding lines (16-18) to be processed.

The concluding line generates the multipole integrals at the final geometry for use in Link 601, which prints the final multipole moments as well as the orbitals and population analysis if so requested. Finally, Link 9999 generates the archive entry and terminates the job step.

Routes for AM1 optimizations are similar, with all but Link 301 omitted from the invocations of overlay 3, Link 402 replacing Link 501, and overlay 7 omitted (the MOPAC code in Link 402 computes the gradient information internally). MP and CI optimizations have the transformation and correlation overlays (8 and 9) and the post-SCF gradient overlays (11 and 10, in that order) inserted before overlay 7. The same two-phase route structure is used for numerical differentiation to produce frequencies or polarizabilities.

The route for **Opt=Restart** is basically just the main loop from the original optimization, with the special lines for the first step omitted. The second invocation of Link 103 is kept and does the actual restarting.

Keywords Related to Non-Standard Routes

ExtraLinks   Enables the inclusion of extra links in an otherwise standard route (the link names are specified as its options). They are always executed after all standard links in that occurrence of the overlay. For example, **ExtraLinks=(L901)** specifies that Link 901 is to be included in every occurrence of overlay 9, after any links in that overlay would be executed anyway.

ExtraOverlays   Provides a mechanism for customizing a route which is somewhat intermediate between using **ExtraLinks** and reading in an entirely new non-standard route. When specified, the program expects one or more lines of input after the blank line following the route section. These are overlay lines as described above. A blank line is then used to separate the last extra overlay line from the title section. The program will parse the standard route and add any extra overlay lines to the route just before the last overlay, Link 99 line: 99//99, generated in the standard route. This provides greater flexibility than the **ExtraLinks** keyword, since the user can provide new options to an additional link, instead of just accepting those which happen to be already there for a given overlay.

Skip   This keyword allows the user to skip past a certain number of overlay lines in a standard route generated by the parser. It can be invoked in two ways:

Skip=Ovn Skip all overlays until the first occurrence of overlay n.
Skip=M Skip the first M overlays.

Use   Allows the user to request an alternative algorithm for certain phases of the calculation. Most of the options are for debugging; they are described in the *Gaussian 98 Programmer's Reference*.

See also the discussion of the **%KJob** Link 0 command in the previous section of this chapter.

4

Efficiency Considerations

Gaussian 98 has been designed to work efficiently given a variety of computer configurations. In general, the program attempts to select the most efficient algorithm given the memory and disk constraints imposed upon it. Since *Gaussian 98* does offer a wide choice of algorithms, an understanding of the possibilities and tradeoffs can help you to achieve optimal performance.

Before proceeding, however, let us emphasize two very important points:

♦   The default algorithms selected by the program give good performance for all but very large jobs. Note that some defaults have changed with *Gaussian 98* to reflect current typical problem sizes. Defaults used in earlier versions of the program were designed for small jobs of under 100 basis functions. The default algorithms used in *Gaussian 98* are generally designed for longer jobs.

♦   For users or sites who routinely run very large jobs, the following defaults placed in the **Default.Route** file (see chapter 6) will produce good general performance:

```
-M-  available-memory
# MaxDisk=available-disk
```

where the amount of available memory and disk are specified as indicated; the default units for each are 8-byte words, and either value may be followed by **KB**, **MB**, **GB**, **KW**, **MW** or **GW** (without intervening spaces) to specify units of kilo-, mega- or giga- bytes or words. Once the **Default.Route** file is set up, for many sites, no other special actions are required for overall efficient program use. The default memory size is 6MW.

Estimating Calculation Memory Requirements

The following formula can be used to estimate the memory requirement of various types of *Gaussian 98* jobs (in 8-byte words):

$$M + 2N_B{}^2$$

where N_B is the number of basis functions used in the calculation, and M is a minimum value that depends on the job type, given in the following table:

Job Type	Highest Angular Momentum Basis Function				
	f functions	g functions	h functions	i functions	j functions
SCF Energies	4 MW	4 MW	9 MW	23 MW	≈60 MW
SCF Gradients	4 MW	5 MW	16 MW	38 MW	
SCF Frequencies	4 MW	9 MW	27 MW		
MP2 Energies	4 MW	5 MW	10 MW	28 MW	≈70 MW
MP2 Gradients	4 MW	6 MW	16 MW	38 MW	
MP2 Frequencies	6 MW	10 MW	28 MW		

For example, on a 32-bit system, a 300 basis function HF geometry optimization using g functions would require about 5.2 MW (≈42 MB) of memory.

Note that 1 MW = 1,048,576 words (= 8,388,608 bytes). The values in the table are for 32-bit computer systems; they would need to be doubled for 64-bit systems (Cray, DEC Alpha running Digital UNIX). They also reflect the use of uncontracted higher angular momentum functions—f and above—which is the default type. Larger amounts of memory may be required for derivatives of contracted high angular momentum functions.

The remainder of this chapter is designed for users who wish to understand more about the tradeoffs inherent in the various choices in order to obtain optimal performance for an individual job, not just good overall performance. Techniques for both very large and small jobs will be covered. Additional, related information may be found in reference [395].

Storage, Transformation, and Recomputation of Integrals

One of the most important performance-related choices is the way in which the program processes the numerous electron repulsion integrals. There are five possible approaches to handling two-electron repulsion integrals implemented in *Gaussian 98*:

AO   The two-electron integrals over the atomic orbitals (AO integrals) are generated once and stored externally on disk. This is the approach used by conventional SCF calculations.

MO   The AO integrals are generated once and stored externally, then transformed to the molecular orbital basis. The transformed (MO) integrals are also stored externally. This is the approach used by earlier versions of *Gaussian* for all correlated energy methods.

Direct   The AO integrals (and possibly integral derivatives) are recomputed as needed. This does not require $O(N^4)$ internal or external storage, but does potentially involve additional computational effort. In some cases, other savings are possible that compensate for this additional effort. In any case, direct methods are the only choice when memory and disk are exhausted and consequently are inevitably used for the largest calculations. In contrast to earlier versions of the program, the direct method is the default for SCF calculations in *Gaussian 98*.

Semi-Direct   The AO integrals (and possibly integral derivatives) are recomputed as needed. In addition, MO quantities are stored temporarily on disk in whatever size chunks fit in the available disk space.

In-Core   The AO integrals are generated once and stored in canonical order in main memory (i.e., including zeroes). This requires large amounts of memory, but allows the integrals to be processed using simple matrix operations and no I/O, and consequently is very fast.

At least two of these approaches are available for all methods in *Gaussian 98*. The default method for a given job is chosen to give good performance on small to medium sized molecules. The various options and tradeoffs for each method are described in the following sections.

SCF Energies and Gradients

The performance issues that arise for SCF calculations include how the integrals are to be handled, and which alternative calculation method to select in the event that the default procedure fails to converge.

Integral Storage

By default, SCF calculations use the direct algorithm. It might seem that direct SCF would be preferred only when disk space is insufficient. However, this is not the case in practice. Because of the use of cutoffs, the cost of direct SCF scales with molecular size as $N^{2.7}$ or better, while conventional SCF scales in practice as $N^{3.5}$ [395]. Consequently, a point is reached fairly quickly where recomputing the integrals (really, only those integrals that are needed) actually consumes less CPU time than relying on external storage. Where this crossover occurs depends on how fast the integral evaluation in direct SCF is, and it varies from machine to machine. However, on modern computer systems, the most efficient strategy is to do an in-core SCF as long as it is feasible, and use the direct algorithm from that point on; the conventional algorithm is virtually never a good choice on such systems.

The change to direct SCF as the default algorithm in *Gaussian 98* was made in consideration of these facts. **SCF=Conven** keyword is only needed on small memory computer systems like the PC.

In-core SCF is also available. Direct SCF calculations that have enough memory to store the integrals are automatically converted to in-core runs. **SCF=InCore** can be requested explicitly, in which case the job will be terminated if insufficient memory is available to store the integrals. Generally, about $N^4/8$ + 500,000 words of memory are necessary for closed-shell in-core SCF, and $N^4/4$ + 500,000 words for UHF or ROHF in-core SCF. This corresponds to about 100 MB for a 100 basis function job, 1.6 GB for a 200 basis function job, and 8.1 GB for a 300 basis function job (closed-shell).

GVB and MCSCF calculations can also be done using direct or in-core algorithms [282]. Memory requirements are similar to the open-shell Hartree-Fock case described above. The primary difference is that many Fock operators must be formed in each iteration. For GVB, there are $2N_{orb}$ operators, where N_{orb} is the number of orbitals in GVB pairs. For MCSCF, there are $N_{active}(N_{active}-1)/2 + 1$ operators, where N_{active} is the number of orbitals in the active space. Consequently:

♦ Cutoffs are less effective than for Hartree-Fock, so the crossover in efficiency is at a larger number of basis functions.

♦ The number of operators can be quite large for larger MCSCF active spaces, so performance can be improved by ensuring that enough memory is available to hold all the density and operator matrices at once. Otherwise, the integrals will be evaluated more than once per iteration.

Direct SCF Procedure

In order to speed up direct HF calculations, the iterations are done in two phases:

♦ The density is converged to about 10^{-5} using integrals accurate to six digits and a modest integration grid in DFT calculations. This step is terminated after 21 iterations even if it is not fully converged. This step is omitted by default if any transition metal atoms are present.

♦ The density is then converged to 10-8 using integrals accurate to ten digits, allowing up to a total of 64 cycles total for the two steps.

This approach is substantially faster than using full integral accuracy throughout without slowing convergence in all cases tested so far. In the event of difficulties, full accuracy of the integrals throughout can be requested using **SCF=NoVarAcc**, at the expense of additional CPU time. See the discussion of the **SCF** keyword in chapter 3 for more details.

Single-Point Direct SCF Convergence
In order to improve performance for single-point direct and in-core SCF calculations, a modification of the default SCF approach is used:

♦ The integrals are done to only 10^{-6} accuracy except for all-electron (non-ECP) calculations involving molecules containing atoms heavier than argon.

♦ The SCF is converged to either 10^{-4} on both the energy and density, or to 10^{-5} on the energy, whichever comes first.

This is sufficient accuracy for the usual uses of single-point SCF calculations, including relative energies, population analysis, multipole moments, electrostatic potentials, and electrostatic potential derived charges. Conventional SCF single points and all jobs other than single points use tight convergence (10^{-8} on the density). The tighter convergence can be applied to single-point direct SCF by requesting **SCF=Tight**. See the discussion of the **SCF** keyword in chapter 3 for more details.

Problem Convergence Cases

If the default SCF approach (iterative diagonalization with DIIS extrapolation [389]) fails to converge, several alternatives are available (labeled by their corresponding keyword):

SCF=VShift[=N] This shifts the energy of the virtual orbitals up by occupieds and virtuals N millihartrees. N defaults to 100. This keyword is useful when occupied and virtual orbitals are being interchanged repeatedly, which is often the case in systems involving transition metals and partially filled d shells. This option is enabled by default for systems containing transition metals.

SCF=QC This is quadratic convergence SCF, based on the method of Bacskay [388]. Since it combines linear minimizations with the Newton-Raphson algorithm suggested by Bacskay, it is guaranteed to reach a stationary point eventually. Typically, **SCF=QC** is about twice as expensive as conventional SCF. Since **SCF=QC** is reliable and can be used for direct SCF, it is usually the first choice if convergence problems are encountered. It can be used for RHF and UHF, but not for complex or ROHF.

Guess=Alter Sometimes convergence difficulties are a warning that the initial guess has occupied the wrong orbitals. The guess should be examined, especially as to the symmetries of the occupied orbitals. **Guess=Alter** can be used to modify the orbitals selected for occupation.

SCF=NoDIIS This implies conventional SCF using the old 3 and 4 point extrapolation. It is not usually a good choice for RHF and UHF, but is sometimes helpful for ROHF, for which there are fewer alternatives. More than 64 cycles may be needed for convergence.

SCF(MaxCyc=N) Increases the total number of SCF iterations to N. Note that merely increasing the number of SCF cycles for the default algorithm is rarely helpful. DIIS either works in 64 cycles or it never converges.

SCF=DM This is the older steepest descent algorithm of Seeger [390]. It can be used for complex HF, but not for direct HF or DFT.

These approaches all tend to force convergence to the closest stationary point in the orbital space, which may not be a minimum with respect to orbital rotations. A stability calculation can be used to verify that a proper SCF solution has been obtained (see the **Stable** keyword in chapter 3). Note also that you should verify that the final wavefunction corresponds to the desired electronic state, especially when using **SCF=VShift** or **Guess=Alter**.

SCF Frequencies

Four alternatives for integral processing are available for Hartree-Fock second derivatives:

Direct The coupled perturbed Hartree-Fock (CPHF) equations are solved using integrals that are recomputed every iteration. Since cutoffs are not as effective for direct CPHF as for direct SCF, the crossover to direct being faster is higher, but even for 100 basis functions, direct frequencies are only about 40% slower than conventional (**AO**). Hence, as for direct SCF, the direct algorithm is preferred above 100 basis functions or so on vector machines and must be used when disk is exhausted on scalar machines. This algorithm is the default.

AO   The CPHF equations are solved using the written-out AO integrals. The petit (symmetry reduced) list can be used. This may be the optimal choice for jobs of up to about 100 basis functions.

MO   The CPHF equations are solved using transformed integrals. This is the only method used in most other electronic structure programs and is a bit faster than using the AO basis for small cases, but it is basically a waste of disk space. It is selected by specifying **CPHF=MO** in the route section. This option is not available for DFT methods.

In-Core   The integrals are stored in memory in canonical order. Memory requirements are the same as for in-core SCF. This is the fastest available method when it can be used. This algorithm is selected using **SCF=InCore**.

By default, during in-core frequencies, the integrals are computed once by each link that needs them. This keeps the disk storage down to the same modest amount as for direct—$O(N^3)$. If $N^4/8$ disk is available, and in-core is being used only for speed, then specifying **SCF=(InCore,Pass)** will cause the integrals to be stored on disk (on the read-write file) after they are computed for the first time, and then read from disk rather than be recomputed by later steps.

HF frequency calculations include prediction of the infrared and Raman vibrational intensities by default. The IR intensities add negligible overhead to the calculation, but the Raman intensities add 10-20%. If the Raman intensities are not of interest, they can be suppressed by specifying **Freq=NoRaman**.

Freq=Raman produces Raman intensities by numerical differentiation for DFT and MP2 frequency calculations. Using this option does not change the calculation's disk requirements, but it will approximately double the CPU time for the job.

While frequency calculations can be done using very modest amounts of memory, performance on very large jobs will be considerably better if enough memory is available to complete the major steps in one pass. Link 1110 must form a "skeleton derivative Fock matrix" for every degree of freedom (i.e., 3 x Number-of-atoms) and if only some of the matrices can be held in memory, it will compute the integral derivatives more than once. Similarly, in every iteration of the CPHF solutions, link 1002 must form updates to all the derivative Fock matrices. Link 1110 requires $3N_AN^2/2$ words of memory, plus a constant amount for the integral derivatives to run optimally. Link 1002 requires $3N_AN^2$ words, plus a constant amount, to run optimally.

The **freqmem** utility program, described in chapter 5, returns the optimal memory size for different parameters of frequency calculation. Here are some typical values:

Atoms	Basis Functions	R/UHF	Optimal Memory (MWords)
10	100	R	1.2
20	100	R	1.3
20	100	U	1.7
30	100	R	1.5
10	200	R	1.7
20	200	R	2.9
20	200	U	5.3
30	200	R	4.1
20	300	R	5.9

MP2 Energies

Four algorithms are available for MP2, but most of the decision-making is done automatically by the program. The critical element of this decision making is the value of **MaxDisk,** which should be set according to your particular system configuration (see chapter 3). It indicates the maximum amount of disk space available in words. If no value is specified for **MaxDisk,** either in the route section or in the **Default.Route** file, *Gaussian 98* will assume that enough disk is available to perform the calculation with no redundant work, which may not be the case for larger runs. *Thus, specifying the amount of available memory and disk is by far the most important way of optimizing performance for MP2 calculations.* Doing so allows the program to decide between the various available algorithms, selecting the optimal one for your particular system configuration. This is best accomplished with -M- directive and **MaxDisk** keyword in the Default.Route file (although **MaxDisk** and **%Mem** may be included in the input file).

The algorithms available for MP2 energies are:

Semi-Direct   The AO integrals are generated as needed. The half-transformed integrals $(ip|\lambda\sigma)$ over one or more occupied orbitals i are sorted on disk. This method can function in as little as $O(N^2)$ memory and N^3 disk and is usually the optimal choice. It is specified with **MP2=SemiDirect.**

In-Core   The AO integrals are generated once and stored in canonical order in memory. $N^4/4$ memory is required. This is very fast if sufficient memory is available. This algorithm can be specified with **MP2=InCore,** which does in-core SCF and MP2.

FullDirect   The AO integrals are recomputed as needed during evaluation of $E^{(2)}$. No external storage is required. The number of integral evaluations depends on the amount of memory available. This is a good method only for machines with *large* amounts of physical memory. It is specified with **MP2=FullDirect.**

Conventional   The AO integrals are written out and transformed, then the MO integrals are antisymmetrized to produce $E^{(2)}$. This was the default algorithm in *Gaussian 88* and earlier versions. The **MP2=Conven** keyword forces this conventional MP2 algorithm. While the new (semi-direct) algorithm can function well for very large N in modest memory, it does have a fixed minimum memory requirement of about one million words for basis sets containing only s, p, and d functions. The old code, which is slower on all machines, can be run in very small memory and may be needed on low-end machines.

Use=L903   The AO integrals are written out, then the transformation and formation of $E^{(2)}$ are done in memory. $N^3/2$ memory is necessary. This was an option in *Gaussian 88* if the energy but not the gradient was desired. This algorithm is selected with **Use=L903**.

In addition, when the direct, semi-direct, and in-core MP2 algorithms are used, the SCF phase can be either conventional, direct, or in-core. The default is direct or in-core SCF.

MP2 Gradients

The choices for MP2 gradients are much the same as for MP2 energies, except:

♦   The conventional algorithm requires the storage of the two-particle density matrix and therefore uses considerably more disk than if only energies are needed. The new methods require no more disk space for gradients than for the corresponding energies.

♦   The modern methods compute the integral derivatives at least twice, once in the E^2 phase and once after the CPHF step. As a result, for small systems (50 basis functions and below) on scalar machines, the conventional algorithm is somewhat faster.

♦   The integral derivative evaluation during E^2 in the new algorithms requires extra main memory if higher than f functions are used.

As for the MP2 energy, the default is to do direct or in-core SCF and then dynamically choose between semi-direct, direct, or in-core E^2.

MP2 Frequencies

Only semi-direct methods are available for analytic MP2 second derivatives. These reduce the disk storage required below what a conventional algorithm requires.

MP2 frequency jobs also require significant amounts of memory. The default of six million words should be increased for larger jobs. If f functions are used, eight million words should be provided for computer systems using 64-bit integers.

Higher Correlated Methods

The correlation methods beyond MP2 (MP3, MP4, CCSD, CISD, QCISD, etc.) all require that some transformed (MO) integrals be stored on disk and thus (unlike MP2 energies and gradients) have disk space requirements that rise quartically with the size of the molecule. There are, however, several alternatives as to how the transformed integrals are generated, how many are stored, and how the remaining terms are computed:

♦ The default in *Gaussian 98* is a semi-direct algorithm. The AO integrals may be written out for use in the SCF phase of the calculation or the SCF may be done directly or in-core. The transformation recomputes the AO integrals as needed and leaves only the minimum number of MO integrals on disk (see below). The remaining terms are computed by recomputing AO integrals.

♦ The conventional algorithm, which was the default in *Gaussian 90*, involves storing the AO integrals on disk, reading them back during the transformation, and forming all of the MO two-electron integrals except those involving four virtual orbitals. The four virtual terms were computed by reading the AO integrals. This procedure can be requested in *Gaussian 98* by specifying **Tran=Conven** in the route section, and it is appropriate for smaller jobs on slower machines.

♦ A full set of MO integrals can be requested with **Tran=Full**. It can save a substantial amount of CPU time when disk space is plentiful. It is useful on machines with fast I/O.

The default algorithm is good for most jobs, providing that the default of two million words of memory is available, and will benefit from more memory for large cases or if f functions are used. **Tran=Conven** is needed on machines with limited memory. The disk requirements of the semi-direct algorithm are much less than those of the conventional. For CID, CISD, CCD, MP4SDQ, QCISD, and BD energies (without triple excitations or gradients), only the integrals involving two occupied and two virtual orbitals are needed, along with some intermediate storage during the transformation.

MaxDisk and Post-SCF Calculations

MP3, MP4, QCISD, CCSD, QCISD(T), and CCSD(T) calculations all now look at **Maxdisk**. If the calculation can be done using a full integral transformation while keeping disk usage under **MaxDisk**, this is done; if not, a partial transformation is done and some terms are computed in the AO basis. Since MP2 obeys MaxDisk as much as possible, the **Stingy**, **NoStingy** and **VeryStingy** options are not needed.

Thus, it is *crucial* for a value for MaxDisk to be specified explicitly for these types of jobs, either within the route section or via a system wide setting in the **Default.Route** file. If **MaxDisk** is left unset, the program now assumes that disk is abundant and performs a full transformation by default, in contrast to G94 where a partial transformation was the default in such cases. If **MaxDisk** is not set and sufficient disk space is not available for a full transformation, the job will fail (where it may have worked in G94).

Excited State Energies and Gradients

In addition to integral storage selection, the judicious use of the restart facilities can improve the economy of CIS and TD calculations.

Integral Storage

Excited states using CI with single excitations can be done using five methods (labeled by their corresponding option to the **CIS** keyword):

Direct   Solve for the specified number of states using iterative diagonalization, forming the product vectors from two-electron integrals computed as needed. This algorithm reduces memory and disk requirements to $O(N^2)$.

InCore   Requests that the AO Raffenetti combinations be held in memory. In-core is quite efficient, but is only practical for small molecular systems or large memory computers as $N^4/4$ words of memory are required.

MO[†]   Solve for the specified number of states using iterative (Davidson) diagonalization, forming the product vectors using MO integrals. This is the fastest method and is the default. This algorithm is an efficient choice up to about 150 basis functions, depending on the number of occupied orbitals. The more occupied orbitals, the sooner the direct algorithm should be used. Since only integrals involving two virtuals are needed (even for gradients) an attempt is made to obey **MaxDisk**. The minimum disk required is about $4O^2N^2$ ($6O^2N^2$ for open-shell).

AO[†]   Solve for the specified number of states using iterative diagonalization, forming the product vectors from written-out AO integrals. This is a slow method and is never the best choice.

ICDiag[†]   The entire CIS Hamiltonian matrix is loaded into core and diagonalized. This produces all possible states, but requires O^2V^2 memory and O^3V^3 CPU time. Accordingly, it is practical only for very small molecular systems and for debugging purposes.

Restarting Jobs and Reuse of Wavefunctions

CIS and TD jobs can be restarted from a *Gaussian 98* checkpoint file. This is of limited use for smaller calculations, which may be performed in the MO basis, as new integrals and transformation must be done, but is invaluable for direct CIS. If a direct CIS job is aborted during the CIS phase, then both **CIS=Restart** and **SCF=Restart** should be specified, as the final SCF wavefunction is not moved to its permanent location (suitable for **Guess=Read**) until the entire job step (or optimization step) completes.

[†] Not available for TD calculations.

CIS Excited State Densities

If only density analysis is desired, and the excited states have already been found, the CIS density can be recovered from the checkpoint file, using **Density=(Check,Current) Guess=Only**, which recovers whatever generalized density was stored for the current method (presumably CIS) and repeats the population analysis. Note that the one-particle (unrelaxed) density as well as the generalized (relaxed) density can be examined, but that dipole moments and other properties at the CIS level are known to be much less accurate if the one-particle density is used (i.e., if the orbital relaxation terms are neglected) [102, 313]. Consequently, the use of the CIS one-particle density is strongly discouraged, except for comparison with the correct density and with other programs that cannot compute the generalized density.

Separate calculations are required to produce the generalized density for several states, since a CPHF calculation must be performed for each state. To do this, first solve for all the states and the density for the first excited state:

```
# CIS=(Root=1,NStates=N) Density=Current
```

if N states are of interest. Then do $N-1$ additional runs, using a route section of the form:

```
CIS=(Read,Root=M,NStates=N) Density=Current
```

for states $M=2$ through N.

Pitfalls for Open-Shell Excited States

Since the UHF reference state is not an eigenfunction of S^2, neither are the excited states produced by CIS or TD[396].

Stability Calculations

Tests of Triplet and Singlet instabilities of RHF and UHF and restricted and unrestricted DFT wavefunctions can be requested using the **Stable** keyword. **MO**, **AO**, **Direct**, and **InCore** options are available, which request the corresponding algorithm. The default is **Direct**. Direct stability calculations can be restarted as described above for **CIS**.

CASSCF

The primary challenge in using the CASSCF method is selecting appropriate active space orbitals. There are several possible tactics:

♦ Use the standard delocalized initial guess orbitals. This is sometimes sufficient, e.g. if the active space consists of all π electrons. Use **Guess=Only** to inspect the orbitals and determine whether any alterations are required before running the actual calculation.

- ♦ Use localized initial guess orbitals. This is useful if specific bond pairs are to be included, since localization separates electron pairs.

- ♦ Use the natural orbitals from the total density from a UHF calculation (CAS-UNO) [290, 291]. For singlets, this requires that one has coaxed the UHF run into converging to a broken symmetry wavefunction (normally with **Guess=Mix**). It is most useful for complex systems in which it is not clear which electrons are most poorly described by doubly-occupied orbitals.

In all cases, a single-point calculation should be performed before any optimization, so that the converged active space can be checked to ensure that the desired electrons have been correlated before proceeding. There are additional considerations in solving for CASSCF wavefunctions for excited states, which are discussed in chapter 3.

CASSCF Frequencies

CASSCF frequencies require large amounts of memory. Increasing the amount of available memory will always improve performance for CASSCF frequency jobs (the same is not true of frequency calculations performed with other methods). These calculations also require O^2N^2 disk space.

5
Utility Programs

This chapter discusses various utility programs included with *Gaussian 98*. The commands to run all the utilities are defined in the *Gaussian 98* initialization files (see chapter 2). The utilities are discussed in alphabetical order within this chapter.

Most utilities are available for both UNIX and Windows versions of *Gaussian*. However, be sure to consult the release notes accompanying the program for information pertaining to specific operating systems.

The following table lists the available utilities and their functions (starred items are included on the *Gaussian 98W* **Utilities** menu):

Utility	*Function*
c8698	Converts checkpoint files from previous program versions to *Gaussian 98* format.
chkchk*	Displays the route and title sections from a checkpoint file.
chkmove*	Converts checkpoint files to and from binary and text formats for transfer between different computer architectures.
clearipc	Releases shared memory segments.
cubegen*	Standalone cube generation utility.
cubman*	Manipulates *Gaussian 98*-produced cubes of electron density and electrostatic potential (allowing them to be added, subtracted, and so on).
formchk*	Converts a binary checkpoint file into an ASCII form suitable for use with visualization programs.
freqchk*	Prints frequency and thermochemistry data from a checkpoint file, or creates a molecule and script file for visualizing normal modes with HyperChem.
freqmem	Determines memory requirements for frequency calculations.
gauopt	Performs optimizations of variables other than molecular coordinates.
ghelp	On-line help for *Gaussian 98*.
newzmat*	Conversion between a variety of molecular geometry specification formats.
testrt*	Route section syntax checker and non-standard route generation.
unfchk*	Convert a formatted checkpoint file back to its binary form.

c8698

The **c8698** utility converts checkpoint files from *Gaussian 86* through *Gaussian 94* to *Gaussian 98* format. It takes the name of the checkpoint file as its argument, and transforms it in place, so that the reformatted file has the same name as the original one. For example, the following command converts the checkpoint file taxol.chk in the *Gaussian* scratch directory to *Gaussian 98* format:

```
$ c8698 $GAUSS_SCRDIR/taxol.chk
```

chkchk

The **chkchk** utility displays the route and title sections from a checkpoint file, and indicates other information that is present within it. It is useful for determining the contents of random checkpoint files whose purpose has been forgotten and whose names are non-descriptive. It takes the name of the checkpoint file as its argument. Here is an example of its use:

```
$ chkchk important
 Checkpoint file important.chk:
 Title: Optimization and frequencies for pentaprismane
 Route: #T BECKE3LYP/6-31+G(D,P) OPT FREQ POP=FULL
 Atomic coordinates present.
 SCF restart data present.
 This file appears to be from the middle of a restartable job.
 Internal force constants may be present.
```

chkmove

This program converts a binary checkpoint file into and out of a text format designed for transfer between different computer operating systems. It is invoked by a command line of the form:

chkmove u|f *chkpt-filename xfer-filename*

where the code letter indicates the direction of the conversion: to the text format (f), or back into the binary format (u), *chkpt-filename* is the name of the checkpoint file to be converted, and *xfer-filename* is the name for the reformatted version.

For example, the following commands might be used to move a checkpoint file from a Sun to an RS/6000:

sun-23> **chkmove f taxol.chk taxol.xfr**
messages indicating successful reformatting
sun-24> **rlogin my_rs6k**
login messages
rs6k-11> **rcp indy:taxol.xfr .**
rs6k-12> **chkmove u taxol.xfr taxol.chk**

The checkpoint file is now ready to use on the second computer system. The conventional extension for text format checkpoint files is .xfr.

The formatted output from **chkmove** is not intended to actually be readable, but rather is intended solely to facilitate moving checkpoint files between different machines; note that **chkmove** is the preferred method for accomplishing such transfers. Use the **formchk** utility to produce human- and program-readable formatted checkpoint files.

RESTRICTIONS

chkmove may be used to convert checkpoint files from completed calculations only. It will not work with checkpoint files from failed jobs or from intermediate calculations such an unconverged optimizations, partially completed IRC's or numerical frequencies.

clearipc

clearipc is a C-shell script which releases shared memory segments used in the shared-memory parallel versions of *Gaussian 98* (for systems which use standard UNIX System V shared memory). Shared memory segments are normally released automatically when a job terminates normally, but may be left allocated if a job aborts. **clearipc** is invoked simply by name:

```
$ clearipc
```

When a normal user invokes **clearipc**, all shared memory segments owned by that user are cleared. When the utility is invoked by root, however, *all* shared memory segments are cleared. Note that this is a change in functionality from the shell script provided with earlier versions of *Gaussian*.

clearipc can safely be run even while *Gaussian* jobs are executing since cleared shared memory segments are not actually released until any process referencing them has terminated. Therefore, we recommended that it be invoked frequently, for example, in each *Gaussian* user's initialization file or periodically via the UNIX **cron** facility, whenever a parallel version of *Gaussian 98* is in use.

The status of shared memory segments can be displayed using the UNIX **ipcs -m** command. **clearipc** uses the UNIX **ipcrm -m** command to clear shared memory segments.

cubegen

Gaussian 98 now offers a standalone utility for generating cubes from the data in a formatted checkpoint file (equivalent to a subset of the functionality of the **Cube** keyword). The utility is named **cubegen**, and it has the following syntax:

cubegen *memory kind fchkfile cubefile npts format*

where the parameters have the following meanings:

memory   Amount of dynamic memory to allocate in words. A value of **0** implies a machine-specific default value.

kind   A keyword specifying the type of cube to generate:

        mo=*n*   Molecular orbital *n*. The keywords **Homo**, **Lumo**, **All**, **OccA** (all alpha occupied), **OccB**, **Valence** and **Virtuals** may also be used in place of a specific orbital number.

        density=*type*   Total density of the specified type.

        spin=*type*   Spin density (difference between α and β densities) of the specified type.

        alpha=*type*   Alpha spin density of the specified type.

        beta=*type*   Beta spin density of the specified type.

        potential=*type* Electrostatic potential using the density of the specified type.

The *type* keyword is one of the single density selection options that are valid with the **Density** keyword: **SCF**, **MP2**, **CI**, **QCI**, and so on (note that **Current** is not supported). The **fdensity**, **falpha** and **fbeta** forms request the use of full instead of frozen-core densities. Note that multiple MO cubes cannot be generated in a single run by this utility.

fchkfile   Name of the formatted checkpoint file (**test.fchk** is the default).

cubefile   Name of the output cube file (**test.cube** is the default).

npts   Number of points per side in the cube. A value of **0** selects the default value of 80; a value of **-1** says to read the cube specification from the input stream. The values **-2**, **-3** and **-4** correspond to the **Cube** keywords **Coarse**, **Medium** and **Fine** and to values of 40, 80 and 100 (respectively). These keyword themselves may also be used.

format   Format of output file: **h** means include header (this is the default); **n** means don't include header.

cubman

The **cubman** program manipulates cubes of values of electron density and electrostatic potential as produced by *Gaussian 98*. The program prompts for an operation to perform, and then the names of the necessary files. The possible operations and their associated subcommands are:

- **add**   Add two cubes to produce a new one.
- **copy**   Copy a cube, possibly converting it from formatted to unformatted or vice versa.
- **diff**   Compute properties of the difference between two cubes, without writing out a new cube.
- **prop**   Computes the properties of a single cube.
- **subtract** Subtracts two cubes to produce a new cube.
- **scale**   Scale a cube by a constant factor, producing a new cube.

All operation subcommands can be abbreviated to the shortest unique form.

Here are some annotated sample runs with **cubman** (user input is shown in boldface type, and output has been condensed slightly due to space considerations):

```
$ cubman
Action [Add, Copy, Difference, Properties, SUbtract, SCale]? p
Input file? b.cube
Is it formatted [no,yes,old]? y          Cube files produced by Gaussian 98 are formatted
Opened special file b.cube.
Input file titles:
First excited state of propellane    Title line from the job
CI Total Density                     Contents of cube file

  SumAP= 13.39263 SumAN= .00000 SumA= 13.39263       Statistics about cube contents
  CAMax=  3.35320 XYZ= .18898 -1.32280 .000004
  CAMin=   .00000 XYZ= -9999.00000 -9999.00000 -9999.00000

  DipAE=  -.8245357658     .7624198057      .1127178115
  DipAN=  -.0000060000    -.0000060000      .0000000000
  DipA=   -.8245417658     .7624138057      .1127178115

$ cubman
Action [Add, Copy, Difference, Properties, SUbtract, SCale]? su
First input? b.cube
Is it formatted [no,yes,old]?  y
Opened special file b.cube.
Second input? a.cube
Is it formatted [no,yes,old]?  y
Opened special file a.cube.
Output file? c.cube                  File to hold the new cube
Should it be formatted [no,yes,old]?  y
Opened special file c.cube.
Input file titles:
First excited state of propellane    Title from first file
CI Total Density                     Contents of first cube
Input file titles:
Propellane HF/6-31G*                 Title from second file
SCF Total Density                    Contents of second cube
Output file titles:                  Composite title used for new file
First excited state of propellane || Propellane HF/6-31G*
CI Total Density - SCF Total Density Difference to be computed

  SumAP= 13.39263 SumAN= .00000 SumA= 13.39263      Statistics for first cube
  CAMax=  3.35320 XYZ=  .18898 -1.32280 .000004
  CAMin=   .00000 XYZ= -9999.00000 -9999.00000 -9999.00000

  SumBP= 13.38168 SumBN= .00000 SumB= 13.38168      Statistics for second cube
  CBMax=  3.39683 CBMin= .00000

  SumOP=   .63453 SumON=-.62358 SumO=   .01094      Statistics for output cube
  COMax=   .49089 COMin=-.39885

  DipAE=  -.8245357658     .7624198057      .1127178115
  DipAN=  -.0000060000    -.0000060000      .0000000000
```

```
DipA=      -.8245417658     .7624138057      .1127178115

DipBE=     -.8306292172     .5490287046      .1243830393
DipBN=     -.0000060000    -.0000060000      .0000000000
DipB=      -.8306352172     .5490227046      .1243830393

DipOE=      .0060934514     .2133911011     -.0116652278
DipON=     -.0000060000    -.0000060000      .0000000000
DipO=       .0060874514     .2133851011     -.0116652278
```

In the output. the input cubes are denoted as A and B, and the output cube is designated by O. Other code letters are N for "negative values" or for "nuclear," depending on the context, P for "positive values," E for "electronic," C for "charge," Dip for "dipole," Sum for "sum," Max for "maximum," and Min for "minimum." Thus, SumAN is the sum over the first input cube, taking the negative values only, and DipON is the nuclear contribution to the dipole moment for the output cube. Similarly, CBMax is the maximum charge for the second input cube, and SumO is the sum of the values in the output cube, including both positive and negative values.

formchk

formchk converts the data in a *Gaussian 98* checkpoint file into a formatted form which is suitable for input into a variety of visualization software.

formchk has the following syntax:

formchk [-c] *chkpt-file formatted-file*

where *chkpt-file* is the name of the binary checkpoint file to be formatted, and *formatted-file* is the name for the resultant output file. For example, the following command will produce the formatted checkpoint file **propell.fchk** from the checkpoint file **propell.chk**:

```
$ formchk propell.chk propell.fchk
```

The conventional extension for formatted checkpoint files is .fchk on UNIX systems and other computers supporting variable-length extensions, and .fck on systems which limit extension to three characters like the PC.

Note that **formchk** is designed to reformat the information stored in a *Gaussian 98* checkpoint file into a format that is easily imported into other programs. It is not designed as a data exchange format between computer platforms; use the **chkmove** utility when you want to move a checkpoint file from one type of computer system to another.

The command **formchk -c** causes the molecular mechanics atom types to appear in the formatted checkpoint file as strings rather than integers.

freqchk

The **freqchk** utility may be used for retrieving frequency and thermochemistry data from a checkpoint file, with optional specification of an alternate temperature, pressure, scale factor, and/or isotope substitutions.

freqchk optionally takes the name of the formatted or unformatted checkpoint file to be processed as its command line argument; it will prompt for it if no argument is given, and it prompts for all other information that it requires. A filename parameter specified without an extension is assumed to be a formatted checkpoint file.

The following annotated sessions illustrate its use (user input is set in boldface type):

```
$ freqchk
 Checkpoint file? solvent.chk
 Write Hyperchem files? n
 Temperature (K)? [0=>298.15] 0 Zero must be entered; return doesn't work
 Pressure (Atm)? [0=>1 atm] 0
 Scale factor for frequencies during thermochemistry? [0=>1/1.12] 0
 Do you want the principal isotope masses? [Y]: Return accepts defaults
Isotopes for each atom are printed
 Full mass-weighted force constant matrix:
 Low frequencies --- -948.3077     .0008      .0020      .0026
 ...
```

Normal Gaussian 98 frequency output follows ...

```
                         1                    2
                        ?A                   ?A
 Frequencies --    1885.3939            3853.5773
 Red. masses --       1.0920               1.0366
 Frc consts  --       2.2871               9.0697
 IR Inten    --      17.3416              21.5997
 Raman Activ --       7.8442              67.0384
 Depolar     --        .7428                .2248
 Atom AN    X      Y      Z        X      Y      Z       Normal modes
   1   8   .06    .00    .04      .04    .00    .02
   2   1  -.70    .00    .03      .01    .00   -.71
   ...
```

```
 -------------------
 - Thermochemistry -
 -------------------
 Temperature   298.150 Kelvin.  Pressure   1.00000 Atm.
 Thermochemistry will use frequencies scaled by  .8929.
 ...
 Zero-point vibrational energy      53494.5 (Joules/Mol)
                                   12.78550 (Kcal/Mol)
 VIBRATIONAL TEMPERATURES:   2422.01  4950.36  5495.38 (KELVIN)
```
Zero-point and thermal corrections:
```
 Zero-point correction=               .020375 (Hartree/Particle)
 Thermal corr to Energy=              .023210
 Thermal corr to Enthalpy=            .024154
 Thermal corr to Gibbs Free Energy=   .045589
```

E=thermal energy; CV=constant volume molar heat capacity; S=entropy

	E	CV	S
	KCAL/MOL	CAL/MOL-KELVIN	CAL/MOL-KELVIN
TOTAL	14.564	6.001	45.114
ELECTRONIC	.000	.000	.000
TRANSLATIONAL	.889	2.981	34.609
ROTATIONAL	.889	2.981	10.500
VIBRATIONAL	12.787	.039	.005

Partition functions

	Q	LOG10(Q)	LN(Q)
TOTAL BOT	.561443D-01	-1.250695	-2.880127
TOTAL V=0	.132155D+09	8.121085	18.699192
VIB (BOT)	.424961D-09	-9.371650	-21.579023
VIB (V=0)	.100030D+01	.000129	.000297
ELECTRONIC	.100000D+01	.000000	.000000
TRANSLATIONAL	.300436D+07	6.477751	14.915574
ROTATIONAL	.439749D+02	1.643204	3.783618

```
$ freqchk solvent.chk        Checkpoint filename can be placed on the command line
Write Hyperchem files? n
Temperature (K)? [0=>298.15] 300        Alternate temperature
Pressure (Atm)? [0=>1 atm] 1.5          Alternate pressure
Scale factor for freqs during thermochem? [0=>1/1.12] 1        No scaling
Do you want to use the principal isotope masses? [Y]: n
For each atom, give the integer mass number.
In each case, the default is the principal isotope.
Atom number 1, atomic number 8: [16]        Return accepts default
Atom number 2, atomic number 1: [1] 2       Specify isotope masses as integers
. . .
```

Frequency output follows, reflecting the values specified above. Note that if scaling is specified, only the thermochemistry data reflects it; the frequencies themselves are not scaled.

freqmem

The **freqmem** utility takes parameters for a frequency calculation and determines the amount of memory required to complete all steps in one pass, for maximum efficiency. All parameters must be provided on the command line, using the following syntax:

freqmem *natoms nbasis* r|u c|d *functions*

where the arguments are:

natoms   Number of atoms in the molecule.

nbasis   Number of basis functions for this system under the desired basis set.

r|u   A one-letter code indicating an RHF (closed shell) or UHF (open shell) calculation, as appropriate.

c | d   A one-letter code indicating whether the calculation will be run using the conventional or direct algorithm.

functions   A string indicating the types of basis functions used in the chosen basis set: sp, spd, spdf, and so on.

Here is an example of its use, estimating the memory resources required for RHF/STO-3G frequencies on taxol (113 atoms):

```
$ freqmem 113 361 r d sp
 RHF direct frequencies with sp functions:
 One pass requires 44.80 megawords.
```

The output indicates that the program will require about 360 MB of memory to complete the frequency calculation in a single pass.

If the amount of memory specified by **freqmem** is not available, a frequency calculation can still be completed using multiple passes. Use the **%Mem** Link 0 command to specify the amount of available memory. Setting this parameter to one half or one third of the amount of memory recommended by **freqmem** is often a good choice.

The number of basis functions required used in a *Gaussian 98* calculation is printed out early in the output file. It may also be calculated by setting up an input file for the job in question, and including the **%KJob=301** Link 0 command, which tells the program to terminate as soon as Link 301 is reached (which is almost immediately). The number of basis functions used for the molecule with the specified basis set may then be retrieved from the log file with a command like this one:

```
$ grep "basis func" name.log
    361 basis functions        1083 primitive gaussians
```

gauopt

The **gauopt** utility performs an optimization by repeatedly executing *Gaussian 98*. In this way, it can optimize any parameter in the input stream, including general or massaged basis functions. It operates by repeatedly creating subprocesses running *Gaussian 98*. **gauopt** is typically used to optimize parameters such as basis functions for which there is no standard optimization method implemented within *Gaussian 98*. It is invoked by its command verb, **gauopt**, and takes its input from standard input.

Input for **gauopt** consists of a template file, in which certain fields are replaced with variables whose values are to be optimized. The template file is used to construct an actual *Gaussian 98* input file containing the current values of the variables for each energy evaluation. The energy is then computed at each step automatically by running a *Gaussian 98* single point calculation. The format for the first line of the template is:

NVar, MaxIt, SaveFlag, Conv, ConvV

using a format 2I3, L2, D9.2. The fields are defined as follows:

NVar	The number of variables.
MaxIt	The maximum number of optimization cycles to perform.
**T	F**	A logical flag indicating whether the intermediate *Gaussian 98* output files are to be saved. These are named fork.com, fork.log, fork.rwf, and so on. They are deleted by default, but can be saved as an aid in debugging the template input.
Conv	Convergence on the RMS change in the variables. A fairly tight default is provided if this parameter is set to 0.0.
ConvV	Convergence on the energy, which defaults to 1 milliHartree when the parameter is set to 0.0.

The next line of the template file has one or more pairs of values using the following syntax:

Value **C | V**   *Repeated n times (no internal spaces)*

where *Value* is the value for the variable, and the second value is a one-character flag which can be set to **C** to constrain the variable (i.e., not optimize it during the current run), or to **V** if the variable is to be optimized. This line uses a format of F14.9, A1 for each pair of values.

The remainder of the template file contains a *Gaussian 98* input file template. Each field in the input file where a previously-defined variable should be inserted should contain either $<n\ x.y>$, indicating that the nth variable should be inserted at that point using format F$x.y$, or $<-n\ x.y>$, indicating that -1 times variable n should be inserted there.

An example will help make all of these concepts clearer. The following **gauopt** template file optimizes the scale factors in the STO-2G expansion of a minimal basis set for water:

```
3   3 T      0.0       0.0
        7.66V         2.25V         1.24V
# RHF/Gen Test

Water RHF/STO-2G basis with optimized scale factors

0.1
O
H,1,r
H,1,r,2,a

r 0.96
a 104.5

1 0
sto 1s 2 <1 12.10>
sto 2sp 2 <2 12.10>
****
2 0
sto 1s 2 <3 12.10>
****
```

```
3  0
sto 1s  2 <3 12.10>
****
```

The scale factors on the two hydrogens are made equal by using the same **gauopt** variable in more than one place; of course, this same effect could also have been accomplished by specifying that the same basis was to be used on every hydrogen atom.

ghelp

ghelp is a hierarchical help facility for *Gaussian 98*. Typing **ghelp** alone will display general information and a list of topics for which help is available. The form **ghelp topics** will display just the list of topics.

Information about *Gaussian 98* keywords and options is available using the format:

ghelp route   *keyword* [*option*]

Information about internal option *m* in overlay *n* (**IOp**(*n*/*m*)) may be obtained using the form:

ghelp route ov*n* **iop**(*m*)

Information about *Gaussian 98* utilities may be accessed using either the utility name as the primary topic or via the topic **utilities**.

newzmat

The **newzmat** utility was designed primarily for converting molecule specifications between a variety of standard formats. It can also perform many related functions, such as extracting molecule specifications from *Gaussian 98* checkpoint files. Its full set of capabilities includes the following:

♦ **newzmat** can convert molecule specifications between a variety of data file formats. This includes generating a Z-matrix (and hence input for *Gaussian 98*) from the files produced by other programs and also converting between the file formats of any of these programs. **newzmat** can thus be used to produce *Gaussian 98* input from the data files of many popular graphics and mechanics packages, allowing them to act as graphical input front-ends to *Gaussian 98*. The resulting data files have the proper symmetry constraints for efficient computation (if applicable).

♦ Given a Z-matrix and a new set of choices for defining bonds, angles, and dihedrals, **newzmat** can generate the values for the internal coordinates following the new scheme, producing the same structure as specified in the old scheme. It thus builds a "new Z-matrix"—hence the utility's name. This capability is useful, for example, in generating a new Z-matrix with fewer symmetry constraints than the original one, as when a frequency calculation has indicated that a high symmetry structure is a saddle point with respect to symmetry breaking.

♦ **newzmat** can also generate *Gaussian 98* checkpoint files from other data files, and (more importantly) generate the data files from checkpoint files. This capability can be used to extract data for display with a visualization package.

♦ **newzmat** can retrieve intermediate structures from a checkpoint file from (or during) a geometry optimization, for reuse or display.

Command Syntax

newzmat has the following general syntax:

newzmat *option(s) input-file output-file*

where *option(s)* is one or more options, specifying the desired operations, *input-file* is the file containing the structure to be converted (or retrieved), and *output-file* is the file in which to place the new molecule specification (or *Gaussian 98* input). Either filename may be replaced by a hyphen to denote standard input or standard output, as appropriate.

If the output filename is omitted, it is given the same base name as the input file, along with a conventional extension denoting its file type. In general, extensions can be omitted from file specifications provided that extension conventions are followed. The default extensions are listed in the following table:

Extension	File Type	Option Form
.bgf	Biograf internal data file	bgf
.cac	CaChe molecule file	cache
.chk	*Gaussian 98* checkpoint file	chk
.com	*Gaussian 98* input file (Z-matrix mol. spec.)	zmat
.com	*Gaussian 98* input file (Cart. coords. mol. spec.)	cart
.con	QUIPU system data file	con
.dat	Model/XModel/MM2 data file	model
.dat	MacroModel data file (may be formatted or unformatted)	mmodel ummodel
.ent	Brookhaven data file (≡PDB)	ent[†]
.inp	MOPAC input file	mopac
.pdb	Protein Data Bank format (≡Brookhaven)	pdb
.ppp	Some PPP program (output only)	ppp
.xyz	Unadorned Cartesian coordinates	xyz
.zin	Ancient version of ZINDO	zindo

[†] **bkv** is an obsolete synonym for **ent**.

Input and Output Options
The options specifying the formats of the input and output molecule specifications are formed from the string **-i** or **-o** (respectively), followed immediately by the appropriate option form string from the preceding table corresponding to the desired molecule specification format (no spaces intervene). For example, **-ipdb** indicates that the input molecule specification is in PDB format and that the extension .pdb should be applied to the input filename if no extension is specified. Similarly, **-oxyz** specifies an

output format of cartesian coordinates along with a default extension of .xyz for the output filename. The default input and output options are **-izmat** and **-ozmat**. Note that **-izmat** and **-icart** are synonyms, and either one of them can read a *Gaussian 98* input file containing any molecule specification format: Z-matrix, Cartesian coordinates, or mixed internal and Cartesian coordinates.

Other Options Related to Input and Output

The following options further specify the input for **newzmat**:

-step *N*   Use the structure from step *N* of the geometry optimization data in a *Gaussian 98* checkpoint file (valid only for the **-ichk** input option).

This option is not available for optimizations in redundant internal coordinates (the default coordinate system). Instead, retrieve the structure from the checkpoint file in a subsequent job by using a route section containing **Geom=(Check,Step=***N***)**.

-ubohr   Input distances in input file are specified in Bohr (the default is Angstroms).

-urad   Input angles in input stream are specified in radians (the default is degrees).

The following options further specify the output file format:

-mof1   Use macromodel format 1 (only valid with **-ommodel**).

-mof2   Use macromodel format 2 (this is default if **-ommodel** is specified).

-optprompt   Prompt for which parameters should be optimized; used when setting up a molecule specification destined for a geometry optimization and **-ozmat** is specified (or no output option is included). By default, all parameters not fixed by symmetry are optimized.

-prompt   Prompt for route section and title section lines and for the charge and multiplicity when using **-ozmat** (or no output option is specified). *Gaussian 98* input files produced by **newzmat** set up HF/6-31G(d) single point energy calculations by default.

Examples

The following command reads the molecule specification from the PDB file **water.pdb** and writes a *Gaussian 98* input file, including the equivalent Z-matrix, to the file **h2o.com**:

```
$ newzmat -ipdb water h2o              -ozmat is the default, so it can be omitted.
  Charge and multiplicity [0,1]?       A return accepts the default values shown.
```

newzmat prompts for the charge and multiplicity for the Z-matrix since these items cannot be determined from the PDB file.

The following command reads the molecule specification from the *Gaussian 98* checkpoint file **G98-11234.chk** and writes the PDB file **propell.hin** (the extension is the one desired by HyperChem):

```
$ newzmat -ichk -opdb G98-11234 propell.hin
```

The following command reads the molecule specification from step 5 of the optimization from the checkpoint file newopt.chk and produces the Mopac file step5.inp:

```
$ newzmat -ichk -omopac -step 5 newopt step5
```

The following command prints the molecule specification found in the checkpoint file mystery.chk and displays it in *Gaussian 98* input file format on the terminal screen (assuming the command is executed interactively):

```
$ newzmat -ichk mystery.chk -
```

The following command creates the checkpoint file quick.chk from the *Gaussian 98* input file that the user types in interactively:

```
$ newzmat -ochk - quick
#

anything

0 1
O
H 1 1.0
H 1 1.0 2 120.

^D
```

Note that the input file must end with a blank line.

The following command reads the molecule specification from the Mopac file newsalt.inp and writes a *Gaussian 98* input file including the equivalent Z-matrix to the file newsalt.com, prompting for the route and title sections and the charge and spin multiplicity for the molecule:

```
$ newzmat -imopac -prompt newsalt
Percent or Route card? # Becke3LYP/6-31G(d,p) Opt
Route card?                              End route section with a blank line.
Titles? Optimization of caffeine at Becke3LYP/6-31G**
Titles?                                  End title section with a blank line.
Charge and Multiplicity? 0,1
```

Selecting an Output Format

In order to communicate with a non-supported visualization system, the first choice of format to try is the PDB file. This format includes the connectivity information and is widely supported. Note that some software packages use the .ent extension, rather than .pdb; the **-ient** and **-oent** options select the former, while **-ipdb** and **-opdb** select the latter. Another commonly used alternative is the Mopac file format.

Specifying a Template for a New Z-matrix

newzmat can optionally read a Z-matrix template in addition to the input file specifying the actual molecular structure when the output file format is a Z-matrix (i.e., when -ozmat or no output option is specified). This template provides information about how to set up the output Z-matrix by specifying the choices of pairs of bonded atoms, triplets defining angles, and quartets defining dihedral angles used to specify the geometry in the output file. By default, no template is read, and the same choices are used in the output file as in the input file, except for the Model and MacroModel input formats for which full connectivity is available.

The template can be read from standard input or from a checkpoint file. In the latter case, the name of the checkpoint file holding the template becomes the final argument to **newzmat**.

The template Z-matrix must be complete: it begins with a charge and multiplicity card, and includes values for any variables used. Frozen variables are treated as constants.

The options relating to Z-matrix templates are listed below:

-tchk
: The template Z-matrix is in Z-matrix format within a *Gaussian 98* checkpoint file. The name of the checkpoint file holding the template follows the output file specification on the command line.

-tmodel
: The template Z-matrix is in **Geom=ModelA** format (as described in Appendix B); it is taken from standard input.

-tnone
: Skip the default rearrangement for Model and MacroModel input files.

-tzmat
: The template Z-matrix is in Z-matrix format and is taken from standard input.

-coince
: Reorder atoms for maximum coincidence (by default, **newzmat** allows the atoms to be specified in a different order in the input and output Z-matrices).

-nocoin
: Do not reorder atoms.

Other newzmat Options

The other options to **newzmat** are concerned with generating connectivity information, with the use of standard geometrical parameters, and with the determination and use of molecular symmetry. A complete connectivity table can be used to generate Z-matrix specifications suitable for inclusion of symmetry constraints. Such a table is also required for output of the data files for the molecular mechanics programs. If one of the input formats which includes full connectivity is used (e.g., MacroModel data files), the connectivity that it provides is used. However, when Z-matrix or MOPAC format input is provided, only the connectivity information which is implied by the internal coordinate specification is available. Thus if a new Z-matrix which incorporates the molecular symmetry is to be generated, the remaining connectivity information must be generated. When cartesian coordinates are read in, naturally, no connectivity information is provided, so the default is to generate the table using the internally stored atomic radii. In addition, when used to generate input structures, the mechanics programs may not generate suitable bond distances and often produce coordinates which are close to but not exactly symmetric. Options control how each of these cases is handled.

-allbonded   In generating new connectivity information, assume all atoms are bonded.

-bmodel   Use standard model B bond lengths along with internal values in determining bond distances.

-density *N*   Generate natural orbitals for density number *N*. This option is only useful if you are generating a CaChe file. *N* should be set to 0 for HF, to 2 for MP2, to 6 for CI, and to 7 for QCISD or CCD.

-fudge   Fudge bond distances to make sure they are reasonable, using internal values. This is the default for model input and is not applicable elsewhere.

-gencon   Generate connectivity information using internal radii.

-getfile   Insist on filename specifications for all arguments, making standard input and output unacceptable.

-lsymm   Use loose cutoffs for determining symmetry. This option implies **-symav**.

-mdensity *M*   Subtract generalized density *M* from that specified with **-density** to make a difference density, which is then converted to natural orbitals.

-nofudge   Do not fudge bond distances. This is the default and only choice for all cases except model input.

-nogetfile   Cancels **-getfile**.

-noround   Turns off rounding of Z-matrix parameters.

-nosymav   Turns off averaging of input coordinates.

-nosymm   Turns off all use of symmetry.

-order   Keeps the order of atoms as close as possible to the input order.

-round   Rounds Z-matrix parameters to 0.01 Å and 1 degree.

-symav   Average input coordinates using approximate symmetry operations to achieve exact symmetry.

-symm   Assign molecular symmetry.

-tsymm   Use tight cutoffs for determining symmetry. The option is the default.

-rebuildzmat   Build a new Z-matrix rather than using the read-in one (as would be the default for Z-matrix or MOPAC input). This option implies **-gencon**, and the option may be abbreviated as **-redoz**.

Known Difficulties with newzmat

♦ **newzmat** works quite reliably when molecular symmetry is not involved. It is also quite reliable for symmetric systems for most point groups. However, since it does not yet have the ability to insert dummy atoms where needed, generating a Z-matrix for molecules having a C_2 axis but not having any atoms on the symmetry axis will result in one which has more variables than appropriate for the symmetry constraints (but which nevertheless does correctly describe the molecular structure).

♦ The symmetry averaging process, which guesses the intended symmetry given coordinates which are only approximately symmetric, does not always achieve the intended symmetry. It will take coordinates printed in a *Gaussian 98* output file to 6 digits and restore symmetry, and it will usually work given coordinates from molecular mechanics provided that the mechanics optimization was converged reasonably far. In generating coordinates with MacroModel, for example, it is sometimes necessary to do a final full Newton-Raphson step after the normal minimization.

♦ When converting from a given structure to a specific Z-matrix (when the user has provided a template Z-matrix), **newzmat** works in a straightforward manner if there are no dummy atoms in the template Z-matrix. It will print an error message if any constants or variable constraints in the template Z-matrix are inconsistent with the specified structure, and it will always work correctly if all template Z-matrix parameters are separate variables, or if the constraints are consistent with the structure. In fact, while a complete template Z-matrix including values for any variables must be provided, the values assigned to the variables are ignored in this case.

However, when dummy atoms are present in the template Z-matrix, their parameters (and those of real atoms which depend on dummy atoms) cannot be assigned directly from the structure provided. In this case, **newzmat** does a least-squares fit to set the parameters in the template Z-matrix to produce a structure which matches the original one. The values of the variables in the template Z-matrix are used as the initial guess in this fit, and consequently these should be reasonable for the system in question. They needn't be very close, but outrageous bond lengths of (0.0 or 10.0 Å, for example) will cause problems.

If your ultimate goal is a geometry optimization, then use the **-oxyz newzmat** option and use the resulting structure for an optimization in redundant internal coordinates (the default procedure).

♦ **newzmat** computes the nuclear repulsion energy of the initial read-in structure and of the final structure as a consistency check. If these disagree, a warning is printed. Substantial disagreement indicates a failure of the program.

♦ **newzmat** is dimensioned with conversion of data files between mechanics programs in mind. Thus it can handle thousands of atoms. This can cause problems on very small memory systems due to the very large virtual address space required. If **newzmat** is to be used *only* for manipulating data for *Gaussian 98*, reduce the the parameter MaxNZ in the **newzmat** source file to 20,000 (the limit imposed by *Gaussian 98*), and then rebuild **newzmat**.

testrt

testrt is a utility which takes a standard *Gaussian 98* route as input and produces the equivalent nonstandard route. The route is usually specified on the command line (enclosed in quotation marks):

```
$ testrt "# rhf/sto-3g"
```

If it is not included on the command line, **testrt** will prompt for the route to be tested.

If the specified route is valid, **testrt** will print out the non-standard route corresponding to it. If syntax errors are present, then error messages will be displayed. Thus, **testrt** can be used to verify the syntactic correctness of route sections even by users who understanding nothing of non-standard routes.

Here are some example runs of **testrt**:

```
$ testrt "# qcisd(modredun)/6-31G* scf=driect"
-----------------------------------
 # qcisd(modredun)/6-31G* scf=driect
-----------------------------------
    QPERR ---- A SYNTAX ERROR WAS DETECTED IN THE INPUT LINE.
   # QCISD(ADDREDUNDANT)
            '           ModRedundant is a valid Gaussian 98 option, but is not valid with  QCISD
 ...
```

```
$ testrt "# mp4 stable"
 ...
 Failure in RteDef: Jtype=25, Iprc1=4, MaxDer=0, JP=1, JD=0.
 ...                     Stability calculations are not available for the MP4 method.
```

```
$ testrt
 Please type in the route spec., terminated with a blank line
 # Opt=QST2/6-31G* Test

 1/5=1,18=20,27=202/1,3;
 2/12=2,17=6,18=5/2;
 ...
```

As the first example indicates, only the first error within the route section is flagged. The second example illustrates the error message from an invalid combination of keywords. The final example shows the output from a successful route test.

Note that **testrt** cannot detect keyword usage errors; it checks only the syntax of the given route section. Thus, it will not warn you that including the **MP2** keyword twice within the route section will have unexpected results (running an MP4 job).

testrt's output can be redirected to a file by standard UNIX output redirection:

```
$ testrt "# rhf/sto-3g" >output-file
```

unfchk

This utility is the opposite number to **FormChk**. It converts a formatted checkpoint file to a binary checkpoint file, in a format appropriate to the local computer system:

```
$ unfchk
 Formatted Checkpoint file? water
 Read formatted file water.fchk
 Write checkpoint file water.chk
```

The utility applies the extension .fch to the specified filename on Windows systems and the extensions .fchk on other computer systems.

6

Installation and Configuration

This chapter discusses the general procedures for installing and configuring *Gaussian 98* on UNIX systems. Be sure to check the instructions and release notes accompanying your version of the program for additional or alternate instructions pertaining to your particular computer system.

System Requirements

♦ The *Gaussian 98* directories will require about 120 MB of disk space after the executables have been built.

♦ Sufficient swap space must be available while the program is building: about 128 MB on the RS/6000, for example.

♦ About 64 MB of swap space should be available for each *Gaussian 98* job executing simultaneously using the default dynamic memory allocation of 48 MB. Of course, additional swap space will be required if more memory is requested in a job by using the **%Mem** Link 0 command, or via the **-M-** command in the **Default.Route** file.

♦ Refer to the distribution handout which comes with the tape, or contact Gaussian, Inc. for specific operating system and compiler requirements.

♦ The build system uses native compilers and the UNIX **make** facility. It *will not work* with the GNU version of **make** except under Intel Linux (where the GNU utilities are native).

Installing *Gaussian 98*

The UNIX distribution tape contains a single **tar** format archive, and it can be read using the **tar** command. For example, the following commands will extract the files from the tape in drive 1 into the proper directory:

```
$ cd location-for-G98-files
$ tar xvf /dev/rmt1
```

This command will create a directory named **g98** under the current working directory.

Running the Installation Script

Next, execute the *Gaussian 98* installation script, using these C shell commands:

```
$  /bin/csh                        Change to the C shell if necessary ...
%  cd location-for-G98-files-as-above
%  setenv g98root 'pwd'
%  cd $g98root/g98
%  chmod +x bsd/install
%  bsd/install
```

If the tape is a binary distribution tape, the program is now ready to run. If it is a source tape, the program should be compiled, using the **bldg98** script:

```
%  bsd/bldg98 >& bldg98.log &
```

This will start the compilation in the background, which will take from minutes to hours to complete (depending on computer speed). Use the UNIX **jobs** command to monitor the job periodically as it runs. You may also examine the log file, bldg98.log, for errors and status messages.

Refer to the distribution handout which comes with the tape, or contact Gaussian, Inc. for operating system and compiler requirements. The build system uses native compilers and the UNIX **make** facility. It *will not work* with the GNU version of **make** except on Linux systems for which it is the native facility.

Setting Up the *Gaussian 98* Execution Environment

Gaussian 98 locates executables and creates scratch files in directories specified by several environment variables. However, the user is responsible for creating two of them:

♦ g98root: Indicates the directory where the g98 directory resides (i.e., the directory above **g98**).

♦ GAUSS_SCRDIR: Indicates the directory which should be used for scratch files.

The *Gaussian 98* initialization files are responsible for initializing other aliases and environment variables as needed (see chapter 2). On-line help for the input and commands to the programs is provided by the **ghelp** utility (as described in chapter 5).

All *Gaussian 98* users need to execute the appropriate *Gaussian 98* initialization file within their UNIX shell-specific initialization file (as discussed in chapter 2).

The environment variables created by g98.**login** and g98.**profile** include:

♦ GAUSS_EXEDIR: **S**pecifies the directories in which the *Gaussian 98* images are stored. By default it includes the main directory $g98root/g98 and several alternate directories.

- ♦ GAUSS_ARCHDIR: Specifies the directory in which the main site-wide archive file is kept, and into which temporary archive files should be placed if the main archive is unavailable. It defaults to $g98root/g98/arch if unset.

- ♦ G98BASIS: The directory which contains files specifying the standard *Gaussian 98* internally stored basis sets, as well as some additional basis sets in the form of general basis set input. This environment variable is provided for convenience and is designed for use with the @ include mechanism (see chapter 3).

Scratch File Considerations

On UNIX systems, *Gaussian 98* generates unique scratch file names based on the process ID when no name has been specified by the user. This mechanism is designed to allow multiple *Gaussian 98* jobs to execute simultaneously using a common scratch directory.

Scratch files are deleted automatically when a job completes successfully or dies cleanly by default. However, scratch files are not deleted when a job is killed externally or otherwise terminates abnormally. Consequently, leftover files may accumulate in the scratch directory.

An easy method for avoiding excessive clutter is to have all users share a common scratch directory, and to have that scratch directory cleared at system boot time by adding an **rm** command to the appropriate system boot script (e.g., /etc/rc). If the NQS batch system is in use, clearing the scratch directory should also be done before NQS is started, ensuring that no jobs are using the directory when it is cleared.

Running *Gaussian 98* Test Jobs

An extensive set of test jobs for *Gaussian 98* are provided, along with their corresponding output files. The input files are found in directory $g98root/g98/tests/com. Output files are in a separate subdirectory under $g98root/g98/tests for each machine, such as tests/rs6k for the RS/6000 files. A command file is provided which runs ranges of test jobs automatically (described below).

We recommend that you run a few of the test jobs to verify that the program has been built correctly. However, it is not usually necessary to run the entire test suite. Test job input files have names of the form test*nnn*.com. Tests 1, 28, 94, 155, 194, 296, and 302 cover a range of *Gaussian 98* capabilities. Note that some test jobs are intended for fast hardware and are quite expensive on smaller, slower computer systems. The file $g98root/g98/tests/tests.idx lists what each test job does, and the reference output files provided with *Gaussian 98* indicate how long the jobs can be expected to take. You can extract this information using the following commands:

```
$ cd $G98root/G98/tests/system-name
$ grep "cpu time" *.log
```

The script $g98root/g98/tests/submit.csh can be used to run test jobs. It accepts two parameters: the numbers of the first and last jobs to run (by default, all of the tests are run). Note that you should run the test jobs from a separate directory to prevent them from clobbering the reference output.

If you choose to run some or all of the *Gaussian 98* test jobs, you will need to make sure that they run with the program's built-in default settings. Therefore, you'll need to rename both the site-wide **Default.Route** file (located in the $g98root/g98 directory) as well as any individual version of the defaults file that you may have prior to running any test job. Note that certain settings in this file can cause some test jobs to fail.

The following commands illustrate the recommended procedure for running a test job, using the directory /chem/newtests as the test job executor area and test job 28 as an example:

```
$ mkdir /chem/newtests; cd /chem/newtests
$ ln -s $g98root/g98/tests/com .
$ mkdir system-name; cd system-name
$ g98 ../com/test028.com ./ &
```

system-name is returned by the utility **gau-machine** on all UNIX platforms. It is a keyword corresponding to the type of computer on which you are running.

After the test job finishes, verify that it completed successfully. Then, compare its current output with the reference output using the UNIX **diff** command. For example:

```
$ diff test028.log $g98root/g98/tests/system-name
```

The differences that appear should be limited to non-substantive items.

Procedure for Building *Gaussian 98* Individual Links

If you want to build an individual *Gaussian 98* link at some later point, then you must do so from the C shell. For example, you would use these commands to build Link 502:

```
$ /bin/csh
% cd $g98root/g98
% source bsd/g98.login
% mg l502.exe
```

Site Customization: The Default.Route File

Depending on the characteristics of a particular computer system, it is sometimes necessary for performance reasons to override some of the defaults built into the program. This can be done by creating a site customization file, named **Default.Route** and residing in $g98root/g98.

The following sections describe the types of information which can be supplied in the defaults file.

Route Defaults

These parameters are introduced by −#− and have the same form as normal route section commands. For example, this line will set the default SCF algorithm to the conventional (non-direct) algorithm:

```
-#- SCF=Conventional
```

There may be more than one −#− line in the file.

Commands listed in **Default.Route** change only the defaults; they are overridden by anything specified in the route section of an input file. Thus, if the **Default.Route** contains:

```
-#- MP2=NoDirect
```

and the route section contains:

```
# MP2 ...
```

then the conventional MP2 algorithm will be used. However, if the route section contains:

```
# MP2=Direct
```

then the direct algorithm will be used.

All sites will want to specify the amount of scratch disk space available via the **MaxDisk** keyword in the **Default.Route** file. For example, the following line sets **MaxDisk** to 800 MB:

```
-#- MaxDisk=800MB
```

This line will have the effect of limiting disk usage in the semi-direct algorithms to the specified amount. Some suitable limit should be defined for your configuration. Keep in mind that the more disk space is available, the faster the evaluation, especially for MP2.

Default.Route Limitations

Not all route section keywords are honored in the **Default.Route** file. In general, the rule is that only options which do not affect the outcome of a calculation (i.e., do not change the values of any predicted quantities) are allowed in the file. Thus, **SCF=Conven**, which changes only the integral storage algorithm, will be honored, while **Int(Grid=3)**, which affects the results of many kinds of calculations, will be ignored.

Rename Existing Default.Route File Before Running Test Jobs

If you choose to run some or all of the *Gaussian* 98 test jobs, you will need to make sure that they run with the program's built-in default settings. Therefore, you'll need to rename both the site-wide **Default.Route** file (located in the **$g98root/g98** directory) as well as any individual version of the defaults file that you may have prior to running any test job. Note that certain settings in this file can cause some test jobs to fail.

Memory Defaults

It is often the case that *Gaussian 98* jobs which unwisely use excessive memory can cause severe difficulties on the system. The **−M−** directive enforces a default dynamic memory limit. For example, the following line sets default memory use to 32 MB:

```
-M- 4000000
```

Note that this limit can be bypassed with the **%Mem** Link 0 command. The value may also be followed by **KB**, **MB**, **GB**, **KW**, **MW** or **GW** to indicate units other than words. The default memory size is 6 MW.

Number of Processors

If your computer system has multiple processors, and parallel processing is supported in your version of *Gaussian 98*, you may specify the default number of processors to use in the **Default.Route** file. For example, the following command sets the default number of processors to 4:

```
-P- 4
```

Normally, the program defaults to execution on only a single processor. The **%NProc** Link 0 command can be used to override the default for a specific job. Clearly, the number of processors requested should not exceed the number of processors available, or a substantial decrease in performance will result.

Site Name

The site name may be specified by the directive, which sets -S- as the site name to be used in archive entries generated by *Gaussian 98*. The default site name is **GINC**. For example, the following line sets the site name to **EXPCONS**:

```
-S- EXPCONS
```

Typical Default Settings

Here are reasonable default settings for various machine configurations:

♦ For a small workstation with 64 MB memory and 1 GB of disk, the default algorithms and memory allocation are fine. **MaxDisk** is all that need be specified.

```
-#- MaxDisk=400MB
```

♦ On a powerful workstation with 8 processors and 128 MB of memory, being used for large jobs, 4 processors should be used by default (2 jobs on 4 processors each gives better throughput than one 8 processor job). Also, more memory should be given to each job:

```
-M- 16MW
-#- MaxDisk=400MB
```

- On a Pentium PC with 32 MB of memory and 500 MB of available disk space, the following directives are recommended:

```
-M- 2MW
-#- MaxDisk=500MB
```

- On a 486 PC with 16 MB of memory and 160 MB of available disk space, the following directives are recommended:

```
-M- 500KW
-#- Tran=(Conven,Old2PDM) SCF=Conven
-#- Int=(Rys1E,Rys2E,Berny,DSRys)
-#- MaxDisk=150MB
```

Note that the name of the *Gaussian 98* defaults file is **Default.Rou** on the PC.

User Defaults Files

Gaussian 98 users may set their own defaults by creating their own **Default.Route** file. *Gaussian 98* checks the current working directory for a file of this name when a job is initiated. Settings in the local file take precedence over those in the site-wide file, and options specified in the route section of the job take precedence over both of them.

A

Summary of Changes Between *Gaussian 98* and *Gaussian 94*

This section briefly summarizes the major differences between *Gaussian 98* and *Gaussian 94*. See earlier sections of the manual for full details on these features.

New Methods and Features

- Vibrational circular dichroism intensities.
- MP2 and DFT Raman intensities.
- Enhanced version of the Polarized Continuum (overlapping spheres) model (PCM) of Tomasi and coworkers for SCRF solvent effects.
- Trajectory calculations.
- Reaction path optimizations.
- The ONIOM facility of Morokuma and coworkers.
- ZINDO and TD excited state energies.
- The IRCMax method for locating/optimizing transition states.
- Molecular mechanics methods using the AMBER, DREIDING and UFF force fields.
- Additional DFT functionals:
    - Exchange functionals: Perdew-Wang 91, Barone's modification of PW91 and Gill 96.
    - Correlation functional: Becke 96.
    - Hybrid functionals: Becke's 1996 one-parameter hybrid functional along with several variations due to Barone and Adamo.
- NMR calculations at the MP2 level.
- **ModRedundant** style changes to the geometry in the input stream are now permitted via **Geom=ModRedundant**.
- Forces, optimizations and frequencies with background point charges.
- Analytic ECP second derivatives.
- Transparent handling of linear dependencies in basis sets.
- Very general choices for internal coordinates in geometry optimizations.
- Additional basis sets: Davidson's modified cc-pDVZ, Stuttgart/Dresden ECP's, MIDI!, Ahlrich's SV, SVP and TZV basis sets, extended atom range for the Stevens/Basch/Krauss ECP pseudopotential and basis set.

Efficiency Improvements

♦ CASSCF calculations may now use an active space of up to 12 orbitals. CASSCF calculations may now use Davidson diagonalization in addition to Lanczos and full diagonalization.

♦ MP2 frequencies require less disk and obey **MaxDisk** more often.

♦ DFT frequencies speed improvements.

♦ Improved efficiency of parallel Hartree-Fock and DFT calculations.

♦ Linearly-scaling performance for large semi-empirical and DFT calculations via the fast multipole method (FMM) and sparse matrix techniques.

Functional Differences Between *Gaussian 98* and *Gaussian 94*

♦ The default memory amount in G98 is 6MW.

♦ **Opt=QST2** and **QST3** input now require a set of redundant internal coordinate modifications following each geometry specification when the **ModRedundant** option is also specified.

♦ The syntax for specifying modifications to redundant internal coordinates has been enhanced.

♦ The PCM method in *Gaussian 94* has been replaced by the code of Tomasi and coworkers. The previous facility is deprecated, but it may be accessed for retrospective comparative purposes using the **SCRF=OldPCM** keyword.

♦ The new **SCF=FON** facility is the default procedure.

♦ The **Charge** keyword now respects the units set by the **Units** keyword.

♦ Charges are now specified in the input orientation.

♦ Stratmann-Scuseria weights are the default for DFT integration.

♦ The **cc-pV*Z** basis sets have had duplicate functions removed and have been rotated [270] in order to increase computational efficiency. As so altered, they produce identical energetic results to the **cc*** basis sets in *Gaussian 94*, but they no longer match those made available on the world wide web by Dunning and coworkers.

♦ MP3, MP4, QCISD, CCSD, QCISD(T), and CCSD(T) calculations all now look at **Maxdisk**. It is *crucial* for a value for MaxDisk to be specified explicitly for these types of jobs, either within the route section or via a system wide setting in the **Default.Route** file. If **MaxDisk** is left unset, the program now assumes that disk is abundant and performs a full transformation by default, in contrast to *Gaussian 94* where a partial transformation was the default in such cases. If **MaxDisk** is not set and sufficient disk space is not available for a full transformation, the job will fail (where it may have worked in G94).

B

Program Limitations

This appendix outlines the various size limitations that exist within *Gaussian 98*. These limitations occur in the form of fixed dimension statements and algorithm design limitations, and their overall effect is to limit the size and types of calculation that can be performed.

Z-matrix Limitations

There are restrictions on the size of a Z-matrix, the maximum number of variables and the maximum number of atoms within a calculation. These are set consistently for a maximum of 20000 real atoms (including ghost but not dummy atoms), and a maximum of 20000 Z-matrix centers (atoms, ghost atoms, and dummy atoms). In addition, the maximum number of variables that can be specified in an optimization is unlimited for Berny optimizations but must not exceed 50 for Murtaugh-Sargent or **Opt=EF** optimizations (30 for Fletcher-Powell optimizations).

Basis Set Limitations

Throughout the *Gaussian 98* system, basis set limitations manifest themselves in two ways. The main restriction is imposed within the integral evaluation programs and limits the number of primitive gaussian functions and how they are combined into atomic orbital basis functions. Secondly, dimensioning requirements limit the total number of basis functions that can be used in a few of the older of the energy evaluation procedures.

Integral Program Limitations

To understand fully the limitations in the integral programs, the reader must have some understanding of the concepts presented in discussion of the **Gen** keyword in chapter 3 (input of non-standard bases). In the terminology introduced there, the limitations are as follows: the maximum total number of primitive shells is 60000; the maximum number of primitive d-shells is 20000; the maximum number of primitive f-shells and higher is 20000; the maximum number of contracted shells is 20000. The maximum degree-of-contraction allowed is 100.

The other major restriction that appears in the integral programs is in the manner in which integral labels are packed. These limits apply only when two-electron integrals are written out and can be avoided entirely by using **SCF=Direct** (which is the default in *Gaussian 98*). Normally, disk space limitations force the use of direct methods before the following limits are reached.

When the conventional integral storage procedure is selected (in contrast to the Raffenetti ("PK") storage modes [397]), the suffixes μ, ν, λ, and σ of the two-electron integral $(\mu\nu|\lambda\sigma)$ are packed into a computer word as 8-bit quantities in the UNIX version, and as 16-bit quantities in the UniCOS version. This in effect limits the number of basis functions to 255 under UNIX and to 65,535 on the Cray (the latter is not much of a limitation!) for conventional calculations in this mode. When the Raffenetti modes are selected (for **SCF=Conventional** except when **Tran=Conventional**, **Stable=Complex**, or **CASSCF** is also specified), the two linearized suffixes $(\mu\nu)$ and $(\lambda\sigma)$ (where $(\mu\nu =(\mu(\mu-1)/2)+\nu)$ are packed into a word. This imposes a theoretical limit of 361 basis functions for conventional calculations on the 32-bit computer systems. *These limits do not apply to direct calculations.*

SCF and Post-SCF Limitations

There are only a few other links which have additional dimensioning limits. There is no further restriction for RHF, UHF, ROHF, DFT, MP, CI, QCISD, CC, or BD calculations using the default algorithms. Complex HF calculations are limited to 180 basis functions, and complex MP2 calculations are effectively limited by a requirement of $O(N^3)$ words of main memory, and are also limited to f functions. The **AIM** properties facility is restricted to spd functions if the **Tight** option is selected. The GVB program is limited to 100 paired orbitals, which is not a restriction in practice.

The remaining restrictions are in some of alternative programs which must be specifically requested. **SCF=DM** is limited to 255 basis functions, although the preferred **SCF=QC** can be used with direct SCF and imposes no dimensioning limits. Link 903 (in-core MP2) requires $O(N^3)$ words of main memory.

C

Constructing Z-Matrices

This appendix presents a brief overview of traditional Z-matrix descriptions of molecular systems.

Using Internal Coordinates

Each line of a Z-matrix gives the internal coordinates for one of the atoms within the molecule. The most-used Z-matrix format uses the following syntax:

Element-label, atom 1, bond-length, atom 2, bond-angle, atom 3, dihedral-angle [*,format-code*]

Although these examples use commas to separate items within a line, any valid separator may be used. *Element-label* is a character string consisting of either the chemical symbol for the atom or its atomic number. If the elemental symbol is used, it may be optionally followed by other alphanumeric characters to create an identifying label for that atom. A common practice is to follow the element name with a secondary identifying integer: C1, C2, etc.

Atom1, atom2, atom3 are the labels for previously-specified atoms and are used to define the current atoms' position. Alternatively, the other atoms' line numbers within the molecule specification section may be used for the values of variables, where the charge and spin multiplicity line is line 0.

The position of the current atom is then specified by giving the length of the bond joining it to *atom1*, the angle formed by this bond and the bond joining *atom1* and *atom2*, and the dihedral (torsion) angle formed by the plane containing *atom1*, *atom2* and *atom3* with the plane containing the current atom, *atom1* and *atom2*. Note that bond angles must be in the range $0° < angle < 180°$. Dihedral angles may take on any value.

The optional *format-code* parameter specifies the format of the Z-matrix input. For the syntax being described here, this code is always **0**. This code is needed only when additional parameters follow the normal Z-matrix specification data, as in an ONIOM calculation.

As an initial example, consider hydrogen peroxide. A Z-matrix for this structure would be:

```
H
O 1 0.9
O 2 1.4 1 105.0
H 3 0.9 2 105.0 1 120.0
```

The first line of the Z-matrix simply specifies a hydrogen. The next line lists an oxygen atom and specifies the internuclear distance between it and the hydrogen as 0.9 Angstroms. The third line defines another oxygen with an O-O distance of 1.4 Angstroms (i.e., from atom 2, the other oxygen) and having an O-O-H angle (with atoms 2 and 1) of 105 degrees. The fourth and final line is the only one for which all three internal coordinates need be given. It defines the other hydrogen as bonded to the second oxygen with an H-O distance of 0.9 Angstroms, an H-O-O angle of 105 degrees and a H-O-O-H dihedral angle of 120 degrees.

Variables may be used to specify some or all of the values within the Z-matrix. Here is another version of the previous Z-matrix:

```
H
O  1  R1
O  2  R2  1  A
H  3  R1  2  A  1  D
   Variables:
R1  0.9
R2  1.4
A  105.0
D  120.0
```

Symmetry constraints on the molecule are reflected in the internal coordinates. The two H-O distances are specified by the same variable, as are the two H-O-O bond angles. When such a Z-matrix is used for a geometry optimization in internal coordinates (**Opt=Z-matrix**), the values of the variables will be optimized to locate the lowest energy structure. For a full optimization (**FOpt**), the variables are required to be linearly independent and include all degrees of freedom in the molecule. For a partial optimization (**POpt**), variables in a second section (often labeled **Constants:**) are held fixed in value while those in the first section are optimized:

```
   Variables:
R1  0.9
R2  1.4
A  105.0
   Constants:
D  120.0
```

See the examples in the discussion of the **Opt** keyword in chapter 3 for more information about optimizations in internal coordinates.

Mixing Internal and Cartesian Coordinates

We noted in chapter 3 that Cartesian coordinates are a special case of the Z-matrix, as in this example:

```
C    0.00    0.00    0.00
C    0.00    0.00    1.52
H    1.02    0.00   -0.39
H   -0.51   -0.88   -0.39
H   -0.51    0.88   -0.39
H   -1.02    0.00    1.92
H    0.51   -0.88    1.92
H    0.51    0.88    1.92
```

It is also possible to use both internal and Cartesian coordinates within the same Z-matrix, as in this example:

```
O 0 xo  0.   zo
C 0 0.   yc  0.
C 0 0.  -yc  0.
N 0 xn  0.   0.
H 2 r1 3 a1 1  b1
H 2 r2 3 a2 1  b2
H 3 r1 2 a1 1 -b1
H 3 r2 2 a2 1 -b2
H 4 r3 2 a3 3  d3
  Variables:
xo -1.
zo  0.
yc  1.
xn  1.
r1 1.08
r2 1.08
r3 1.02
a1 125.
a2 125.
d3 160.
b1  90.
b2 -90.
```

This Z-matrix has several features worth noting:

◆   The variable names for the Cartesian coordinates are given symbolically in the same manner as for internal coordinate variables.

◆   The integer 0 after the atomic symbol indicates symbolic Cartesian coordinates to follow.

◆   Cartesian coordinates can be related by a sign change just as dihedral angles can.

Alternate Z-matrix Format

An alternative Z-matrix format allows nuclear positions to be specified using two bond angles rather than a bond angle and a dihedral angle. This is indicated by a **1** in an additional field following the second angle (this field defaults to **0**, which indicates a dihedral angle as the third component):

```
C4 O1 0.9 C2 120.3 O2 180.0 0
C5 O1 1.0 C2 110.4 C4 105.4 1
C6 O1 R C2 A1 C3 A2 1
```

The first line uses a dihedral angle while the latter two use a second bond angle.

Using Dummy Atoms

This section will illustrate the use of dummy atoms within Z-matrices, which are represented by the pseudo atomic symbol **X**. The following example illustrates the use of a dummy atom to fix the three-fold axis in C_{3v} ammonia:

```
N
X 1 1.
H 1 nh 2 hnx
H 1 nh 2 hnx 3   120.0
H 1 nh 2 hnx 3  -120.0

nh 1.0
hnx 70.0
```

The position of the dummy on the axis is irrelevant, and the distance 1.0 used could have been replaced by any other positive number. hnx is the angle between an NH bond and the threefold axis.

Here is a Z-matrix for oxirane:

```
X
C1   X halfcc
O    X      ox C1 90.
C2   X halfcc  O 90. C1 180.0
H1 C1       ch  X hcc  O  hcco
H2 C1       ch  X hcc  O -hcco
H3 C2       ch  X hcc  O  hcco
H4 C2       ch  X hcc  O -hcco

halfcc    0.75
ox        1.0
ch        1.08
hcc     130.0
hcco    130.0
```

This example illustrates two points. First, a dummy atom is placed at the center of the C-C bond to help constrain the cco triangle to be isosceles. ox is then the perpendicular distance from O to the C-C bond, and the angles oxc are held at 90 degrees. Second, some of the entries in the Z-matrix are represented by the negative of the dihedral angle variable hcco.

The following examples illustrate the use of dummy atoms for specifying linear bonds. Geometry optimizations in internal coordinates are unable to handle bond angles of 180 degrees which occur in linear molecular fragments, such as acetylene or the C_4 chain in butatriene. Difficulties may also be encountered in nearly linear situations such as ethynyl groups in unsymmetrical molecules. These situations can be avoided by introducing dummy atoms along the angle bisector and using the half-angle as the variable or constant:

```
N
C 1 cn
X 2 1. 1 90.
H 2 ch 3 90. 1 180.

cn 1.20
ch 1.06
```

Similarly, in this Z-matrix intended for a geometry optimization, half represents half of the NCO angle which is expected to be close to linear. Note that a value of half less than 90 degrees corresponds to a cis arrangement:

```
N
C 1 cn
X 2 1. 1 half
O 2 co 3 half 1 180.0
H 4 oh 2  coh 3   0.0

cn 1.20
co 1.3
oh 1.0
half 80.0
coh 105.
```

Using Ghost Atoms

Ghost atoms provide a convenient way to request arbitrary points at which to compute electrostatic properties. They are represented in the Z-matrix by the symbol **Bq** [398]. These points can be specified directly in Cartesian coordinates in the standard orientation. It is sometimes easier to specify the points in internal coordinates, and, since properties are automatically computed at all nuclear coordinates, ghost atoms can be added to the Z-matrix at points of interest.

Ghost atoms may also be used for a counterpoise calculation for an estimate of the magnitude of basis set superposition error (as has been repeatedly shown [399, 400], *counterpoise corrections provide only a crude estimate and not an upper bound on the error*). A counterpoise correction can be achieved by specifying the dimer structure with the atomic symbol for one monomer replaced by a ghost atom. Since ghost atoms have no basis functions by default, they must be explicitly added via the **ExtraBasis** facility or a general basis set. See also the discussion of **Massage** in chapter 3.

Model Builder Geometry Specifications

The model builder is another facility within *Gaussian 98* for quickly specifying certain sorts of molecular systems. It is requested with the **ModelA** or **ModelB** options to the **Geom** keyword, and it requires additional input in a separate section within the job file.

The basic input to the model builder is called a *short formula matrix*, a collection of lines, each of which defines an atom (by atomic symbol) and its connectivity, by up to six more entries. Each of these can be either an integer, which is the number of the line defining another explicitly specified atom to which the current atom is bonded, or an atomic symbol (e.g. H, F) to which the current atom is connected by a terminal bond, or a symbol for a terminal functional group which is bonded to the current atom. The functional groups currently available are OH, NH_2, Me, Et, NPr, IPr, NBu, IBu, and TBu.

The short formula matrix also implicitly defines the rotational geometry about each bond in the following manner. Suppose atoms X and Y are explicitly specified. Then X will appear in row Y and Y will appear in row X. Let *I* be the atom to the right of X in row Y and *J* be the atom to the right of Y in row X. Then atoms *I* and *J* are put in the trans orientation about the X-Y bond. The short formula matrix may be followed by optional lines modifying the generated structure. There are zero or more of each of the following lines, which must be grouped together in the order given here:

AtomGeom,*I,Geom*   Normally the local geometry about an atom is defined by the number and types of bond about the atom (e.g., carbon in methane is tetrahedral, in ethylene is trigonal, etc.). All bond angles at one center must be are equal. The **AtomGeom** line changes the value of the bonds at center *I*. *Geom* may be the angle as a floating point number, or one of the strings **Tetr**, **Pyra**, **Trig**, **Bent**, or **Line**.

BondRot,*I,J,K,L,Geom*   This changes the orientations of the *I-J* and *K-L* bonds about the *J-K* bond. *Geom* is either the dihedral angle or one of the strings **Cis** (≥0), **Trans** (≥180), **Gaup** (≥+60), or **Gaum** (≥-60).

BondLen,*I,J,NewLen*   This sets the length of the *I-J* bond to *NewLen* (a floating point value).

The model builder can only build structures with atoms in their normal valencies. If a radical is desired, its extra valence can be "tied down" using dummy atoms, which are specified by a minus sign before the atomic symbol (e.g., -H). Only terminal atoms can be dummy atoms.

The two available models (A and B) differ in that model A takes into account the type (single, double, triple, etc.) of a bond in assigning bond lengths, while model B bond lengths depend only on the types of the atoms involved. Model B is available for all atoms from H to Cl except He and Ne. If Model A is requested and an atom is used for which no Model A bond length is defined, the appropriate Model B bond length is used instead.

D

Additional Keywords

This appendix lists three types of keywords not included in the main discussion in chapter 3:

♦ Obsolete keywords and options for which preferred synonyms exist.
♦ Keywords and options for deprecated features supported for backward compatibility only.
♦ Keywords and options useful to programmers but not recommended for production use.

Each of these classes will be discussed below.

Obsolete Keywords

The following table lists obsolete keywords used by previous versions of *Gaussian*. While all of them are still supported by *Gaussian 98*, we strongly recommend converting to the up-to-date equivalents given in the table.

Obsolete Keyword	Replacement Keyword & Option
Alter	Guess=Alter
BD-T	BD(T)
BeckeHalfandHalf	BHandH
Camp-King	SCF=Camp-King
CCSD-T	CCSD(T)
CubeDensity	Cube=Density
Cube=Divergence	Cube=Laplacian
DIIS	SCF=DIIS
Direct	SCF=Direct
GridDensity	Cube=Density
Guess=Restart	SCF=Restart
NoDIIS	SCF=NoDIIS
NoExtrap	SCF=NoExtrap
NoRaff	Int=NoRaff
Opt=AddRedundant	Opt=ModRedundant
OptCyc=n	Opt(MaxCyc=n)
OSS	GVB(OSS)

Obsolete Keyword	Replacement Keyword & Option
PlotDensity	Cube=Density
Prop=Grid	Cube=Density
QCID	CCD
QCISD-T	QCISD(T)
QCSCF	SCF=QC
Raff	Int=NoRaff
Save	none (Save is a no-op)
SCFCon=n	SCF(Conver=n)
SCFCyc=n	SCF(MaxCyc=n)
SCFDM	SCF=DM
SCFQC	SCF=QC
VShift[=n]	SCF(VShift[=n])

Deprecated Features

CCD+STCCD   Specifies a coupled cluster calculation using double substitutions and evaluation of the contribution of single and triple excitations through fourth order using the CCD wavefunction. It is superseded by **CCSD(T)**. **ST4CCD** is a synonym for **CCD+STCCD**.

CPHF=DirInv   Invert the A-matrix directly. The default is to invert directly whenever possible.

Geom=Coord   Indicates that the geometry specification is in Cartesian coordinates.

LST *and* **LSTCyc**   Requests that an initial guess for a transition structure be generated using Linear Synchronous Transit [401]. The LST procedure locates a maximum along a path connecting two structures and thus provides a guess for the transition structure connecting them. **LST** is not valid with **AM1**.

Note that an LST calculation does not actually locate a proper transition state. However, the structure resulting from an LST calculation may be suitable as input for a subsequent **Opt=TS**.

The LST method has been superseded by **Opt=QST2**.

OldConstants   The latest and most accurate values of physical constants are stored in *Gaussian 98* for conversion between internal quantities (in atomic units) and more common units (these constants are listed inside the back cover of this manual). Between the releases of *Gaussian 86* and *Gaussian 88*, the best estimates of several of these constants changed more than had been previously expected.

In order to facilitate reproducing values produced with earlier versions of the program, the **OldConstants** keyword requests the values of physical constants used in *Gaussian 86*. Note that **OldConstants** should *not* be used for *any other purpose*. **NewConstants** is the opposite to **OldConstants** and is the default. **OldPhyCon** is a synonym for **OldConstants**, and **NewPhyCon** is a synonym for **NewConstants**.

Opt=EnOnly   Requests an optimization using a pseudo-Newton-Raphson method with a fixed Hessian and numerical differentiation of energies to produce gradients. This option requires that the Hessian be read in via **ReadFC** or **RCFC**. It can be used to locate transition structures and higher saddle points. It is the default for transition state optimizations using methods for which analytic gradients are not available, although **EF** is a good alternative.

Opt=FP   Requests the Fletcher-Powell optimization algorithm [123], which does not require analytic gradients.

Opt=Grad   Requests a gradient optimization, using the default method unless another option is specified. This is the default whenever analytic gradients are available and is invalid otherwise.

Opt=MNDOFC   Requests that the MNDO (or AM1, if possible) force constants be computed and used to start the (presumably ab initio) optimization.

Opt=MS   Specifies the Murtaugh-Sargent optimization algorithm [124]. The Murtaugh-Sargent optimization method is an obsolete alternative, and is retained in *Gaussian 98* only for backwards compatibility.

Opt=StarOnly Specifies that the specified force constants are to be estimated numerically but that no optimization is to be done. This has *nothing* to do with computation of vibrational frequencies. In order to pass force constants estimated in this way to the Murtaugh-Sargent program, it is necessary to do one run with **Opt=StarOnly** to produce the force constants, and then run the actual optimization with **Opt(MS,ReadFC)**.

Opt=UnitFC   Requests that a unit matrix be used instead of the usual valence force field guess for the Hessian.

SCRF=OldPCM   The PCM model present in *Gaussian 94* may be accessed using this option to **SCRF**. It requires the dielectric constant of the solvent and the number of points per sphere as input. The radii of the spheres may optionally be specified for each atom type by including the **ReadRadii** option. Alternate radii for each atom for use in fitting potentials may be input via the **ReadAtRadii** option.

%SCR   Used to specify the location of the .SCR scratch file.

Program Development-Related Keywords

The following keywords, useful for developing new methods and other debugging purposes, but not recommended for production level calculations, are described in the *Gaussian 98 Programmer's Reference*.

♦   **ExtraLinks**
♦   **ExtraOverlays**

- **FullCI**
- **IOp2** and its synonyms **MDV** and **Core**
- **IOp33**
- **Restart**
- **Skip**
- **Use**

The *Gaussian 98 Programmer's Reference* also documents all internal options (**IOp**s). They are also documented on our web site: www.gaussian.com/iops.htm.

References

1   W. J. Hehre, W. A. Lathan, R. Ditchfield, M. D. Newton and J. A. Pople, *Gaussian 70* (Quantum Chemistry Program Exchange, Program No. 237, 1970).

2   J. S. Binkley, R. A. Whiteside, P. C. Hariharan, R. Seeger, J. A. Pople, W. J. Hehre and M. D. Newton, *Gaussian 76* (Carnegie-Mellon University, Pittsburgh, PA, 1976).

3   J. S. Binkley, R. A. Whiteside, R. Krishnan, R. Seeger, D. J. Defrees, H. B. Schlegel, S. Topiol, L. R. Kahn and J. A. Pople, *Gaussian 80* (Carnegie-Mellon Quantum Chemistry Publishing Unit, Pittsburgh, PA, 1980).

4   J. S. Binkley, M. J. Frisch, D. J. Defrees, R. Krishnan, R. A. Whiteside, H. B. Schlegel, E. M. Fluder and J. A. Pople, *Gaussian 82* (Carnegie-Mellon Quantum Chemistry Publishing Unit, Pittsburgh, PA, 1982).

5   M. J. Frisch, J. S. Binkley, H. B. Schlegel, K. Raghavachari, C. F. Melius, R. L. Martin, J. J. P. Stewart, F. W. Bobrowicz, C. M. Rohlfing, L. R. Kahn, D. J. Defrees, R. Seeger, R. A. Whiteside, D. J. Fox, E. M. Fluder and J. A. Pople, *Gaussian 86* (Gaussian, Inc., Pittsburgh, PA, 1986).

6   M. J. Frisch, M. Head-Gordon, H. B. Schlegel, K. Raghavachari, J. S. Binkley, C. Gonzalez, D. J. Defrees, D. J. Fox, R. A. Whiteside, R. Seeger, C. F. Melius, J. Baker, L. R. Kahn, J. J. P. Stewart, E. M. Fluder, S. Topiol and J. A. Pople, *Gaussian 88* (Gaussian, Inc., Pittsburgh, PA, 1988).

7   M. J. Frisch, M. Head-Gordon, G. W. Trucks, J. B. Foresman, K. Raghavachari, H. B. Schlegel, M. Robb, J. S. Binkley, C. Gonzalez, D. J. Defrees, D. J. Fox, R. A. Whiteside, R. Seeger, C. F. Melius, J. Baker, L. R. Kahn, J. J. P. Stewart, E. M. Fluder, S. Topiol and J. A. Pople, *Gaussian 90* (Gaussian, Inc., Pittsburgh, PA, 1990).

8   M. J. Frisch, G. W. Trucks, M. Head-Gordon, P. M. W. Gill, M. W. Wong, J. B. Foresman, B. G. Johnson, H. B. Schlegel, M. A. Robb, E. S. Replogle, R. Gomperts, J. L. Andres, K. Raghavachari, J. S. Binkley, C. Gonzalez, R. L. Martin, D. J. Fox, D. J. Defrees, J. Baker, J. J. P. Stewart and J. A. Pople, *Gaussian 92* (Gaussian, Inc., Pittsburgh, PA, 1992).

9   M. J. Frisch, G. W. Trucks, H. B. Schlegel, P. M. W. Gill, B. G. Johnson, M. W. Wong, J. B. Foresman, M. A. Robb, M. Head-Gordon, E. S. Replogle, R. Gomperts, J. L. Andres, K. Raghavachari, J. S. Binkley, C. Gonzalez, R. L. Martin, D. J. Fox, D. J. Defrees, J. Baker, J. J. P. Stewart and J. A. Pople, *Gaussian 92/DFT* (Gaussian, Inc., Pittsburgh, PA, 1993).

10 M. J. Frisch, G. W. Trucks, H. B. Schlegel, P. M. W. Gill, B. G. Johnson, M. A. Robb, J. R. Cheeseman, T. A. Keith, G. A. Petersson, J. A. Montgomery, K. Raghavachari, M. A. Al-Laham, V. G. Zakrzewski, J. V. Ortiz, J. B. Foresman, J. Cioslowski, B. B. Stefanov, A. Nanayakkara, M. Challacombe, C. Y. Peng, P. Y. Ayala, W. Chen, M. W. Wong, J. L. Andres, E. S. Replogle, R. Gomperts, R. L. Martin, D. J. Fox, J. S. Binkley, D. J. Defrees, J. Baker, J. P. Stewart, M. Head-Gordon, C. Gonzalez and J. A. Pople, *Gaussian 94* (Gaussian, Inc., Pittsburgh, PA, 1995).

11 J. E. Carpenter and F. Weinhold, *J. Mol. Struct. (Theochem)* **169**, 41 (1988).

12 J. E. Carpenter, PhD thesis, University of Wisconsin (Madison, WI), 1987 .

13 J. P. Foster and F. Weinhold, *J. Amer. Chem. Soc.* **102**, 7211 (1980).

14 A. E. Reed and F. Weinhold, *J. Chem. Phys.* **78**, 4066 (1983).

15 A. E. Reed and F. Weinhold, *J. Chem. Phys.*, 1736 (1983).

16 A. E. Reed, R. B. Weinstock and F. Weinhold, *J. Chem. Phys.* **83**, 735 (1985).

17 A. E. Reed, L. A. Curtiss and F. Weinhold, *Chem. Rev.* **88**, 899 (1988).

18   F. Weinhold and J. E. Carpenter, "The Structure of Small Molecules and Ions," *Plenum*, 227 (1988).

19   M. J. Frisch, M. Head-Gordon and J. A. Pople, *J. Chem. Phys.* **141**, 189 (1990).

20   M. Head-Gordon, J. A. Pople and M. J. Frisch, *Chem. Phys. Lett.* **153**, 503 (1988).

21   M. J. Frisch, M. Head-Gordon and J. A. Pople, *Chem. Phys. Lett.* **166**, 275 (1990).

22   M. J. Frisch, M. Head-Gordon and J. A. Pople, *Chem. Phys. Lett.* **166**, 281 (1990).

23   J. Almloff, K. Korsell and K. Faegri, Jr., *J. Comp. Chem.* **3**, 385 (1982).

24   M. Head-Gordon and T. Head-Gordon, "Analytic MP2 Frequencies Without Fifth Order Storage: Theory and Application to Bifurcated Hydrogen Bonds in the Water Hexamer," *Chem. Phys. Lett.* **220**, 122 (1994).

25   G. W. Trucks, M. J. Frisch, J. L. Andres and H. B. Schlegel, "An Efficient Theory and Implementation of MP2 Second Derivatives," in prep. (1998).

26   M. Head-Gordon and J. A. Pople, "A Method for Two-Electron Gaussian Integral and Integral Derivative Evaluation Using Recurrence Relations," *J. Chem. Phys.* **89**, 5777 (1988).

27   P. M. W. Gill, "Molecular Integrals over Gaussian Basis Functions," *Adv. Quant. Chem.* **25**, 143 (1994).

28   P. R. Taylor, *Int. J. Quant. Chem.* **31**, 521 (1987).

29   J. M. Millam and G. E. Scuseria, *J. Chem. Phys.* **106**, 5569 (1997).

30   J. C. Burant, G. E. Scuseria and M. J. Frisch, *J. Chem. Phys.* **195**, 8969 (1996).

31   J. C. Burant, M. C. Strain, G. E. Scuseria and M. J. Frisch, "Kohn-Sham Analytic Energy Second Derivatives with the Gaussian Very Fast Multipole Method (GvFMM)," *CPL* **258**, 45 (1996).

32   J. C. Burant, M. C. Strain, G. E. Scuseria and M. J. Frisch, "Analytic Energy Gradients for the Gaussian Very Fast Multipole Method (GvFMM)," *Chem. Phys. Lett.* **248**, 43 (1996).

33   M. C. Strain, G. E. Scuseria and M. J. Frisch, "Achieving Linear Scaling for the Electronic Quantum Coulomb Problem," *Science* **271**, 51 (1996).

34   A. D. Daniels, J. M. Millam and G. E. Scuseria, "Semiempirical methods with conjugate gradient density matrix search to replace diagonalization for molecular systems containing thousands of atoms," *J. Chem. Phys.* **107**, 425 (1997).

35   W. D. Cornell, P. Cieplak, C. I. Bayly, I. R. Gould, K. M. Merz Jr., D. M. Ferguson, D. C. Spellmeyer, T. Fox, J. W. Caldwell and P. A. Kollman, *J. Am. Chem. Soc.* **117**, 5179 (1995).

36   S. L. Mayo, B. D. Olafson and W. A. Goddard, *J. Phys. Chem.* **94**, 8897 (1990).

37   A. K. Rappé, C. J. Casewit, K. S. Colwell, W. A. Goddard III and W. M. Skiff, *J. Am. Chem. Soc.* **114**, 10024 (1992).

38   A. K. Rappé and W. A. Goddard III, *J. Phys. Chem.* **95**, 3358 (1991).

39   G. Segal and J. Pople, *J. Chem. Phys.* **44**, 3289 (1966).

40   J. A. Pople, D. Beveridge and P. Dobosh, *J. Chem. Phys.* **47**, 2026 (1967).

41   M. Dewar and W. Thiel, *J. Amer. Chem. Soc.* **99**, 4499 (1977).

42   R. C. Bingham and M. Dewar, *J. Am. Chem. Soc.* **97**, 1285 (1975).

43   M. J. S. Dewar and W. Thiel, "Ground States of Molecules. 38. The MNDO Method. Approximations and Parameters," *J. Amer. Chem. Soc.* **99**, 4899 (1977).

44   M. J. S. Dewar and H. S. Rzepa, *J. Am. Chem. Soc.* **100**, 777 (1978).

45   M. J. S. Dewar and M. L. McKee, *J. Comp. Chem.* **4**, 84 (1983).

46   L. P. Davis, et. al., *J. Comp. Chem.* **2**, 433 (1981).

47   M. J. S. Dewar, M. L. McKee and H. S. Rzepa, *J. Am. Chem. Soc.* **100**, 3607 (1978).

48   M. J. S. Dewar and E. F. Healy, *J. Comp. Chem.* **4**, 542 (1983).

49   M. J. S. Dewar, G. L. Grady and J. J. P. Stewart, *J. Am. Chem. Soc.* **106**, 6771 (1984).

50   M. J. S. Dewar, et. al., *Organometallics* **4**, 1964 (1985).

51   M. J. S. Dewar, E. G. Zoebisch and E. F. Healy, "AM1: A New General Purpose Quantum Mechanical Molecular Model," *J. Amer. Chem. Soc.* **107**, 3902 (1985).

52   M. J. S. Dewar and C. H. Reynolds, *J. Comp. Chem.* **2**, 140 (1986).

53   J. J. P. Stewart, *J. Comp. Chem.* **10**, 209 (1989).

54   J. J. P. Stewart, *J. Comp. Chem.* **10**, 221 (1989).

55   C. C. J. Roothan, "New Developments in Molecular Orbital Theory," *Rev. Mod. Phys.* **23**, 69 (1951).

56   J. A. Pople and R. K. Nesbet, "Self-Consistent Orbitals for Radicals," *J. Chem. Phys.* **22**, 571 (1954).

57   R. McWeeny and G. Dierksen, *J. Chem. Phys.* **49**, 4852 (1968).

58   C. Møller and M. S. Plesset, *Phys. Rev.* **46**, 618 (1934).

59   J. A. Pople, R. Seeger and R. Krishnan, "Variational Configuration Interaction Methods and Comparison with Perturbation Theory," *Int. J. Quant. Chem. Symp.* **11**, 149 (1977).

60   R. Krishnan and J. A. Pople, *Int. J. Quant. Chem.* **14**, 91 (1978).

61   R. Krishnan, M. J. Frisch and J. A. Pople, "Contribution of triple substitutions to the electron correlation energy in fourth-order perturbation theory," *J. Chem. Phys.* **72**, 4244 (1980).

62   K. Raghavachari, J. A. Pople, E. S. Replogle and M. Head-Gordon, "Fifth-Order Møller-Plesset Perturbation Theory: Comparison of Existing Correlation Methods and Implementation of New Methods Correct to Fifth-Order," *J. Phys. Chem.* **94**, 5579 (1990).

63   S. Saebo and J. Almlof, *Chem. Phys. Lett.* **154**, 83 (1989).

64   J. A. Pople, J. S. Binkley and R. Seeger, "Theoretical Models Incorporating Electron Correlation," *Int. J. Quant. Chem. Symp.* **10**, 1 (1976).

65   J. A. Pople, R. Krishnan, H. B. Schlegel and J. S. Binkley, "Electron Correlation Theories and Their Application to the Study of Simple Reaction Potential Surfaces," *Int. J. Quant. Chem.* **XIV**, 545 (1978).

66   J. Cizek, *Adv. Chem. Phys.* **14**, 35 (1969).

67   G. D. Purvis and R. J. Bartlett, *J. Chem. Phys.* **76**, 1910 (1982).

68   G. E. Scuseria, C. L. Janssen and H. F. Schaefer, III, *J. Chem. Phys.* **89**, 7382 (1988).

69   G. E. Scuseria and H. F. Schaefer, III, *J. Chem. Phys.* **90**, 3700 (1989).

70   J. A. Pople, M. Head-Gordon and K. Raghavachari, *J. Chem. Phys.* **87**, 5968 (1987).

71   N. C. Handy, J. A. Pople, M. Head-Gordon, K. Raghavachari and G. W. Trucks, *Chem. Phys. Lett.* **164**, 185 (1989).

72   C. E. Dykstra, *Chem. Phys. Lett.* **45**, 466 (1977).

73   P. Hohenberg and W. Kohn, "Inhomogeneous Electron Gas," *Physical Review* **136**, B864 (1964).

74   W. Kohn and L. J. Sham, "Self-Consistent Equations Including Exchange and Correlation Effects," *Physical Review* **140**, A1133 (1965).

75   J. C. Slater, *Quantum Theory of Molecular and Solids. Vol. 4: The Self-Consistent Field for Molecular and Solids* (McGraw-Hill, New York, 1974).

76   J. A. Pople, P. M. W. Gill and B. G. Johnson, "Kohn-Sham density-functional theory within a finite basis set," *Chemical Physics Letters* **199**, 557 (1992).

77   C. Lee, W. Yang and R. G. Parr, "Development of the Colle-Salvetti correlation-energy formula into a functional of the electron density," *Physical Review B* **37**, 785 (1988).

78   A. D. Becke, *Phys. Rev. A* **38**, 3098 (1988).

79   B. Miehlich, A. Savin, H. Stoll and H. Preuss, *Chem. Phys. Lett.* **157**, 200 (1989).

80   A. D. Becke, "Density-functional thermochemistry. III. The role of exact exchange," *J. Chem. Phys.* **98**, 5648 (1993).

81   A. D. Becke, *J. Chem. Phys.* **104**, 1040 (1996).

82   C. Adamo and V. Barone, *Chem. Phys. Lett.* **274**, 242 (1997).

83   C. Adamo and V. Barone, *J. Comp. Chem.* **19**, 419 (1998).

84   J. A. Pople, M. Head-Gordon, D. J. Fox, K. Raghavachari and L. A. Curtiss, "Gaussian-1 theory: A general procedure for prediction of molecular energies," *J. Chem. Phys.* **90**, 5622 (1989).

85   L. A. Curtiss, C. Jones, G. W. Trucks, K. Raghavachari and J. A. Pople, "Gaussian-1 theory of molecular energies for second-row compounds," *J. Chem. Phys.* **93**, 2537 (1990).

86   L. A. Curtiss, K. Raghavachari, G. W. Trucks and J. A. Pople, "Gaussian-2 theory for molecular energies of first- and second-row compounds," *J. Chem. Phys.* **94**, 7221 (1991).

87   L. A. Curtiss, K. Raghavachari and J. A. Pople, "Gaussian-2 theory using reduced Møller-Plesset orders," *J. Chem. Phys.* **98**, 1293 (1993).

88   M. R. Nyden and G. A. Petersson, "Complete basis set correlation energies. I. The asymptotic convergence of pair natural orbital expansions," *J. Chem. Phys.* **75**, 1843 (1981).

89   G. A. Petersson and M. A. Al-Laham, "A complete basis set model chemistry. II. Open-shell systems and the total energyes of the first-row atoms," *J. Chem. Phys.* **94**, 6081 (1991).

90   G. A. Petersson, T. G. Tensfeldt and J. A. Montgomery Jr., "A complete basis set model chemistry. III. The complete basis set-quadratic configuration interaction family of methods," *J. Chem. Phys.* **94**, 6091 (1991).

91   J. A. Montgomery Jr., J. W. Ochterski and G. A. Petersson, "A complete basis set model chemistry. IV. An improved atomic pair natural orbital method," *J. Chem. Phys.* **101**, 5900 (1994).

92   J. W. Ochterski, G. A. Petersson and J. A. Montgomery Jr., "A complete basis set model chemistry. V. Extensions to six or more heavy atoms," *J. Chem. Phys.* **104**, 2598 (1996).

93   J. A. Montgomery Jr, M. J. Frisch, J. W. Ochterski and G. A. Petersson, "A complete basis set model chemistry. VI. Use of density functional geometries and frequencies," in prep. (1998).

94   D. Hegarty and M. A. Robb, *Mol. Phys.* **38**, 1795 (1979).

95   R. H. E. Eade and M. A. Robb, *Chem. Phys. Lett.* **83**, 362 (1981).

96   J. J. McDouall, K. Peasley and M. A. Robb, "A Simple MC-SCF Perturbation Theory: Orthogonal Valence Bond Møller-Plesset 2 (OVB-MP2)," *Chem. Phys. Lett.* **148**, 183 (1988).

97   E. M. Siegbahn, *Chem. Phys. Lett.* **109**, 417 (1984).

98   M. A. Robb and U. Niazi, *Reports in Molecular Theory* **1**, 23 (1990).

99   F. W. Bobrowicz and W. A. Goddard, III, "The Self-Consistent Field Equations for Generalized Valence Bond and Open-Shell Hartree-Fock Wave Functions," in *Methods of Electronic Structure Theory,* Ed. H. F. Schaefer, III (Plenum, New York, 1977), vol. 3, 79.

100   R. Seeger and J. A. Pople, "Self-Consistent Molecular Orbital Methods. XVIII. Constraints and Stability in Hartree-Fock Theory," *J. Chem. Phys.* **66** (1977).

101   R. Bauernschmitt and R. Ahlrichs, "Stability analysis for solutions of the closed shell Kohn-Sham equation," *J. Chem. Phys.* **104**, 9047 (1996).

102   J. B. Foresman, M. Head-Gordon, J. A. Pople and M. J. Frisch, "Toward a Systematic Molecular Orbital Theory for Excited States," *J. Phys. Chem.* **96**, 135 (1992).

103   R. E. Stratmann, G. E. Scuseria and M. J. Frisch, *J. Chem. Phys.*, submitted (1998).

104   R. Bauernschmitt and R. Ahlrichs, *Chem. Phys. Lett.* **256**, 454 (1996).

105   M. E. Casida, C. Jamorski, K. C. Casida and D. R. Salahub, *J. Chem. Phys.* **108**, 4439 (1998).

106   A. D. Bacon and M. C. Zerner, "An Intermediate Neglect of Differential Overlap Theory for Transition Metal Complexes: Fe, Co, and Cu Chlorides," *Theo. Chim. Acta* **53**, 21 (1979).

107   W. P. Anderson, W. D. Edwards and M. C. Zerner, "Calculated Spectra of Hydrated Ions of the First Transition-Metal   Series," *Inorganic Chem.* **25**, 2728 (1986).

108   M. C. Zerner, G. H. Lowe, R. F. Kirchner and U. T. Mueller-Westerhoff, "An Intermediate Neglect of Differential Overlap Technique   for Spectroscopy of Transition-Metal Complexes. Ferrocene," *J. Am. Chem. Soc.* **102**, 589 (1980).

109   J. E. Ridley and M. C. Zerner, "An Intermediate Neglect of Differential Overlap Technique for Spectroscopy: Pyrrole and the Azines," *Theo. Chim. Acta.* **32**, 111 (1973).

110   J. E. Ridley and M. C. Zerner, "Triplet states via Intermediate Neglect of Differential Overlap: Benzene, Pyridine, and the Diazines," *Theo. Chim. Acta.* **42**, 223 (1976).

111   M. A. Thompson and M. C. Zerner, "The Electronic Structure and Spectroscopy of the Photosynthetic Reaction Center from Rhodopseudomonas viridis," *J. Am. Chem. Soc.* **113**, 8210 (1991).

112   M. C. Zerner, "Semi Empirical Molecular Orbital Methods," in *Reviews of Computational Chemistry,* Ed. K. B. Lipkowitz and D. B. Boyd (VCH Publishing, New York, 1991), vol. 2, 313.

113   M. C. Zerner, P. Correa de Mello and M. Hehenberger, "On the Convergence of the Self Consistent Field Method to Excited States," *Int. J. Quant. Chem.* **21**, 251 (1982).

114   L. K. Hanson, J. Fajer, M. A. Thompson and M. C. Zerner, "Enviromental Effects on the Properties of Bacteriachlorphylls in Photosynthetic Reaction Centers: Theoretical Models," *J. Amer. Chem. Soc.* **109**, 4728 (1987).

115   H. B. Schlegel, "Optimization of Equilibrium Geometries and Transition Structures," *J. Comp. Chem.* **3**, 214 (1982).

116   H. B. Schlegel and M. A. Robb, *Chem. Phys. Lett.* **93**, 43 (1982).

117   F. Bernardi, A. Bottini, J. J. W. McDougall, M. A. Robb and H. B. Schlegel, *Far. Symp. Chem. Soc.* **19**, 137 (1984).

118   J. A. Pople, R. Krishnan, H. B. Schlegel and J. S. Binkley, *Int. J. Quant. Chem., Quant. Chem. Symp.* **13**, 325 (1979).

119   N. C. Handy and H. F. Schaefer, III, *J. Chem. Phys.* **81**, 5031 (1984).

120   G. W. Trucks, E. A. Salter, C. Sosa and R. J. Bartlett, "Theory and Implementation of the MBPT Density Matrix. An Application to One-Electron Properties," *Chem. Phys. Lett.* **147**, 359 (1988).

121   G. W. Trucks, J. D. Watts, E. A. Salter and R. J. Bartlett, "Analytic MBPT(4) Gradients," *Chem. Phys. Lett.* **153**, 490 (1988).

122   R. Krishnan, H. B. Schlegel and J. A. Pople, *J. Chem. Phys.* **72**, 4654 (1980).

123   R. Fletcher and M. J. D. Powell, "A Rapidly Convergent Descent Method for Minimization," *Comput. J.* **6**, 163 (1963).

124   B. A. Murtaugh and R. W. H. Sargent, "Computational Experience with Quadratically Convergent Minimization Methods," *Comput. J.* **13**, 185 (1970).

125   J. Baker, *J. Comp. Chem.* **7**, 385 (1986).

126   J. Baker, *J. Comp. Chem.* **8**, 563 (1987).

127   H. B. Schlegel, in *New Theoretical Concepts for Understanding Organic Reactions,* Ed. J. Bertran (Kluwer Academic, The Netherlands, 1989) 33.

128   C. Peng, P. Y. Ayala, H. B. Schlegel and M. J. Frisch, "Using redundant internal coordinates to optimize geometries and transition states," *J. Comp. Chem.* **17**, 49 (1996).

129   C. Peng and H. B. Schlegel, "Combining Synchronous Transit and Quasi-Newton Methods for Finding Transition States," *Israel J. Chem.* **33**, 449 (1994).

130   C. Gonzalez and H. B. Schlegel, "An Improved Algorithm for Reaction Path Following," *J. Chem. Phys.* **90**, 2154 (1989).

131   C. Gonzalez and H. B. Schlegel, "Reaction Path Following in Mass-Weighted Internal Coordinates," *J. Phys. Chem.* **94**, 5523 (1990).

132   S. Dapprich, I. Komaromi, K. S. Byun, K. Morokuma and M. J. Frisch, "A New ONIOM Implementation for the Calculation of Energies, Gradients and Higher Derivatives Using Mechanical and Electronic Embedding I," *Theo. Chem. Act.*, in prep. (1998).

133   I. Komaromi, S. Dapprich, K. S. Byun, K. Morokuma and M. J. Frisch, "A New ONIOM Implementation for the Calculation of Energies, Gradients and Higher Derivatives Using Mechanical and Electronic Embedding II," *Theo. Chem. Act.*, in prep. (1998).

134   S. Humbel, S. Sieber and K. Morokuma, *J. Chem. Phys.* **105**, 1959 (1996).

135   F. Maseras and K. Morokuma, *J. Comp. Chem.* **16**, 1170 (1995).

136   T. Matsubara, S. Sieber and K. Morokuma, "A Test of the New "Integrated MO + MM" (IMOMM) Method for the Conformational Energy of Ethane and n-Butane," *Int. Journal of Quantum Chemistry* **60**, 1101 (1996).

137   M. Svensson, S. Humbel, R. D. J. Froese, T. Matsubara, S. Sieber and K. Morokuma, *J. Phys. Chem.* **100**, 19357 (1996).

138   P. Y. Ayala and H. B. Schlegel, "A combined method for determining reaction paths, minima and transition state geometries," *J. Chem. Phys* **107**, 375 (1997).

139   M. J. Bearpark, M. A. Robb and H. B. Schlegel, "A Direct Method for the Location of the Lowest Energy Point on a Potential Surface Crossing," *Chem. Phys. Lett.* **223**, 269 (1994).

140   I. N. Ragazos, M. A. Robb, F. Bernardi and M. Olivucci, "Optimization and Characterization of the Lowest Energy Point on a Conical Intersection using an MC-SCF Lagrangian," *Chem. Phys. Lett.* **197**, 217 (1992).

141   F. Bernardi, M. A. Robb and M. Olivucci, *Chem. Soc. Reviews* **25**, 321 (1996).

142   D. K. Malick, G. A. Petersson and J. A. Montgomery Jr., "Transition States for Chemical Reactions. I. Geometry and Barrier Height," *J. Chem. Phys.* **108**, 5704 (1998).

143   B. C. Garrett, D. G. Truhlar, R. S. Grev and A. D. Magnusson, "Improved treatment of threshold contributions in variational transition state theory," *J. Phys. Chem.* **84** (1980).

144   G. A. Petersson, "Complete Basis Set Thermochemistry and Kinetics," in *Computational Thermochemistry,* Ed. K. K. Irikura and D. J. Frurip (Amer. Chem. Soc., Washington, DC, 1998) 237.

145   M. Schwartz, P. Marshall, R. J. Berry, C. J. Ehlers and G. A. Petersson, "Computational Study of the Kinetics of Hydrogen Abstraction from Fluoromethanes by the Hydroxyl Radical," *J. Phys. Chem.*, submitted (1998).

146   G. A. Petersson, D. K. Malick, W. G. Wilson, J. W. Ochterski, J. A. Montgomery Jr. and M. J. Frisch, "Calibration and comparison of the G2, CBS, and DFT methods forcomputational thermochemistry," *J. Chem. Phys.*, submitted (1998).

147   H. Eyring, "The activated complex in chemical reactions," *J. Chem Phys.* **3**, 107 (1935).

148   D. G. Truhlar, "Adiabatic Theory of Chemical Reactions," *J. Chem. Phys.* **53**, 2041 (1970).

149   D. G. Truhlar and A. Kuppermann, "Exact tunneling calculations," *J. Am. Chem. Soc.* **93**, 1840 (1971).

150   R. T. Skodje, D. G. Truhlar and B. C. Garrett, "Vibrationally adiabatic models for reactive tunneling," *J. Chem. Phys.* **77**, 5955 (1982).

151   W. Chen, W. L. Hase and H. B. Schlegel, "Ab initio classical trajectory study of $H_2CO \rightarrow H_2 + CO$ dissociation," *Chem. Phys. Lett.* **228**, 436 (1994).

152 H. B. Schlegel, J. S. Binkley and J. A. Pople, "First and Second Derivatives of Two Electron Integrals over Cartesian Gaussians using Rys Polynomials," *J. Chem. Phys.* **80**, 1976 (1984).

153 Y. Yamaguchi, M. J. Frisch, J. Gaw, H. F. Schaefer, III and J. S.Binkley, "Analytic computation and basis set dependence of Intensities of Infrared Spectra," *J. Chem. Phys.* **84**, 2262 (1986).

154 M. J. Frisch, Y. Yamaguchi, H. F. Schaefer, III and J. S. Binkley, "Analytic Calculation of Raman Intensities for Closed-Shell Wavefunctions," *J. Chem. Phys.* **84**, 531 (1986).

155 N. Yamamoto, T. Vreven, M. A. Robb, M. J. Frisch and H. B. Schlegel, "A Direct Derivative MC-SCF Procedure," *Chem. Phys. Lett.* **250**, 373 (1996).

156 R. D. Amos, *Chem. Phys. Lett.* **108**, 185 (1984).

157 B. G. Johnson and M. J. Frisch, "An implementation of analytic second derivatives of the gradient-corrected density functional energy," *J. Chem. Phys.* **100**, 7429 (1994).

158 B. G. Johnson and M. J. Frisch, "Analytic second derivatives of the gradient-corrected density functional energy: Effect of quadrature weight derivatives," *Chem. Phys. Lett.* **216**, 133 (1993).

159 R. E. Stratmann, J. C. Burant, G. E. Scuseria and M. J. Frisch, *J. Chem. Phys.* **106**, 10175 (1997).

160 G. W. Trucks and M. J. Frisch, "Analytic Second Derivatives of Excited States: Configuration Interaction Singles Theory and Application," in prep. (1998).

161 A. Kormornicki and R. L. Jaffe, *J. Chem. Phys.* **71**, 2150 (1979).

162 P. Pulay and W. Meyer, *J. Chem. Phys.* **57**, 3337 (1972).

163 K. Raghavachari and J. A. Pople, *Int. J. Quant. Chem.* **20**, 167 (1981).

164 J. E. Gready, G. B. Bacskay and N. S. Hush, *J. Chem. Phys.* **90**, 467 (1978).

165 R. S. Mulliken, "Electronic Populations Analysis on LCAO-MO Molecular Wave Functions," *J. Chem. Phys.* **23**, 1833 (1955).

166 B. H. Besler, K. M. Merz, Jr. and P. A. Kollman, *J. Comp. Chem.* **11**, 431 (1990).

167 U. C. Singh and P. A. Kollman, *J. Comp. Chem.* **5**, 129 (1984).

168 L. E. Chirlian and M. M. Francl, *J. Comp. Chem.* **8**, 894 (1987).

169 C. M. Breneman and K. B. Wiberg, *J. Comp. Chem.* **11**, 361 (1990).

170 J. R. Cheeseman, M. J. Frisch, G. W. Trucks and T. A. Keith, "A Comparison of Models for Calculation Nuclear Magnetic Resonance Shielding Tensors," *J. Chem. Phys.* **104**, 5497 (1996).

171 T. A. Keith and R. F. W. Bader, "Calculation of magnetic response properties using a continuous set of gauge transformations," *Chem. Phys. Lett.* **210**, 223 (1993).

172 T. A. Keith and R. F. W. Bader, "Calculation of magnetic response properties using atoms in molecules," *Chem. Phys. Lett.* **194**, 1 (1992).

173 K. Wolinski, J. F. Hilton and P. Pulay, "Efficient Implementation of the Gauge-Independent Atomic Orbital Method for NMR Chemical Shift Calculations," *J. Am. Chem. Soc.* **112**, 8251 (1990).

174 J. L. Dodds, R. McWeeny and A. J. Sadlej, *Mol. Phys.* **41**, 1419 (1980).

175 R. Ditchfield, "Self-consistent perturbation theory of diamagnetism I. A gauge-invariant LCAO method for N.M.R. chemical shifts," *Mol. Phys.* **27**, 789 (1974).

176 R. McWeeny, *Phys. Rev.* **126**, 1028 (1962).

177 F. London, *J. Phys. Radium, Paris* **8**, 397 (1937).

178 J. R. Cheeseman, M. J. Frisch, F. J. Devlin and P. J. Stephens, "Ab Initio Calculation of Atomic Axial Tensors and Vibrational Rotational Strengths Using Density Functional Theory," *Chem. Phys. Lett.* **252**, 211 (1996).

179 R. F. W. Bader, *Atoms in Molecules: A Quantum Theory* (Oxford Univ. Press, Oxford, 1990).

180   J. Cioslowski, A. Nanayakkara and M. Challacombe, "Rapid evaluation of atomic properties with mixed analytical/numerical integration," *Chem. Phys. Lett.* **203**, 137 (1993).

181   J. Cioslowski and P. R. Surjan, "An observable-based interpretation of electronic wavefunctions: application to "hypervalent" molecules," *J. Mol. Struc.* **255**, 9 (1992).

182   J. Cioslowski and B. B. Stefanov, "Variational Determination of the Zero-Flux Surface of Atoms in Molecules," *Mol. Phys.* **84**, 707 (1995).

183   B. B. Stefanov and J. R. Cioslowski, "An Efficient Approach to Calculation of Zero-Flux Atomic Surfaces and Generation of Atomic Integration Data," *J. Comp. Chem.* **16**, 1394 (1995).

184   J. V. Ortiz, *J. Chem. Phys.* **89**, 6348 (1988).

185   L. S. Cederbaum, *J. Phys.* **B8**, 290 (1975).

186   W. von Niessen, J. Schirmer and L. S. Cederbaum, *Comp. Phys. Rep.* **1**, 57 (1984).

187   V. G. Zakrzewski and W. von Niessen, *J. Comp. Chem.* **14**, 13 (1993).

188   V. G. Zakrzewski and J. V. Ortiz, *Int. J. Quantum Chem.*, in press (1994).

189   J. V. Ortiz, *Int. J. Quant. Chem., Quant. Chem. Symp.* **22**, 431 (1988).

190   J. V. Ortiz, *Int. J. Quant. Chem., Quant. Chem. Symp.* **23**, 321 (1989).

191   Walker, *J. Chem. Phys.* **52**, 1311 (1970).

192   P. W. Abegg and T.-K. Ha, *Mol. Phys.* **27**, 763 (1974).

193   R. Cimiraglia, M. Persico and J. Tomasi, *Chem. Phys. Lett.* **76**, 169 (1980).

194   S. Koseki, M. W. Schmidt and M. S. Gordon, *J. Phys. Chem.* **96**, 10768 (1992).

195   P. W. Abegg, *Mol. Phys.* **30**, 579 (1975).

196   M. W. Wong, M. J. Frisch and K. B. Wiberg, "Solvent Effects 1. The Mediation of Electrostatic Effects by Solvents," *J. Amer. Chem. Soc.* **113**, 4776 (1991).

197   M. W. Wong, K. B. Wiberg and M. J. Frisch, "Solvent Effects 2. Medium Effect on the Structure, Energy, Charge Density, and Vibrational Frequencies of Sulfamic Acid," *J. Amer. Chem. Soc.* **114**, 523 (1992).

198   M. W. Wong, K. B. Wiberg and M. J. Frisch, "SCF Second Derivatives and Electric Field Properties in a Reaction Field," *J. Chem. Phys.* **95**, 8991 (1991).

199   M. W. Wong, K. B. Wiberg and M. J. Frisch, "Solvent Effects 3. Tautomeric Equilibria of Formamide and 2-Pyridone in the Gas Phase and Solution: An ab inition SCRF Study," *J. Amer. Chem. Soc.* **114**, 1645 (1992).

200   S. Miertus, E. Scrocco and J. Tomasi, "Electrostatic Interaction of a Solute with a Continuum. A Direct Utilization of ab initio Molecular Potentials for the Prevision of Solvent Effects," *Chem. Phys.* **55**, 117 (1981).

201   S. Miertus and J. Tomasi, "Approximate Evaluations of the Electrostatic Free Energy and Internal Energy Changes in Solution Processes," *Chem. Phys.* **65**, 239 (1982).

202   M. Cossi, V. Barone, R. Cammi and J. Tomasi, *Chem. Phys. Lett.* **255**, 327 (1996).

203   M. T. Cances, V. Mennucci and J. Tomasi, *J. Chem. Phys.* **107**, 3032 (1997).

204   V. Barone, M. Cossi, B. Mennucci and J. Tomasi, *J. Chem. Phys.* **107**, 3210 (1997).

205   M. Cossi, V. Barone, B. Mennucci and J. Tomasi, *Chem. Phys. Lett.* **286**, 253 (1998).

206   V. Barone, M. Cossi and J. Tomasi, *J. Comp. Chem.* **19**, 404 (1998).

207   V. Barone and M. Cossi, *J. Phys. Chem.* **A 102**, 1995 (1998).

208   B. Mennucci and J.Tomasi, *J. Chem. Phys.*, in press (1998).

209   J. B. Foresman, T. A. Keith, K. B. Wiberg, J. Snoonian and M. J. Frisch, "Solvent Effects. 5. The Influence of Cavity Shape, Truncation of Electrostatics, and Electron Correlation on Ab Initio Reaction Field Calculations," *J. Phys. Chem.* **100**, 16098 (1996).

210 J. B. Foresman and Æ. Frisch, *Exploring Chemistry with Electronic Structure Methods,* 2nd edition, (Gaussian, Inc., Pittsburgh, PA, 1996).

211 W. J. Hehre, R. F. Stewart and J. A. Pople, *J. Chem. Phys.* **51**, 2657 (1969).

212 J. B. Collins, P. v. R. Schleyer, J. S. Binkley and J. A. Pople, "Self-Consistent Molecular Orbital Methods. 17. Geometries and binding energies of second-row molecules. A comparison of three basis sets," *J. Chem. Phys.* **64**, 5142 (1976).

213 J. S. Binkley, J. A. Pople and W. J. Hehre, "Self-Consistent Molecular Orbital Methods. 21. Small Split-Valence Basis Sets for First-Row Elements," *J. Amer. Chem. Soc.* **102**, 939 (1980).

214 M. S. Gordon, J. S. Binkley, J. A. Pople, W. J. Pietro and W. J. Hehre, "Self-Consistent Molecular-Orbital Methods. 22: Small Split-Valence Basis Sets for Second-Row Elements," *J. Amer. Chem. Soc.* **104**, 2797 (1982).

215 W. J. Pietro, M. M. Francl, W. J. Hehre, D. J. Defrees, J. A. Pople and J. S. Binkley, *J. Amer. Chem. Soc.* **104**, 5039 (1982).

216 K. D. Dobbs and W. J. Hehre, *J. Comp. Chem.* **7**, 359 (1986).

217 K. D. Dobbs and W. J. Hehre, *J. Comp. Chem.* **8**, 861 (1987).

218 K. D. Dobbs and W. J. Hehre, *J. Comp. Chem.* **8**, 880 (1987).

219 R. Ditchfield, W. J. Hehre and J. A. Pople, *J. Chem. Phys.* **54**, 724 (1971).

220 W. J. Hehre, R. Ditchfield and J. A. Pople, *J. Chem. Phys.* **56**, 2257 (1972).

221 P. C. Hariharan and J. A. Pople, *Mol. Phys.* **27**, 209 (1974).

222 M. S. Gordon, *Chem. Phys. Lett.* **76**, 163 (1980).

223 P. C. Hariharan and J. A. Pople, *Theo. Chim. Acta.* **28**, 213 (1973).

224 R. C. Binning Jr. and L. A. Curtiss, *J. Comp. Chem.* **11**, 1206 (1990).

225 G. A. Petersson, A. Bennett, T. G. Tensfeldt, M. A. Al-Laham, W. A. Shirley and J. Mantzaris, "A complete basis set model chemistry. I. The total energies of closed-shell atoms and hydrides of the first-row atoms," *J. Chem. Phys.* **89**, 2193 (1988).

226 A. D. McLean and G. S. Chandler, *J. Chem. Phys.* **72**, 5639 (1980).

227 R. Krishnan, J. S. Binkley, R. Seeger and J. A. Pople, *J. Chem. Phys.* **72**, 650 (1980).

228 A. J. H. Wachters, *J. Chem. Phys.* **52**, 1033 (1970).

229 P. J. Hay, *J. Chem. Phys.* **66**, 4377 (1977).

230 K. Raghavachari and G. W. Trucks, "Highly correlated systems. Excitation energies of first row transition metals Sc-Cu," *J. Chem. Phys.* **91**, 1062 (1989).

231 L. A. Curtiss, M. P. McGrath, J.-P. Blaudeau, N. E. Davis, R. C. Binning Jr. and L. Radom, *J. Chem. Phys.* **103**, 6104 (1995).

232 M. P. McGrath and L. Radom, *J. Chem. Phys.* **94**, 511 (1991).

233 T. H. Dunning Jr. and P. J. Hay, in *Modern Theoretical Chemistry,* Ed. H. F. Schaefer, III (Plenum, New York, 1976), vol. 3, 1.

234 A. K. Rappé, T. Smedly and W. A. Goddard, III, "The Shape and Hamiltonian Consistent (SHC) Effective Potentials," *J. Phys. Chem.* **85**, 1662 (1981).

235 W. Stevens, H. Basch and J. Krauss, *J. Chem. Phys.* **81**, 6026 (1984).

236 W. J. Stevens, M. Krauss, H. Basch and P. G. Jasien, *Can. J. Chem.* **70**, 612 (1992).

237 T. R. Cundari and W. J. Stevens, *J. Chem. Phys.* **98**, 5555 (1993).

238 P. J. Hay and W. R. Wadt, *J. Chem. Phys.* **82**, 270 (1985).

239 W. R. Wadt and P. J. Hay, *J. Chem. Phys.* **82**, 284 (1985).

240 P. J. Hay and W. R. Wadt, *J. Chem. Phys.* **82**, 299 (1985).

241 P. Fuentealba, H. Preuss, H. Stoll and L. v. Szentpaly, *Chem. Phys. Lett.* **89**, 418 (1989).

242 L. v. Szentpaly, P. Fuentealba, H. Preuss and H. Stoll, *Chem. Phys. Lett.* **93**, 555 (1982).

243 P. Fuentealba, H. Stoll, L. v. Szentpaly, P. Schwerdtfeger and H. Preuss, *J. Phys. B* **16**, 1323 (1983).

244 H. Stoll, P. Fuentealba, P. Schwerdtfeger, J. Flad, L. v. Szentpaly and H. Preuss, *J. Chem. Phys.* **81**, 2732 (1984).

245 P. Fuentealba, L. v. Szentpaly, H. Preuss and H. Stoll, *J. Phys. B* **18**, 1287 (1985).

246 U. Wedig, M. Dolg, H. Stoll and H. Preuss, in *Quantum Chemistry: The Challenge of Transition Metals and Coordination Chemistry,* Ed. A. Veillard, Reidel and Dordrecht (1986) 79.

247 M. Dolg, U. Wedig, H. Stoll and H. Preuss, *J. Chem. Phys.* **86**, 866 (1987).

248 G. Igel-Mann, H. Stoll and H. Preuss, *Mol. Phys.* **65**, 1321 (1988).

249 M. Dolg, H. Stoll and H. Preuss, *J. Chem. Phys.* **90**, 1730 (1989).

250 P. Schwerdtfeger, M. Dolg, W. H. E. Schwarz, G. A. Bowmaker and P. D. W. Boyd, *J. Chem. Phys.* **91**, 1762 (1989).

251 M. Dolg, H. Stoll, A. Savin and H. Preuss, *Theor. Chim. Acta* **75**, 173 (1989).

252 D. Andrae, U. Haeussermann, M. Dolg, H. Stoll and H. Preuss, *Theor. Chim. Acta* **77**, 123 (1990).

253 M. Kaupp, P. v. R. Schleyer, H. Stoll and H. Preuss, *J. Chem. Phys.* **94**, 1360 (1991).

254 W. Kuechle, M. Dolg, H. Stoll and H. Preuss, *Mol. Phys.* **74**, 1245 (1991).

255 M. Dolg, P. Fulde, W. Kuechle, C.-S. Neumann and H. Stoll, *J. Chem. Phys.* **94**, 3011 (1991).

256 M. Dolg, H. Stoll, H.-J. Flad and H. Preuss, *J. Chem. Phys.* **97**, 1162 (1992).

257 A. Bergner, M. Dolg, W. Kuechle, H. Stoll and H. Preuss, *Mol. Phys.* **80**, 1431 (1993).

258 M. Dolg, H. Stoll and H. Preuss, *Theor. Chim. Acta* **85**, 441 (1993).

259 M. Dolg, H. Stoll, H. Preuss and R. M. Pitzer, *J. Phys. Chem.* **97**, 5852 (1993).

260 U. Haeussermann, M. Dolg, H. Stoll and H. Preuss, *Mol. Phys.* **78**, 1211 (1993).

261 W. Kuechle, M. Dolg, H. Stoll and H. Preuss, *J. Chem. Phys.* **100**, 7535 (1994).

262 A. Nicklass, M. Dolg, H. Stoll and H. Preuss, *J. Chem. Phys.* **102**, 8942 (1995).

263 T. Leininger, A. Nicklass, H. Stoll, M. Dolg and P. Schwerdtfeger, *J. Chem. Phys.* **105**, 1052 (1996).

264 T. Leininger, in prep. (1998).

265 D. E. Woon and T. H. Dunning Jr., *J. Chem. Phys.* **98**, 1358 (1993).

266 R. A. Kendall, T. H. Dunning Jr. and R. J. Harrison, *J. Chem. Phys.* **96**, 6796 (1992).

267 T. H. Dunning Jr., *J. Chem. Phys.* **90**, 1007 (1989).

268 K. A. Peterson, D. E. Woon and T. H. Dunning Jr., *J. Chem. Phys.* **100**, 7410 (1994).

269 A. Wilson, T. van Mourik and T. H. Dunning Jr., *J. Mol. Struct. (Theochem)* **388**, 339 (1997).

270 E. R. Davidson, *Chem. Phys. Lett.* **220**, 514 (1996).

271 A. Schaefer, H. Horn and R. Ahlrichs, *J. Chem. Phys.* **97**, 2571 (1992).

272 A. Schaefer, C. Huber and R. Ahlrichs, *J. Chem. Phys.* **100**, 5829 (1994).

273 R. E. Easton, D. J. Giesen, A. Welch, C. J. Cramer and D. G. Truhlar, *Theor. Chim. Acta* **93**, 281 (1996).

274 V. Barone, in *Recent Advances in Density Functional Methods, Part I,* Ed. D. P. Chong (World Scientific Publ. Co., Singapore, 1996).

275 T. Clark, J. Chandrasekhar, G. W. Spitznagel and P. v. R. Schleyer, *J. Comp. Chem.* **4**, 294 (1983).

276 M. J. Frisch, J. A. Pople and J. S. Binkley, "Self-Consistent Molecular Orbital Methods 25: Supplementary Functions for Gaussian Basis Sets," *J. Chem. Phys.* **80**, 3265 (1984).

277 H. B. Schlegel and M. J. Frisch, *Int. J. Quantum Chem.* **54**, 83 (1995).

278   J. Cioslowski, "Isopycnic Orbital Transformations and Localization of Natural Orbitals," *Int. J. Quant. Chem. Quant. Chem. Symp.* **24**, 15 (1990).

279   J. Cioslowski and S. T. Mixon, "Covalent Bond Orders in the Topological Theory of Atoms in Molecules," *JACS* **113**, 4142 (1991).

280   J. Cioslowski, "An efficient evaluation of atomic properties using a vectorized numerical integration with dynamic thresholding," *Chem. Phys. Lett.* **194**, 73 (1992).

281   J. Cioslowski, *Chem. Phys. Lett.* **219**, 151 (1994).

282   M. J. Frisch, I. N. Ragazos, M. A. Robb and H. B. Schlegel, "An Evaluation of 3 Direct MCSCF Procedures," *Chem. Phys. Lett.* **189**, 524 (1992).

283   F. Bernardi, A. Bottoni, M. J. Field, M. F. Guest, I. H. Hillier, M. A. Robb and A. Venturini, "Study of the Diehls-Alder Reaction Between Ethylene and Butadiene," *J. Am. Chem. Soc.* **110**, 3050 (1988).

284   F. Bernardi, A. Bottoni, M. Olivucci, M. A. Robb, H. B. Schlegel and G. Tonachini, "Supra-Antara Paths Really Exist for 2+2 Cycloaddition Reactions? Analytical Computation of the MC-SCF Hessians for Transition States of C2H4 with C2H4, Singlet O2 and Ketene," *J. Am. Chem. Soc.* **110**, 5993 (1988).

285   F. Bernardi, A. Bottoni, M. A. Robb and A. Venturini, "MC-SCF study of the cycloaddition reaction between ketene and ethylene," *J. Am. Chem. Soc.* **112**, 2106 (1990).

286   F. Bernardi, M. Olivucci, I. Palmer and M. A. Robb, "An MC-SCF study of the thermal and photochemical cycloaddition of Dewar benzene," *J. Org. Chem.* **57**, 5081 (1992).

287   I. J. Palmer, F. Bernardi, M. Olivucci, I. N. Ragazos and M. A. Robb, "An MC-SCF study of the (photochemical) Paterno-Buchi reaction," *J. Am. Chem. Soc.* **116**, 2121 (1994).

288   G. Tonachini, H. B. Schlegel, F. Bernardi and M. A. Robb, "MC-SCF Study of the Addition Reaction of the $^1\Delta_g$ Oxygen Molecule to Ethene," *J. Am. Chem. Soc.* **112**, 483 (1990).

289   T. Vreven, F. Bernardi, M. Garavelli, M. Olivucci, M. A. Robb and H. B. Schlegel, *J. Am. Chem. Soc.* **119**, 12687 (1997).

290   J. M. Bofill and P. Pulay, *J. Chem. Phys.* **90**, 3637 (1989).

291   T. P. Hamilton and P. Pulay, *J. Chem. Phys.* **88**, 4926 (1988).

292   S. Clifford, M. J. Bearpark and M. A. Robb, *Chem. Phys. Lett.* **255**, 320 (1996).

293   J. Pipek and P. G. Mezey, "A fast intrinsic localization procedure applicable for ab initio and semiempirical linear combination of atomic orbital wave functions," *J. Chem. Phys.* **90**, 4916 (1989).

294   S. F. Boys, in *Quantum Theory of Atoms, Molecules and the Solid State,* Ed. P. O. Löwdin (Academic Press, New York, 1966) 253.

295   J. M. Foster and S. F. Boys, *Rev. Mod. Phys.* **32**, 300 (1960).

296   S. F. Boys, "Construction of Molecular Orbitals to be Approximately Invariant for Changes from One Molecule to Another," *Rev. Mod. Phys.* **32**, 296 (1960).

297   R. J. Bartlett and G. D. Purvis, *Int. J. Quant. Chem.* **14**, 516 (1978).

298   T. J. Lee and P. R. Taylor, *Int. J. Quantum Chem. Symp.* **23**, 199 (1989).

299   G. G. Hall and C. M. Smith, *Int. J. Quant. Chem.* **25**, 881 (1984).

300   C. M. Smith and G. G. Hall, *Theo. Chim. Acta.* **69**, 63 (1986).

301   J. Gerratt and I. M. Mills, *J. Chem. Phys.* **49**, 1719 (1968).

302   P. Pulay, *J. Chem. Phys.* **78**, 5043 (1983).

303   R. McWeeny, *Rev. Mod. Phys.* **32**, 335 (1960).

304   R. McWeeny, *Phys. Rev.* **128**, 1028 (1961).

305   R. M. Stevens, R. M. Pitzer and W. N. Lipscomb, *J. Chem. Phys.* **38**, 550 (1963).

306   J. L. Dodds, R. McWeeny, W. T. Raynes and J. P. Riley, *Mol. Phys.* **33**, 611 (1977).

307   J. L. Dodds, R. McWeeny and A. J. Sadlej, *Mol. Phys.* **34**, 1779 (1977).

308   Y. Osamura, Y. Yamaguchi and H. F. Schaefer, III, *J. Chem. Phys.* **75**, 2919 (1981).

309   Y. Osamura, Y. Yamaguchi and H. F. Schaefer, III, *J. Chem. Phys.* **77**, 383 (1982).

310   C. E. Dykstra and P. G. Jasien, *Chem. Phys. Lett.* **109**, 388 (1984).

311   Diercksen, Roos and Sadlej, *Chem. Phys.* **59**, 29 (1981).

312   Diercksen and Sadlej, *J. Chem. Phys.* **75**, 1253 (1981).

313   K. B. Wiberg, C. M. Hadad, T. J. LePage, C. M. Breneman and M. J. Frisch, "An Analysis of the Effect of Electron Correlation on Charge Density Distributions," *J. Phys. Chem.* **96**, 671 (1992).

314   D. R. Salahub and M. C. Zerner, Eds., *The Challenge of d and f Electrons* (ACS, Washington, D.C., 1989).

315   R. G. Parr and W. Yang, *Density-functional theory of atoms and molecules* (Oxford Univ. Press, Oxford, 1989).

316   J. P. Perdew and Y. Wang, "Accurate and Simple Analytic Representation of the Electron Gas Correlation Energy," *Phys. Rev. B* **45**, 13244 (1992).

317   J. P. Perdew, J. A. Chevary, S. H. Vosko, K. A. Jackson, M. R. Pederson, D. J. Singh and C. Fiolhais, "Atoms, molecules, solids, and surgaces: Applications of the generalized gradient approximation for exchange and correlation," *Physical Review B* **46**, 6671 (1992).

318   J. K. Labanowski and J. W. Andzelm, Eds., *Density Functional Methods in Chemistry* (Springer-Verlag, New York, 1991).

319   C. Sosa and C. Lee, *J. Chem. Phys.* **98**, 8004 (1993).

320   J. Andzelm and E. Wimmer, "Density functional Gaussian-type-orbital approach to molecular geometries, vibrations, and reaction energies," *J. Chem. Phys.* **96**, 1280 (1992).

321   G. E. Scuseria, "Comparison of coupled-cluster results with a hybrid of Hartree-Fock and density functional theory," *J. Chem. Phys.* **97**, 7528 (1992).

322   A. D. Becke, "Density-functional thermochemistry. II. The effect of the Perdew-Wang generalized-gradient correlation correction," *J. Chem. Phys.* **97**, 9173 (1992).

323   A. D. Becke, "Density-functional thermochemistry. I. The effect of the exchange-only gradient correction," *J. Chem. Phys.* **96**, 2155 (1992).

324   P. M. W. Gill, B. G. Johnson, J. A. Pople and M. J. Frisch, "The performance of the Becke-Lee-Yang-Parr (B-LYP) density functional theory with various basis sets," *Chemical Physics Letters* **197**, 499 (1992).

325   P. J. Stephens, F. J. Devlin, C. S. Ashvar, C. F. Chabalowski and M. J. Frisch, "Theoretical Calculation of Vibrational Circular Dichroism Spectra," *Faraday Discuss.* **99**, 103 (1994).

326   P. J. Stephens, F. J. Devlin, M. J. Frisch and C. F. Chabalowski, "Ab Initio Calculations of Vibrational Absorption and Circular Dichroism Spectra Using SCF, MP2, and Density Functional Theory Force Fields," *J. Phys. Chem.* **98**, 11623 (1994).

327   A. Ricca and C. W. Bauschlicher Jr., "On the successive binding energies of Fe(CO)5+," *J. Phys. Chem.* **99**, 9003 (1995).

328   K. Burke, J. P. Perdew and Y. Wang, in *Electronic Density Functional Theory: Recent Progress and New Directions*, Ed. J. F. Dobson, G. Vignale and M. P. Das (Plenum, 1998).

329   J. P. Perdew, in *Electronic Structure of Solids '91*, Ed. P. Ziesche and H. Eschrig (Akademie Verlag, Berlin, 1991) 11.

330   J. P. Perdew, J. A. Chevary, S. H. Vosko, K. A. Jackson, M. R. Pederson, D. J. Singh and C. Fiolhais, *Phys. Rev. B* **46** (1992).

331 J. P. Perdew, J. A. Chevary, S. H. Vosko, K. A. Jackson, M. R. Pederson, D. J. Singh and C. Fiolhais, *Phys. Rev. B* **48** (1993).

332 J. P. Perdew, K. Burke and Y. Wang, *Phys. Rev. B* **54**, 16533 (1996).

333 C. Adamo and V. Barone, *J. Chem. Phys.* **108**, 664 (1998).

334 P. M. W. Gill, *Mol. Phys.* **89**, 433 (1996).

335 S. H. Vosko, L. Wilk and M. Nusair, "Accurate spin-dependent electron liquid correlation energies for local spin density calculations: a critical analysis," *Canadian J. Phys.* **58**, 1200 (1980).

336 J. P. Perdew and A. Zunger, *Phys. Rev. B* **23**, 5048 (1981).

337 J. P. Perdew, "Density-functional approximation for the correlation energy of the inhomogeneous electron gas," *Phys. Rev. B* **33**, 8822 (1986).

338 L. Greengard and V. Rokhlin, *J. Comput. Phys.* **73**, 325 (1987).

339 L. Greengard, *The Rapid Evaluation of Potential Fields in Particle Systems* (MIT Press, Cambridge, MA, 1988).

340 L. Greengard, *Science* **265**, 909 (1994).

341 A. G. Baboul and H. B. Schlegel, "Improved Method for Calculating Projected Frequencies along a Reaction Path," *J. Chem. Phys.* (1997).

342 P. Y. Ayala and H. B. Schlegel, *J. Chem. Phys.*, in press (1998).

343 D. A. McQuarrie, *Statistical Thermodynamics* (Harper and Row, New York, 1973).

344 S. W. Benson, *Thermochemical Kinetics* (Wiley and Sons, New York, 1968).

345 J. A. Pople and M. S. Gordon, *J. Amer. Chem. Soc.* **89**, 4253 (1967).

346 W. A. Goddard, III and L. B. Harding, "The Description of Chemical Bonding from Ab Initio Calculations," *Ann. Rev. Phys. Chem.*, 363 (1978).

347 G. W. Trucks and M. J. Frisch, "Rotational Invariance Properties of Pruned Grids for Numerical Integration," in prep. (1998).

348 M. Krack and A. M. Koster, *J. Chem. Phys.* **108**, 3226 (1998).

349 V. I. Lebedev, *Zh. Vychisl. Mat. Mat. Fiz.* **15**, 48 (1975).

350 A. D. McLaren, *Math. Comp.* **17**, 361 (1963).

351 V. I. Lebedev, *Zh. Vychisl. Mat. Mat. Fiz.* **16**, 293 (1976).

352 V. I. Lebedev, "Theory of Cubature of Formulas and Numerical Mathematics," in *Proc. Conf. Diff. Eqn. Numer. Math., Novosibirsk, 1978*, Ed. S. L. Sobolev (Nauka, Novosibivsk, 1980) 110.

353 V. I. Lebedev, *Russian Acad. Sci. Dokl. Math.* **45**, 587 (1992).

354 E. Stratmann, G. E. Scuseria and M. J. Frisch, *Chem. Phys. Lett.* **257**, 213 (1996).

355 H. F. King and M. Dupuis, "Numerical Integration Using Rys Polynomials," *J. Comp. Phys.* **21**, 144 (1976).

356 M. Dupuis, J. Rys and H. F. King, *J. Chem. Phys.* **65**, 111 (1976).

357 J. Rys, M. Dupuis and H. F. King, *J. Comp. Chem.* **4**, 154 (1983).

358 J. R. Cheeseman, G. W. Trucks and M. J. Frisch, in prep. (1998).

359 H. B. Schlegel, "Geometry Optimization on Potential Energy Surfaces," in *Modern Electronic Structure Theory*, Ed. D. R. Yarkony (World Scientific Publishing, Singapore, 1995).

360 O. Farkas and H. B. Schlegel, "An O(N2) method for solving the sequence of linear equations arising in the geometry optimization of large molecules using internal coordinates," in prep. (1998).

361 J. Simons, P. Jorgensen, H. Taylor and J. Ozment, "Walking on Potential Energy Surfaces," *J. Phys. Chem.* **87**, 2745 (1983).

362 P. Csaszar and P. Pulay, *J. Mol. Struct. (THEOCHEM)* **114**, 31 (1984).

363   O. Farkas, PhD (CsC) thesis, Eotvos University of Budapest (Budapest, Hungary), 1995 [in Hungarian].

364   O. Farkas and H. B. Schlegel, in prep. (1998).

365   J. T. Golab, D. L. Yeager and P. Jorgensen, *Chem. Phys.* **78**, 175 (1983).

366   C. J. Cerjan and W. H. Miller, "On Finding Transition States," *J. Chem. Phys.* **75**, 2800 (1981).

367   A. Bannerjee, N. Adams, J. Simons and R. Shepard, "Search for Stationary Points on Surfaces," *J. Phys. Chem.* **89**, 52 (1985).

368   J. Baker and W. J. Hehre, "The Death of the Z-Matrix," *J. Comp. Chem.* **12**, 606 (1991).

369   H. B. Schlegel, "A Comparison of Geometry Optimization with Mixed Cartesian and Internal Coordinates," *Int. J. Quant. Chem.: Quant. Chem. Symp.* **26**, 243 (1992).

370   P. Pulay, G. Fogarasi, F. Pang and J. E. Boggs, *J. Am. Chem. Soc.* **101**, 2550 (1979).

371   P. Pulay and G. Fogarasi, *J. Chem. Phys.* **96**, 2856 (1992).

372   G. Fogarasi, X. Zhou, P. Taylor and P. Pulay, *J. Am. Chem. Soc.* **114**, 8191 (1992).

373   J. Baker, *J. Comp. Chem.* **14**, 1085 (1993).

374   H. B. Schlegel, *Theor. Chim. Acta.* **66**, 33 (1984).

375   R. Fletcher, *Practical Methods of Optimization* (Wiley, New York, 1980).

376   J. M. Bofill, *J. Comp. Chem.* **15**, 1 (1994).

377   J. M. Bofill and M. Comajuan, *J. Comp. Chem.* **16**, 1326 (1995).

378   G. Veress, R. Hargitai and O. Farkas, "A method for the construction of non-redundant valence bond coordinates for complex fused ring systems," in prep. (1998).

379   J. V. Ortiz, V. G. Zakrzewski and O. Dolgounircheva, "One-Electron Pictures of Electronic Structures: Propagator Calculations of Photoelectron Spectra of Aromatic Molecules," in *Conceptual Perspectives in Quantum Chemistry,* Ed. J.-L. Calais and E. Kryachko (Kluwer Academic, 1997) 465.

380   B. G. Johnson, P. M. W. Gill and J. A. Pople, "Computing Molecular Electrostatic Potentials with the PRISM Algorithm," *Chem. Phys. Lett.*, submitted (1991).

381   N. Rega, M. Cossi and V. Barone, *J. Chem. Phys.* **105**, 11060 (1996).

382   V. Barone, *Chem. Phys. Lett.* **262**, 201 (1996).

383   J. Gauss and C. Cremer, *Chem. Phys. Lett.* **150**, 280 (1988).

384   G. W. Trucks and M. J. Frisch, "Semi-Direct QCI Gradients," in prep. (1998).

385   E. A. Salter, G. W. Trucks and R. J. Bartlett, "Analytic Energy Derivatives in Many-Body Methods I. First Derivatives," *J. Chem. Phys.* **90**, 1752 (1989).

386   T. J. Lee, A. P. Rendell and P. R. Taylor, "Comparison of the Quadratic Configuration Interaction and Coupled-Cluster Approaches to Electron Correlation Including the Effect of Triple Excitations," *J. Phys. Chem.* **94**, 5463 (1990).

387   H. B. Schlegel and J. J. McDouall, in *Computational Advances in Organic Chemistry,* Ed. C. Ogretir and I. G. Csizmadia (Kluwer Academic, The Netherlands, 1991) 167.

388   G. B. Bacskay, "A Quadratically Convergent Hartree-Fock (QC-SCF) Method. Application to Closed Systems," *Chem. Phys.* **61**, 385 (1981).

389   P. Pulay, *J. Comp. Chem.* **3**, 556 (1982).

390   R. Seeger and J. A. Pople, *J. Chem. Phys.* **65**, 265 (1976).

391   J. G. Kirkwood, *J. Chem. Phys.* **2**, 351 (1934).

392   L. Onsager, "Electric Moments of Molecules in Liquids," **58**, 1486 (1936).

393   P. Carsky and E. Hubak, "Restricted and Unrestricted Hartree-Fock Reference States in MBPT: a critical comparison of the two approaches," *Theo. Chim. Acta.* **80**, 407 (1991).

394   W. L. Hase, R. J. Duchovic, X. Hu, A. Komornicki, K. F. Lim, D.-H. Lu, G. H. Peslherbe, K. N. Swamy, S. R. V. Linde, A. Varandas, H. Wang and R. J. Wolfe, "VENUS96: A General Chemical Dynamics Computer Program," *Quantum Chem. Program Exchange* **16**, 671 (1996).

395   H. B. Schlegel and M. J. Frisch, "Computational Bottlenecks in Molecular Orbital Calculations," in *Theoretical and Computational Models for Organic Chemistry,* Ed. J. S. Formosinho, I. G. Csizmadia and L. G. Arnaut (Kluwer Academic, The Netherlands, 1991) 5.

396   J. B. Foresman and H. B. Schlegel, "Application of the CI-Singles method in predicting the energy, properties and reactivity of molecules in their excited states," in *Recent experimental and computational advances in molecular spectroscopy,* Ed. R. Fausto and J. M. Hollas (Kluwer Academic, The Netherlands, 1993) 11.

397   R. C. Raffenetti, "Preprocessing Two-Electron Integrals for Efficient Utilization in Many-Electron Self-Consistent Field Calculations," *Chem. Phys. Lett.* **20**, 335 (1973).

398   W. Shakespeare, *Macbeth*, III.iv.40-107, London, c.1606-1611.

399   M. J. Frisch, J. E. Del Bene, J. S. Binkley and H. F. Schaefer, III, *J. Chem. Phys.* **84**, 2279 (1986).

400   D. W. Schwenke and D. G. Truhlar, *J. Chem. Phys.* **82**, 2418 (1985).

401   T. A. Halgren and W. N. Lipscomb, "The Synchronous Transit Method for Determining Reaction Pathways and Locating Transition States," *Chem. Phys. Lett.* **49**, 225 (1977).

402   E. R. Cohen and B. N. Taylor, *The 1986 Adjustment of the Fundamental Physical Constants,* CODATA Bulletin (Pergamon, Elmsford, NY, 1986), vol. 63.

403   *Pure and Applied Chemistry* **2**, 717 (1973).

404   R. C. Weast, *CRC Handbook of Chemistry and Physics* (Chemical Rubber Company, Boca Raton, FL, 1980).

405   *Pure and Applied Chemistry* **51**, 1 (1979).

Index

F

G

G* keywords
  ReadIsotopes option · 87
  Restart option · 88
G1 keyword · 33
G1 method · 87
G2 keyword · 33
G2 method · 87
G2(MP2) method · 87
G2* keyword
  StartMP2 option · 88
G2MP2 keyword · 33
g98 command · 21
g98.login file · 19
G98.login file · 230
g98.profile file · 19
G98.profile file · 230
G98basis environment variable · 231
G98root environment variable · 230
GAMESS · 164
gauge · 126
Gauge-Independant Atomic Orbital method · 126
gauopt utility · 217
gauss_archdir · 231
gauss_archdir environment variable · 231
gauss_exedir environment variable · 230
GAUSS_SCRDIR environment variable · 17, 230
Gaussian 86
  constants used in · 248
Gaussian 94 Programmer's Reference · 250
Gaussian 98
  citation · 10
  documentation set · 15
  features · 9, 11
Gaussian 98 Programmer's Reference · 15
gaussian functions · 89
Gaussian NEWS · 15
Gaussian-1 method · 87
Gaussian-2 method · 87
Gen keyword · 29
general basis sets · 89
General Valence Bond method · 103
Geom keyword
  AllCheck option · 37
  AllCheckpoint option · 94
  Angle option · 96
  CAngle option · 96
  CDihedral option · 96
  Checkpoint option · 93
  CheckPoint option · 37
  Connect option · 96
  Coord option · 248
  Crowd option · 97
  Dihedral option · 96
  Distance option · 96

Independent option · 97
KeepConstants option · 97
KeepDefinition option · 97
ModConnect option · 96
Model options · 245
ModelA option · 97
ModelB option · 97
Modify option · 95
Modify option · 149
ModRedundant option · 94
NewDefinition option · 97
Print option · 97
Step option · 94
geometry optimizations · 128
  coordinate systems and · 136
GFInput keyword · 89
GFPrint keyword · 89
ghelp utility · 219
ghost atoms · 245
GIAO method · 126
Gibbs free energy · 56, 86, 88
GNU make facility
  not supported · 229
gradient norm · 66
GridDensity keyword · 247
grids · 107, 136
  (99,302) for CBS · 57
  and DFT methods · 76
  default · 107
  high accuracy · 108
Guess keyword · 29
  Alter option · 98
  Always option · 98
  Cards option · 99
  Core option · 99
  Huckel option · 99
  Local option · 99
  LowSymm option · 99
  Mix option · 99
  NoSymm option · 99
  Only option · 100
  Read option · 98
  Restart option · 247
  Save option · 100
  Translate option · 99
GVB calculations · 180
GVB keyword · 29
  Freeze option · 104
  InHam option · 104
  NPair option · 104
  OpenShellSinglet option · 104
  OSS option · 104
  with Field keyword · 79
GVBCAS · 50

Q

R